Guide to the
Alaska
Highway

Your Complete Driving Guide

3rd Edition

RON DALBY

MENASHA RIDGE PRESS
BIRMINGHAM, ALABAMA

Guide to the Alaska Highway

Third Edition

Copyright © 2017 by Ron Dalby
All rights reserved
Published by Menasha Ridge Press
Distributed by Publishers Group West
Printed in China
Third edition, third printing 2019

Cover and interior design: Lora Westberg
Cover and interior photographs: Ron Dalby and stock
Cartography: Steve Jones
Indexer: Ann Cassar

Library of Congress Cataloging-in-Publication Data:
Names: Dalby, Ron, 1949- author.
Title: Guide to the Alaska highway / Ron Dalby.
Description: Third edition. | Birmingham, Alabama : Menasha Ridge Press, 2017.
Identifiers: LCCN 2016039863 | ISBN 9781634040884 (paperback)
Subjects: LCSH: Alaska—Guidebooks. | Alaska Highway—Guidebooks. |
    Automobile travel—Alaska Highway—Guidebooks. | Northwest,
    Canadian—Guidebooks. | BISAC: TRAVEL / United States / West / Pacific
    (AK, CA, HI, NV, OR, WA). | TRANSPORTATION / Navigation.
Classification: LCC F902.3 .D354 2017 | DDC 917.9804/5—dc23
LC record available at https://lccn.loc.gov/2016039863

ISBN 978-1-63404-088-4; eISBN 978-1-63404-089-1

🦋 **Menasha Ridge Press**
    An imprint of AdventureKEEN
    2204 First Ave. S., Suite 102
    Birmingham, AL 35233
    800-443-7227, fax 205-326-1012

Visit menasharidge.com for a complete listing of our books and for ordering information. Contact us at our website, at facebook.com/menasharidge, or at twitter.com/menasharidge with questions or comments. To find out more about who we are and what we're doing, visit blog.menasharidge.com.

Dedication

To Chris Dalby, who rests forever in the Yukon near our favorite fishing hole.

Table of Contents

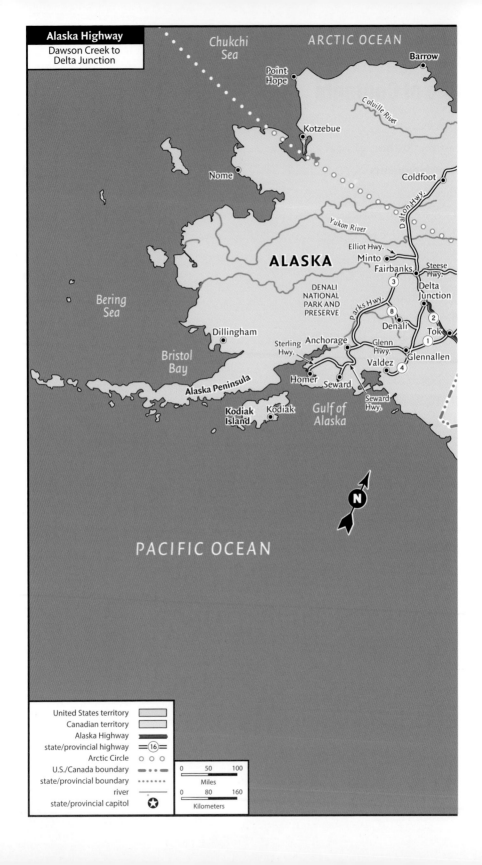

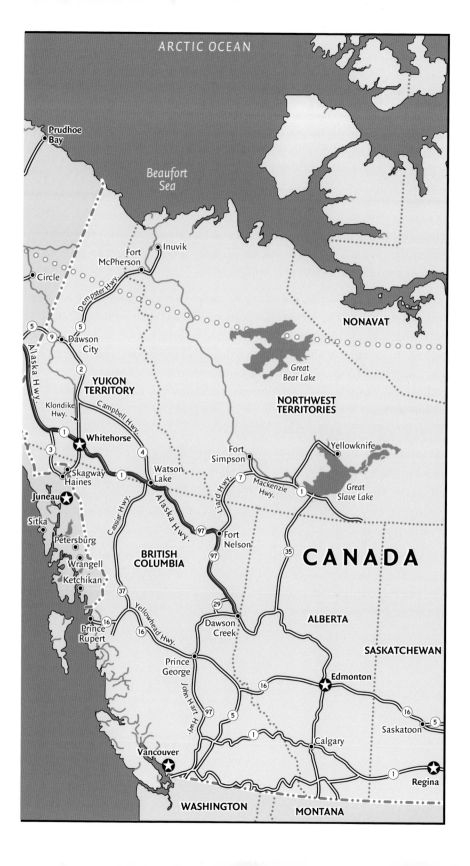

About the Author

Ron Dalby grew up on the American road. He was but a year old in 1950 when he made his first trip down the Alaska Highway. Throughout the rest of his formative years, he crisscrossed the United States countless times as his father, a career army officer, moved from assignment to assignment.

The urge to travel America's roads never left him. Annual forays in Ron's RV have led from his home in Alaska to as far away as Florida and almost everywhere in between. The RV is a perfect match for his itchy foot, and over the years he has owned or used one of every type available.

Ron has worked as a writer and editor for nearly three decades, both as a freelancer and on the staff of various publications. He served as editor of *Alaska Magazine* during the most successful period in its long history and has authored thousands of newspaper and magazine articles and five books. His most successful book, *The Alaska Highway: An Insider's Guide,* though out of print for nearly a decade, is still available on Amazon.com's used book list. This early-1990s book has been replaced with this *Guide to the Alaska Highway.* All of his writings are illustrated by photos he has taken himself.

As a young adult, Ron served two tours as a helicopter pilot in Vietnam and later worked in Alaska as a military test pilot. He has made dramatic rescues of injured climbers on Mount McKinley (officially renamed Denali in 2015) and flown thousands of hours throughout the wilderness of Alaska, both in the military and as a civilian pilot.

He has been married for 46 years to the former Jennifer Durland of Milwaukie, Oregon. She shares his love of travel and adventure and has more than once picked up on stories he might otherwise have missed. They have two grown children, Eric and Tiffany, four granddaughters, and a grandson.

Acknowledgments

This book, like most others, has a single name on the cover as the author. However, just about anyone who has ever written a book will tell you that an author has a lot of help. Without that help, there wouldn't be many books.

Starting with the first edition of this book, which came out in 1991, I've been helped along the way by people of every description. Certainly those thousands of people I've met along the Alaska Highway in the past 44 years contributed in some way—large or small—to this book. Even if I could remember all of their names, there isn't space to list them here. Without these people the Alaska Highway would be just another road. Let it suffice to say that I've never had a negative experience with any of the people I've met along the road in Canada and Alaska. And if the highlight of any travel experience is the people you meet, these folks make my travels along the Alaska Highway the grandest experiences of my life.

The one person I can't get away from listing by name is my daughter, Tiffany. As a teenager she kept the running logs and notes as I drove some 6,000 miles of often less-than-perfect roads. Now, as an adult and a competent writer/editor in her own right, she edited Dad's copy and in general provided the push needed to get this book into the hands of the people who need and want to read it. She is truly the one person besides the author who brought this book to reality.

Finally, there is my wife, Jennifer. She puts up with a lot (me) without ever losing her sense of humor or sense of adventure.

Preface

I first saw the Alaska Highway—then almost universally known as the Alcan—in August 1950, from the backseat of a two-door, black Studebaker Champion. Being 13 months old at the time, I remember absolutely nothing of the trip, though over the years my mother has assured me that I had a great time.

Undoubtedly, my great time came at her expense. Dad did the driving; mother wrestled with my tantrums, diapers, and anything else that came up. This, too, was before the advent of functional disposable diapers, so I suppose her chores were the toughest of the lot.

At any rate, we succeeded in reaching Nebraska so I could meet my grandparents and in plenty of time for the birth of my brother. Yes, indeed, mother must have had quite a trip, being eight months pregnant—in those days, doctors were even farther apart than gas pumps. Campgrounds were wide spots on the road or gravel pits created by the building of the highway, and help in the event of an emergency was usually a long distance away.

Significantly, I can't recall either of my parents mentioning many problems from that trip, not so much as a flat tire. To the end of his days, Dad looked upon it as one of the greatest adventures he'd ever had. Mother still grins when she spins a yarn about her 1950 trek from Alaska to Nebraska. Yet I'm certain they must have had a few tense moments or minor breakdowns.

I find myself acting much the same way. Certainly I've had my share of flat tires (seven in one trip), chipped windshields, and loose bolts, but I have to force myself to remember these things. I've simply had too much fun driving back and forth on the Alaska Highway since 1972. When I think of the Alaska Highway, I think of friends from Whitehorse, Yukon, met by chance in the Squanga Lake Campground, or the largest lake trout I've ever seen surfacing at the end of my son's line after a 40-minute battle. Sunsets, vivid beyond belief, come to mind, as do mountain sheep grazing at roadside. Those are the things that make driving the Alaska Highway such an adventure, an adventure available to anyone with a driver's license and access to a vehicle.

Over the years I've learned to take a few simple precautions that will assure a relatively trouble-free trip, save for an unpredictable accident. That's what part of this book is about. Driving to Alaska needn't be any more nerve-wracking than driving across the contiguous United States. It should, in fact, be a lot more relaxing because there's a lot less traffic. All it takes is a little planning and preparation ahead of time.

The balance of this book describes some of the adventures promised by the words "Alaska Highway." Unfortunately, there's not room for all of them in a book of any size. Besides the nuts and bolts of where to go and what to see, anecdotes from my own experiences and those of others are included. Laugh with me, cry with me, even cuss with me as I detail some of the triumphs and problems overcome in nearly four decades of vacationing along the Alaska Highway.

And for me there are never enough trips on the Alaska Highway. We're already thinking about next year's trip down the road, our 40th in 39 years. You see, I feel duty bound to investigate and report on some intriguing big fish stories from the Yukon that have reached my desk in the past few months . . . .

Like all writers, I may have made some errors when I put my notes, pictures, and memories from the Alaska Highway together in book form. Please feel free to send me an e-mail setting me straight or otherwise commenting on what you find in this book. With your help, the next edition can be even better than this one.

Ron Dalby
Palmer, Alaska
rdcomm@gci.net

CHAPTER 1
A Road to Alaska

The dust had barely settled over Pearl Harbor's sunken battleships in December 1941, when the US Government decided to build a road from Dawson Creek, British Columbia, Canada, through Yukon Territory, Canada, to the US Territory of Alaska.

The connection between Japan's blasting the Pacific Fleet into rubble and a road to Alaska isn't immediately obvious, unless you're staring at the globe Adolf Hitler and his minions might have prepared in late 1941. Save for England, Hitler basically ruled Europe, his armies poised at the gates of Moscow. Hitler's Axis partner, Japan, was gobbling up Pacific islands and Asian mainland bases in southeast Asia and China. Japan and Germany, allied with Italy, looked all but unbeatable in late 1941 to many observers.

Only three countries of sufficient resources retained the independence necessary to prosecute World War II against one or both of the aggressors: Great Britain, the Soviet Union, and the United States.

The only place where any two of these three diverse nations come close together is the Bering Strait, a narrow neck of water separating Alaska and Siberia. This distant but tenuous link in the far north looked mighty good indeed to the Allied powers in 1941. Frankly, there weren't many other places to look at the time.

There was one immediate and pressing problem—in December 1941, there was no guarantee that Alaska could be supplied. No roads led to Alaska. Shipping was thought too dangerous because of the threat of Japanese naval forces. A new road seemed the obvious answer, a road built far enough inland to be out of range of the airplanes carried by Japanese aircraft carriers. With few preliminaries, the US Army Corps of Engineers was sent to build the Alcan Highway, the road known today as the Alaska Highway.

This being wartime, a few proprieties were initially overlooked. Canada and the United States are separate countries, and even though both were warring against the Axis, things were a bit strained when several trains filled with US soldiers and equipment began unloading in Dawson Creek, British Columbia, one winter day, somewhat ahead of any agreement being signed granting the United States the right to build the road.

Both countries, though, took things in stride, having been friendly nations for more than a century. American soldiers just bulldozed ahead, figuring that the inevitable paperwork would catch up sooner or later, and the Canadians,

Vehicles abandoned after construction of the Alaska Highway can still be found in northern forests.

while rushing to fill out the forms, politely allowed the Americans to get started. A few weeks later an agreement was announced, and the few ruffled feathers settled down. Ultimately, the Canadians won big; they were able to purchase most of the road from the Americans for about half its cost when the war ended—not a bad bargain by anyone's standards.

But the American GI who started overland from Dawson Creek in the middle of winter, generally heading northwest to Fairbanks, didn't think he got much of a bargain. It gets right cold in that part of the world in winter. And winter lasts a long time. Not only that, but the officers running this show were in a hurry. As the surveyors walked along flagging a route across creeks, rivers, plains, and mountains, they were rarely out of earshot of the bull-dozers—often within sight of the big metal beasts.

> Not much attention was paid to grades. If the surveyors hiked up or down a particularly steep hill, the bulldozers simply followed them. In fact, a sign just prior to a particularly treacherous downhill stretch called Suicide Hill warned drivers to prepare to meet their maker. This plunge caused several major accidents before it was leveled out.

Even as they pushed rapidly across this wilderness, it became evident that militarily minded men had preceded them. Gravel airstrips suitable for military interceptors and bombers were already operating in places such as Fort Nelson, Watson Lake, and Whitehorse; the new road just tied them all together. During the building of the road, these airstrips provided vital links for communications and transportation.

Once the soldiers started northwest from Dawson Creek and southeast from Alaska, the road came together quickly. In October 1942, just eight months and 12 days after they started, soldiers held a celebration near Kluane Lake—about 150 miles northwest of Whitehorse—commemorating the completion of the project.

If that sounds a little fantastic for finishing a road across 1,500 miles of wilderness, it was. What was then called a road was described by men of great vision with limited functional eyesight. The army had to station engineers with bulldozers along lengthy stretches of single-lane, muddy trails, trails gradually sinking below ground level as the just-bared permafrost under the topsoil melted into mud the consistency of quicksand. The big tractors pulled trucks through these spots during the summer months.

Civilian construction crews from Canada worked throughout 1943 and into 1944 straightening out hairpin curves, leveling grades, and reinforcing muddy surfaces with gravel so that the word "road" could be a reasonable description of this meandering path to Alaska. By then, though, they were working at a much lower priority than those who pioneered the route. By late 1943, Japanese forces were being chased out of Alaskan waters, and the perceived need for the road was markedly reduced.

As the war wound down in 1945, the Alcan gradually became deserving of being described as a road. And what a road it was. Suddenly, large parts of the Canadian North were open to the people of North America. And the few people who lived in the region suddenly had access to the outside world, called the civilized world by those they met when they first ventured along the route. Tourists, first the heady adventurers, then later the calmer, saner folks, began looking north to the last great wilderness on the continent.

The Canadians took control of most of the road in 1946—about 1,200 miles of the 1,512 miles from Dawson Creek to Fairbanks are in Canada. Still, though, driving to Alaska required the permission of the American military. This held for all of 1947 as well. In 1948, the road was opened briefly to the public but was soon closed again because of the number of vehicles pounded to pieces en route to Alaska. Not until 1949 was the road opened to the public on a year-round basis. Ever since, more facilities for travelers—gas stations, motels, restaurants, and camp-grounds—have opened every year. By the late 1970s, travelers were never more than 50 miles or so from at least a small service station, though there are still some exceptions on side roads leading off into the Canadian wilderness. By the mid-1980s, most of the Alaska Highway was paved, though the quality of the pavement varied considerably.

Spur roads began opening shortly after the highway was built. The first of these joined Haines, Alaska, near the northern end of the Alaska Panhandle, to the Alaska Highway at a point about 100 miles northwest of Whitehorse, Yukon Territory. It was completed in December 1943. Soon after the war, it became possible to drive from Whitehorse to Dawson City, Yukon, the latter the scene of the Klondike gold rush of 1898. Yukon's capital moved from Dawson to Whitehorse in 1953, tacit recognition that Whitehorse had eclipsed Dawson as the territory's population and business center. The Alaska Highway played a major role in that switch.

In the last three decades, sufficient spur roads have opened to make it possible to travel from Canada to Alaska while only driving on about 24 miles of the actual Alaska Highway. Thus you could argue that now there are two routes north. Additionally, the Liard Highway, running north from Fort Nelson, links the Alaska

Highway to Northwest Territories, one of Canada's most remote territories. Another road near Dawson leads north to Inuvik, a First Nations village at the apex of the MacKenzie River delta, north of the Arctic Circle. Gradually, but ever so steadily, villages throughout northwestern Canada are being connected to North America's road system. All these various roads increase the potential for adventure for those driving to Alaska.

There is, without a doubt, a lot to see and do in Canada. The Alaska Highway, as it is officially known, provides a path to some of the most thrilling outdoor recreation opportunities in North America. Grizzly bears roam the tundra at roadside, black bears amble in the forests, Stone sheep

Canadians will quickly tell you that you can spend the whole summer exploring northern British Columbia, Yukon, and Northwest Territories without ever entering Alaska. That alone is as much fun or even more fun than driving to Alaska. Maybe you'd better plan to spend two summers up north.

feed on the road shoulder where it crosses the Rocky Mountains, and grizzled trappers still wander the land in solitude, coming out only when necessary to buy supplies or to sell their furs.

The Alaska Highway leads you back in time, back to when the world was a simpler place, a wilder place, and, to some, a more enchanting place. It gives you a glimpse of the way we were, and it shows the careful observer some of the steps we took to get where we are today.

Denali,
Denali National Park

CHAPTER 2
Why Drive to Alaska?

THE WILDERNESS

Ask any tourist you meet on the streets of Anchorage, Juneau, or Fairbanks why he or she came to Alaska, and the answer isn't to see the city you're standing in. The response usually starts out firmly with words such as "glaciers," "mountains," "grizzlies," "whales," or "salmon," and then the respondent's voice trails off like he or she didn't understand the question. Either that or it suddenly seems like a ridiculous thing to ask.

With few exceptions, travelers venture to Alaska to see the wilderness for which this state is so justly famed. They want to touch that wilderness, to breathe its clean air—most claim they can smell the freshness in the air—and to experience this kind of place just one time in their lives. After all, this is as far as we can travel in North America. Our centuries-old westward movement to the frontier has no place left to go. We've finally run out of continent.

That's not to say that this "last frontier" we call Alaska is in any great danger of disappearing soon, though certainly there are arguments every year over various parts of the state, as different groups try to tap resources with which this state is so richly blessed and others pull out all the stops to prevent them from doing so.

This also is not meant to say that we shouldn't have miners, loggers, and oil drillers —even rabid environmentalists. Alaska does harbor magnificent natural resources, resources that provide jobs for people and raw materials to build products. The major question is this: Where do you draw the line? The only obvious reply is that "all or nothing" is not a suitable answer for either side of the debate.

Wilderness as a resource takes many forms. There's the obvious—a home for diverse species of wildlife in significant numbers, an unspoiled place for Alaska natives to practice traditional lifestyles, vast deposits of minerals, and expansive forests that can provide lumber and pulp. Then there's the less-than-obvious. The wilderness that is Alaska's natural depository of minerals and timber is also the wilderness that lures travelers to the north. Tourism in Alaska, though not an extraction industry per se, depends every bit as much on vast forests and untouched backcountry as do the loggers, the miners, and the oil drillers. What travelers would venture to Alaska if every mountainside was clear cut, if every fjord held an oil platform, and if open-pit mines scarred all the broad vistas of the Interior?

Arguments on this subject rage back and forth through every newspaper in the country, mostly because determined people on both sides refuse to seek compromise. All of the industries named here can exist in Alaska—do exist now, in fact. And all can be safely expanded without destroying the last great wilderness region in the United States. Significantly, many of the people voicing positions on either side have never seen or experienced the wilderness they are arguing about. Truly, they do not realize the scope—the vastness—of this land.

Thus Alaskans, and the people who visit Alaska, often find themselves in the middle of a variety of emotional environmental debates, most of which could be settled via open discussion and education instead of through the courts, which is the usual avenue these days.

Take, for example, the grounding of the Exxon Valdez in Prince William Sound in March 1989, which was an absolutely inexcusable accident, no doubt about it. Sticky crude oil leached from the tanker and blackened hundreds and hundreds of miles of pristine shoreline, killing tens of thousands of seabirds, scores of eagles, and hundreds if not thousands of sea otters. That was industry at its worst, and the effects of this spill will be with us for a long time.

Yet, in the years since the accident, the sound has gradually come back. It is once again my favorite fishing hole, oyster farmers are raising succulent treats in its sheltered harbors, and oil tankers still sail across it on an almost daily basis. To be sure, there are still some biological problems thought to be resulting from the spill involving species as diverse as herring and killer whales, but I believe that with time even these situations will gradually be resolved. One key fact must be kept in mind: however big a mess it made, crude oil is still a natural part of the world-wide ecosystem.

Alaska remains a splendid destination for travelers, even Prince William Sound. Much of the sound remains untouched by oil, including the two most visited parts, Columbia Glacier and College Fjord. Although crude oil damaged a lot of coast-line, it still touched barely 2 percent of Alaska's shores.

This is certainly not meant to dampen the outrage and liability Exxon faced or in any way lessen the seriousness of the spill, but it does demonstrate that Alaska can still offer an unparalleled wilderness adventure to travelers, even in the midst of an industrial travesty. Those who drive to Alaska have the greatest opportunity to touch that wilderness and be a part of it for a brief interlude.

Why We Live in Alaska

There are, I suppose, drawbacks to living in Alaska, not the least of which are winter days with, at best, a couple hours of daylight. Then, too, there's the cold, particularly in the Interior around Fairbanks. It's not uncommon in Fairbanks to have weeks of bracing temperatures of 40 below zero and colder—that's actual air temperature, not wind-chill temperature. We have, on several occasions, seen temperatures of 60 below zero in Fairbanks.

Funny things happen to vehicles when the weather turns cold like that. Basically, they just don't like to run and only do so reluctantly, with much pleading and prodding from their owners. But that's another part of the challenge accepted by people who live in the North.

It's challenges like the cold that make this a special place and the people who live here the kind who are equal to almost any occasion—like the local wag in McGrath during the 1989 Iditarod who told a national television reporter from New York, "If it gets any warmer, we could grow bananas." It was a balmy 24 below zero at the time, and the reporter was doing a good bit of complaining. Most of McGrath was happy to see that particular reporter leave town to follow the race west.

Later that same day, after dark, a once-in-10-years display of the aurora borealis (northern lights) lit the night sky with reds, greens, and purples. As the temperature grew ever colder, I joined a group of bundled-up people who stared at the heavens for hours. That was one of those moments when we really knew why we lived in Alaska, the cold and the dark notwithstanding.

THE PEOPLE

Driving to Alaska also affords you the best way to get close to its people. Alaska is a special place, and its residents are special people. Only when you have met them and stayed with them will you know what I mean. Different writers have tried to describe these things for nearly a century now. The two who probably succeeded best are Jack London and Robert Service. Yet you can only get so much from words, regardless of who writes them. Alaska is still the stuff of legends and dreams; you have to experience it to believe it. Only then can you bring these stranger-than-fiction, larger-than-life tales to your unbelieving friends.

THE FIRSTHAND EXPERIENCE

Essentially there are three ways to get to Alaska: drive, fly, or take a cruise. Cruise ship passengers see a lot of wilderness passing by their windows, but they stay in a pampered, luxurious environment, with few options to actually experience the wilderness. Airliners fly 6 or 7 miles above the wilderness and deposit travelers in cities. Only drivers and their passengers, particularly those camping in either an RV or a tent, get firsthand experience actually living as part of the land. And only people driving to Alaska get a true

Mount Hunter, Denali National Park

Lake Louise, Banff National Park, Alberta, Canada

feeling for the vastness of the American North. Alaska itself is only one part of that vastness. To put Alaska in its proper perspective, one must first cross Canada's seemingly endless horizons.

It's one thing to see a temperate rain forest from the deck of a cruise ship, and quite another thing to drive through it, shaded by towering trees with a misty rain dampening your windshield.

It's one thing to see a glacier from a ship and marvel at the size of it, and quite another thing to park near a glacier, walk up to it, and chip ice for the cooler. As glacier ice melts, it makes a faint fizzing or snapping sound caused by the release of tiny air bubbles locked in the ice for untold centuries.

It's one thing to be told by the pilot of an airliner that you are flying over the last great wilderness on the continent, and quite another thing to stop at roadside and wander briefly on the edge of the wilderness, perhaps picking a handful of tart blueberries for tomorrow morning's pancakes, all the while looking over your shoulder for a bear that might consider this his berry patch.

It's one thing to see a bear at great distance along the shoreline of a fjord, and quite another thing to have one dart across the road in front of your car or wander through your campground in the evening. And yes, being that close to a bear should certainly make you edgy. That, too, is part of the wilderness, the knowledge that you don't fully control all you survey.

It's one thing to see a bright, sparkling stream from the air and be told that it's the purest water on Earth, and quite another thing to pull a feisty, glittering arctic grayling from that stream for your supper.

These differences—and others of similar ilk but too numerous to mention—are the reasons for overland travel to Alaska. To sail on a cruise ship or fly in an airliner is to miss out on the very experiences travelers seek in the North. And, most significantly, only those who drive can even begin to make an attempt at putting this majestic land in perspective.

CHAPTER 3
Selecting a Vehicle

Ultimately, the choice of a vehicle for an Alaska Highway adventure boils down to two deceptively simple questions: What do you want to do on the Alaska Highway, and how much money do you want to spend? One other consideration, of course, is the vehicle you currently own.

The first question can get complicated, particularly if you're sitting at home several thousand miles away from the Alaska Highway and planning your first trip. Do you want to drive straight through to Alaska in the shortest possible time? Do you want to linger at places along the way, places you can either plan for in advance or those you won't know until you see them? Is money a major factor—do you, for instance, have to get to Alaska and back cheaply? Who are your traveling companions—what do they want to do? Will you have a lot of luggage? Everybody who has ever planned a major driving trip has questions like these, which in this case all wrap neatly into the heading of what you want to accomplish on a trip to Alaska. Answers to these questions and others lead to the decisions made before the trip.

The money question is even more difficult because it seems so straightforward. Unfortunately, it isn't. The cost of driving the Alaska Highway may actually be cheaper for someone driving a big motorhome with its lousy gas mileage rather than for someone in an economy car stopping at a hotel or lodge each evening and dining in restaurants. The purchase price of the vehicle involved may be the overriding difference in this situation.

In terms of what not to drive to Alaska, the list is pretty simple. Stay away from the exotic. Though the odds are pretty good that any car made today will make it to Alaska, some are pretty much functionless along the highway and hard to obtain parts for if something goes wrong. Among these are vehicles such as Corvettes and other two-seat sports cars. At the other end of the scale are the Bentleys and Rolls-Royces. Getting parts to repair any of these kinds of vehicles on short notice would prove almost impossible in northwestern Canada and most of Alaska, outside of Anchorage and maybe Fairbanks if you're really lucky.

Insider's Tip

If you want to pull a trailer to carry extra equipment, avoid the small, single-wheel utility trailers that hold a couple hundred pounds of gear. These things routinely end up in roadside junkyards, mostly after the tiny tire goes flat, an event unnoticed by most drivers until the trailer has destroyed itself bouncing down the road on its frame.

Is there a happy medium in terms of cost, experiences, and comfort? Probably, though again the answer keeps coming back to your own aspirations for a driving trip to Alaska. A review of different categories of vehicles may offer some ideas when matched against your own wants and needs—and the vehicle you currently own.

Specialized Vehicle?

At different points in this chapter, I make specific recommendations for vehicles and campers I am familiar with. These recommendations are for those who may be thinking of purchasing a vehicle for an Alaska Highway trip. However, the strongest message I want this chapter to deliver is that a specialized vehicle is not necessary for the Alaska Highway. Virtually any vehicle sold in North America can handle the drive to and from Alaska, and each kind of vehicle offers different options for the trip. Also please note that all costs given in this chapter are figured in US currency.

ECONOMY CARS AND SMALL PICKUPS

People driving these kinds of vehicles have two options for overnighting—tent camping or motels. Both offer advantages and disadvantages.

The motel option allows for the greatest amount of driving time in any single day—there's no unpacking and repacking of the car each day and no wrestling with the pots and pans and stoves necessary to cook in camp. It also means you have to transport less equipment. However, staying in motels and eating in restaurants quickly eats up any cost savings derived from the great gas mileage offered by the vehicle. Staying in motels also reduces flexibility. You have to plan to be in a built-up area every night.

Tent campers won't go as far in a day as the motel stoppers, but the price will certainly be cheaper. Public campgrounds along the Alaska Highway run about $15–$20 a night. Private campgrounds—those with showers—average $25–$50 and occasionally require a handful of coins for a shower. Motels, on the other hand, start at about $75 a night for a room and go up from there. You're probably safe to figure on an average of $100–$125 a night with a little shopping around for cheaper places to stay.

Remember, too, that a motel, hotel, or lodge in Yukon Territory or rural Alaska is not likely to resemble a Holiday Inn along the Interstate in the lower 48. Away from the population centers, there's probably less than a 50-50 chance of having a television in your room. Bathrooms may be separate rooms down the hall shared by several guests—even outhouses in rare instances. You can, as a general rule, count on rooms being warm and reasonably clean. If you don't expect more than that, then you'll be pleasantly surprised at whatever else an enterprising owner is able to provide.

As for those staying under canvas, the major argument against tent camping is time. It takes a fair amount of effort each evening setting up camp and preparing meals, then again in the morning for breakfast and putting things away. Tent campers, unless they get up very early, rarely get on the road before late morning. This is particularly true if there are children in the party, which forces mom and dad to do a little extra work for the youngsters—things such as rolling up more sleeping bags, pitching the extra tent or a bigger tent, doing more dishes, and so on.

But camping is almost always worth the extra effort. People venture to northwestern Canada and Alaska because it is wilderness, because it's unlike anything they've ever seen before. Camping puts you right in the middle of what most people travel the Alaska Highway to see and do; camping makes you a part of the wilderness you've come to experience.

As for vehicles, any of the small, four-cylinder pickups on the market would be just fine for two adults either staying in motels or tent camping. Don't try to squeeze three people into one of these trucks, even if you routinely do so for buzzing around town back home. It's just too crowded for too long in the front seat of a mini-pickup with three adults crammed inside for a trip to Alaska. And, if you get one of these mini-pickups with an extended cab, don't even consider trying to put a third or even a fourth member of your party on the little fold-down jump seats that are normally supplied with these sorts of vehicles. Whoever gets sentenced to these jump seats for any length of time will quickly come to hate you, probably within the first 100 miles. The best mini-pickup I know of with seats for more than two people is the four-door Chevrolet Colorado and its GMC equivalent. You can actually seat up to four adults in reasonable comfort in one of these vehicles.

As for economy cars, a hatchback is better than a sedan and a station wagon is better than a hatchback. A trip to Alaska is a long trek, and you'll want to carry extra gear, generally much more than can be carried in the trunk of a small sedan. Manufacturers whose small cars are popular in the North include Subaru, Nissan, Toyota, and Ford. Small cars by other manufacturers will serve quite well, but these four brands are the ones most often seen around Fairbanks and Anchorage.

Besides clothing and other personal gear, drivers of small vehicles can carry along a car-top canoe or other small boat propelled by oars or paddles. Those with small pickups can also add a small outboard motor and the paraphernalia that goes along with it. Outboards and their fuel tanks are best left out of the interiors of small automobiles.

Mini-pickups can tow a lightweight trailer with relative ease, something on the order of a folding tent trailer or perhaps a lightweight boat. A word of caution, though: Gas mileage goes down when towing a trailer, usually a lot. Trailers also mean that you'll have to carry an additional spare tire and other equipment.

Don't Overload Your Vehicle

The major problem that small-vehicle operators should look out for is overloading the vehicle, particularly a small car. Overloading is almost certainly the biggest single cause of flat tires and broken suspension systems along the Alaska Highway. It is easily avoided.

Insider's Tip

Make sure your spare tire is exactly like the four on the ground. The small donut spares popular as a means of reducing weight in small cars are utterly worthless on the Alaska Highway. You need a full-size spare tire.

Molded into the rubber on the sidewall of your car's tires is the load capacity of the tire. Assuming you have the same tires on all four wheels, the load that can be safely carried by your car is four times the load capacity listed on one of the tires. This is the total weight of the car and its contents; the latter includes the people riding in the car. If your loaded car is going to exceed that capacity, replace your tires with tires designed to carry a greater load. Any competent tire dealer should be able to assist in selecting tires of greater load capacity for your vehicle.

If the car sags significantly when loaded, add heavy-duty shocks or air shocks, even heavier springs if necessary. These are fairly routine things that shouldn't take a mechanic more than a couple of hours. The relatively few hours and the minimal funds spent on getting just the right tires and reinforcing your suspension system are solid insurance against flat tires and broken suspension systems.

Also in regard to weight, every vehicle made has a gross vehicle rating, or GVR. This number can usually be found on a placard mounted on the inside of the driver's door. No matter what tires or other after-market accessories you might add, this weight should never be exceeded.

How Much Will It Cost?

Gas costs for a small car going from Dawson Creek to Fairbanks, roughly 1,500 miles, should be less than $200 (US). That's figuring 30 miles per gallon and an average price of $3.50 (US) per gallon of fuel. This fuel price and others in this chapter are based on gas costs along the Alaska Highway in the summer of 2016. At the time, most stations along the Alaska Highway were charging $1.259 cents (Canadian) per liter. Converting liters to gallons and Canadian currency to US dollars and costs worked out as described here. Appendix J offers a simple formula for converting liters and Canadian dollars into gallons and US dollars.

Five nights in a motel for two people plus three restaurant meals a day will total about $700, one way from Dawson Creek to Fairbanks. Five nights in a campground will run about $60, possibly less, plus $200 or so for groceries along the way. Tent campers should throw in a couple of extra bucks for a shower now and then.

Recommendations

MINI-PICKUP: Chevrolet Colorado or its GMC equivalent, four doors, four-cylinder engine, automatic transmission, with or without four-wheel drive. Relatively indestructible. Will deliver about 20–22 miles per gallon with four-wheel drive, a couple extra miles per gallon for two-wheel-drive models.

SMALL CAR: Subaru station wagon, manual transmission, four doors. Lots of value and reliable performance for the money. About 30 miles per gallon.

PICKUP TRUCKS

Far and away the favorite vehicles of northern residents are pickup trucks of any size or brand, usually four-wheel drive. The reason for this is simple: in a

Marl Brown, curator of the Fort Nelson Museum, sits behind the wheel of his operational 1908 Oldsmobile. In 2008 he drove it to Whitehorse and back, about 1,200 miles.

rugged environment, a stoutly built pickup offers multiple uses and requires no more care than a car.

Northerners haul firewood, moose meat, friends, snow machines, and all-terrain vehicles in the back of pickups. They drive them to work, they drive them to fishing holes, they pull trailers with pickups. Everything a car could do for them, a pickup can usually do better. Many veteran travelers on the Alaska Highway would make the same argument.

We're talking now about the mid-size or full-size pickups, pickups designed to haul or pull heavy loads, pickups that can be purchased with extended cabs to haul big loads and lots of people at the same time.

When it comes to selecting a pickup, once a pretty straightforward operation, things can get pretty confusing these days. American manufacturers offer three basic sizes: mini, mid-size, and full-size. Japanese manufacturers, on the other hand, may only offer one basic size in terms of outside dimensions, but the way a particular mini is built might upgrade its capabilities so they're similar to larger-size pickups. Essentially, these are the same pickups recommended as a mini-pickup elsewhere in this chapter, but the extra capabilities mean a larger engine, heavier construction, and a greater load-carrying capacity. Toyota, and now Nissan, have begun offering larger and larger pickups with powerful V-6 and V-8 engines. These offerings seem to be edging the Japanese automakers to the point where they will soon compete in what until now has been the last bastion of automotive engineering for American companies—the full-size, heavy-duty pickups. These are pretty much on a par with full-size American-made pickups, though not yet on a par with American pickups for hauling large cab-over campers.

If the various sizes alone aren't enough to confuse potential buyers, the variety of engine, transmission, and axle ratios available ought to be enough to drive anyone to the local tavern for some attitude adjustment. Pickups identical in appearance can vary in gas mileage from 10 or less to as much as 20 miles per gallon depending on engine and axle-ratio combinations.

Tire Choices

Then, too, there are those who live to see how far off the road they can get in their trucks. Four-wheel drive, big tires, and just about any other option imaginable are for them. They have a lot of fun and get to a lot of places in summer. The big tires, though, are lousy on ice. It's hard to stop a truck wearing that kind of rubber when the roads are icy. Narrow tires are much better on ice, providing the most pounds-per-square-inch on the road, which translates to better stopping power. Wide tires tend to "float" quite a bit on gravel roads at speeds above 40 miles per hour, which tends to make the truck weave from side to side. Unless you're a serious summer mud-bogger, stay away from the after-market wide tires.

Inside the dealer's showroom, when looking for a full-size pickup, three options are immediately apparent: half-ton, three-quarter-ton, and one-ton models. Supposedly these descriptions are based on load capacities. Things get goofy when the dealer tells you about heavy-duty three-quarter tons that can carry a ton and a half or more, or one-tonners that can carry two-ton loads, and so on.

How do you sort this all out? First, be certain in your mind ahead of time what you want a pickup to do. If you're not going to carry a big cab-over camper or pull a heavy trailer, smaller engines in half-ton trucks will do the job nicely, particularly in newer rigs that offer engine and transmission combinations that deliver 20 miles per gallon or more.

On the other end of the scale are the heavy haulers, the heavy-duty, three-quarter-ton and larger rigs, pickups with load range E tires, reinforced suspensions, and big engines. Gas mileage on these rigs can be much less than 10 miles per gallon up to around 15 miles per gallon, depending on the engine and axle ratio you select and the load you are going to carry or pull. These rigs will carry anything you're likely to put in them and pull trailers weighing 9,000 pounds or more.

The easiest way to sort out the axle-ratio problem is to remember that the smaller the number, the better the gas mileage. Take Chevrolet, for example. A three-quarter-ton Chevy pickup with a 350-cubic-inch engine (now known as a Vortec 5700 engine) is commonly available with three axle ratios: 3.43, 3.73, and 4.10. One of these numbers will be printed on the factory invoice provided with the truck. Given otherwise similar equipment, the 3.43 axle provides better mileage than the 3.73, the 3.73 better mileage than the 4.10. However, the 4.10 axle handles the bigger loads with much less effort. If you're going to haul a big camper or pull a big trailer with a pickup equipped with this engine, the 4.10 axle is probably the better choice; otherwise, you will find yourself operating in lower gears whenever there are hills to climb, the kind of driving that burns a lot of gas in just a few miles.

Another factor in selecting large pickups in recent years has been the increased popularity of diesel engines. A diesel engine will raise the purchase price of a three-quarter-ton or one-ton pickup by $4,500 or more. The tradeoff is better gas mileage. Diesel fuel generally runs 3–5 percent cheaper than regular gasoline in Canada. Diesel engines generally deliver at least 10–20 percent better mileage than gasoline engines, often even more. Also, if you plan to keep your pickup for a long time and put a lot of miles on it, diesel engines last much longer than gasoline engines.

It all boils down to the question of what you want out of your truck. Be sure of what you want before you wind up in a dealer's showroom talking to a salesman—and don't let the salesman talk you into more truck than you need.

Unless you already own one, purchasing one of the heavier-duty pickups is a waste of money if you just want to drive north in it and haul a couple of suitcases. In that situation, you're better off with a mini-pickup or even a passenger car.

If, however, you plan on some serious backcountry exploring, pulling a trailer, hauling a camper, or hunting moose, then a big truck is for you. Any of those items requires the power and the capacity that only a full-size, three-quarter-ton or larger pickup can offer.

Do you need four-wheel drive? Probably not, unless your trip extends into the winter months or you plan to do a lot of off-road driving. Given a choice, most Alaskans buying a pickup will opt for four-wheel drive if they have sufficient money—it does add about $2,500 to the cost of a full-size pickup. But these are people who spend six months or more driving on snow and ice where four-wheel drive makes a lot of difference in the daily commute.

Commonly, pickup trucks seen along the Alaska Highway, both two-wheel and four-wheel drive, carry campers of various shapes and sizes. The most basic camper is little more than a shell rigged over the truck bed in which the owner has built a simple bed and perhaps a couple of other conveniences. Top-of-the-line cab-over models may extend 3 feet past the rear bumper with a 7-foot or longer extension over the cab of the truck. These latter campers can be purchased with almost every convenience imaginable, including generators for 110-volt power, air conditioners, full-fledged showers with hot and cold water, and microwave ovens. (Who needs 110-volt power, you say? Just ask any teenager who has just stepped out of the shower with wet hair.)

While the camper shells will fit on trucks of any load capacity, it takes absolutely the biggest three-quarter-ton or one-ton models to safely haul the big cab-overs—that means Ford, Chevy, or Dodge. Each of these manufacturers will have options such as a camper-special package, reinforced springs, air-bag shock absorbers, transmission coolers, spare batteries with isolators, and so on. If you're planning to haul a big camper (or tow a heavy trailer), get them all—literally anything that says heavy duty. Getting them furnished with the pickup saves having to put them on later, and with some 3,000 pounds or more of camper, you'll want all these things sooner or later.

Installing a camper will require some minor modifications to your pickup truck; any competent camper dealer can make these easily. If you buy a used camper to install on your truck, your best option is engaging a camper dealer to make the modifications to your truck and to get everything in working order. At a minimum, you will need extended rear-view mirrors, a wiring harness for the camper, braces to hold the camper to the truck, some sort of trailer hitch system outside the bumper hitch on your pickup, and folding steps for entering the camper. Doing all this and doing it right is quite a chore for the first-time camper owner.

How Much Will It Cost?

Gas costs for a full-size pickup going from Dawson Creek to Fairbanks (about 1,500 miles) should be about $300 with no trailer or camper. With either a camper or trailer, gas costs will increase to about $500 or slightly more. Subtract about 15 percent from these costs for diesel-powered rigs when factoring in the increased mileage and cheaper cost for fuel in Canada.

Recommendations

FULL-SIZE PICKUP: Dodge Ram 3500 dual-wheel pickup with the Cummins diesel engine, automatic transmission, and cruise control. This pickup will deliver as much as 20 mpg when lightly loaded. It will carry the largest camper with ease and still deliver around 14 mpg while doing so. Chevy and Ford offer comparable pickups, and over the years I've owned one of each. However, I relied on the Dodge for more years than the other two combined.

PICKUP CAMPERS: Lance in Los Angeles builds probably the best line of pickup campers on the market today. Tightly built campers to fit pickups of all sizes are available. Prices may be slightly higher than other national brands, but Lance campers are definitely worth the extra money. Visit lancecamper.com for information.

TRAVEL TRAILERS

This category can encompass just about anything pulled behind a car or pickup, including fifth-wheel trailers. For our discussion, though, we'll stick with trailers designed for living aboard during your trip.

Far and away, sleep-aboard RVs are among the most popular vehicles on the Alaska Highway. Some would argue that in the past 30 years the Alaska Highway has been redesigned and rebuilt for RVs. Though that may be stretching things a bit, it's not hard to see that many campgrounds and side roads have been fixed up to allow for easier passage of these long, wide rigs.

Key things to look for in a trailer are tandem (two or even three) axles and all piping—water, propane, and sewer—tucked out of the way of flying gravel. The tandem axles are a safety requirement. Travel trailers can be somewhat top-heavy, and a sudden flat tire on a single-axle trailer may cause it to flip over.

Travel trailers come in two basic models, the first being a standard trailer with a square front that can be pulled by any vehicle, car or truck, with a suitable hitch and sufficient power and weight. The other kind would be the fifth-wheel trailer, increasingly seen following pickups to Alaska and across the lower 48 as well. The hitch for a fifth-wheel trailer sits in the middle of a pickup truck bed, and part of the living space inside the trailer, usually a bedroom, is accessed by stairs leading to a compartment above the trailer hitch.

Trailers range from the most basic with a couple of beds, a stove, and a hand-pump water system to the ultimate in luxury, fully carpeted with bathtubs, central heating, air-conditioning, and all the conveniences attainable. You'll see both the basic and the luxurious—and everything in between—on any given day along the Alaska Highway. And, very quickly, you'll realize the half-truth behind a favorite highway joke: the bigger the rig, the fewer people sleeping in it. Retired couples who spend much of their lives on the road generally have the biggest and most luxuriously appointed trailers. Younger couples with children and probably limited disposable income cram everybody inside a tiny trailer. Both groups have lots of fun on the Alaska Highway.

Recommendations

CAMPING TRAILERS: A 20- to 26-foot fifth-wheel or standard trailer made by one of the larger manufacturers. Stay away from the lesser-known brands whose warranties may not be accepted in the North's rural areas. The trailer should hold plenty of fresh water (25 gallons or more) and have holding tank capacity for all the water on board. Dump stations are infrequent along the highway. If you have the option, choose vinyl floors rather than carpeting; mud and dirt are much easier to clean off vinyl.

TOW VEHICLES: Any full-size pickup will suffice as a tow vehicle. Other capable tow vehicles include Chevrolet Suburbans, full-size Chevrolet Blazers, Ford

Broncos, and Dodge Durangos. Full-size automobiles with big engines will also work quite well, though these are increasingly rare. For smaller trailers, mid-size pickups and the scaled down versions of the Bronco, Blazer, and Durango are adequate, as are some downsized vans. Rear-wheel drive is much better for trailer towing than front-wheel drive.

MOTORHOMES

There are three basic configurations of motorhomes: Class C (mini), Class B (van conversions), and Class A. Class A motorhomes are the flat-fronted rigs that closely resemble buses. Class C motorhomes have a Ford or Chevy van front end with a cab-over compartment like a pickup camper. From behind the cab to the rear they are as wide, tall, and boxy looking as Class A motorhomes. Class B van conversions are standard, full-size vans with higher roof lines and as much camping gear as it's possible to stuff inside. Probably the original Class B motorhomes were the early Volkswagon van campers with the pop-up ceilings.

Class C motorhomes are available in lengths to 28 feet (commonly) or 32 feet (rarely), the shortest being 19 or 20 feet long. Class A motorhomes start at about 20 feet and go up from there all the way to Greyhound bus size—about 45 feet long. Rigs in the 32-foot to 40-foot length are the most common Class A motorhomes seen on the Alaska Highway. Class C motorhomes of 24 or 26 feet are the most frequently seen in this model. Class C motorhomes of this size are also the most commonly available vehicles from RV rental agencies in Alaska.

The most limiting factor on Class A and Class C motorhomes is the amount of overhang behind the rear wheels. The greater the overhang, the fewer places a rig can go—it will drag going through shallow ditches on campground turnoffs or swing out on a turn, possibly snagging on rocks or brush alongside narrow campground roads. Generally speaking, the longer the motorhome, the greater the overhang.

The most limiting factor for Class B motorhomes is storage space. Let's face it: by the time you cram in a double bed—probably a dinette that converts

Class A motorhome dry-camping at Teklanika Campground in Denali National Park

for sleeping—a tiny refrigerator, a cramped bathroom, a minuscule pantry, possibly a TV and a microwave, there just isn't a lot

of room left over. While gas mileage will almost certainly be better, living in one of these vehicles for an Alaska Highway trip will be an extreme exercise in togetherness for the people onboard.

If you do decide on a motorhome, be sure to hang mud flaps behind the rear wheels before starting north. Gravel kicked up by these wheels will quickly make the rear quarter panels look like the victims of several shotgun blasts if mud flaps are not used.

How Much Will It Cost?

Gas mileage on the bigger rigs is, you guessed it, lousy—about 7 miles per gallon. The reasons are quite simple: big engines and lots of weight. However, there's a lot of truth to a bumper sticker seen along the Alaska Highway: "Sure it gets lousy gas mileage for a car, but it gets great mileage for a house."

At 7 miles per gallon, it will cost about $750 just for the gas to drive from Dawson Creek to Fairbanks. But there are no hotel fees. Throw in $200 for food and $75 for campgrounds in the same period, and you can actually drive a motorhome from Dawson Creek to Fairbanks for about the same amount of money as folks in a small car who are staying in motels and eating in restaurants. Sounds ridiculous, but it's the truth.

The problem is the cost of the vehicle to start with. Well-equipped small cars and mini-pickups can be purchased new for $22,000–$28,000. Well-equipped motorhomes start at more than $75,000 and go up from there into the seven-figure range.

Recommendation

A 26-foot Class C motorhome from one of the major manufacturers should offer most of the comfort that motorhomes are prized for, yet it does so in a small enough package that you won't be overly limited in where you can go. Get the biggest engine available, an automatic transmission, and cruise control. You'll find these are easy rigs to drive.

WHICH OPTION IS BEST

Besides the pickups, small cars, and recreational vehicles described in this chapter, there are a multitude of other options available for those driving to Alaska. Broncos and Blazers, mentioned briefly, are quite popular. So are Jeep Cherokees,

Dodge Durangos, and a host of other vehicles, both foreign and domestic. As long as you stay away from the exotic, any vehicle made these days should handle the trip safely.

However, after 44 years of driving the highway, and using every one of these kinds of vehicles at least once (Nissan pickup, Jeep Wagoneer, Dodge Ramcharger, Winnebago Class A motorhome, Georgie Boy Class C motorhome, Ford F250 pickup, Dodge half-ton pickup, and Dodge one-ton pickup), if I were buying a rig just for an Alaska Highway trip, my preference would be a heavy-duty, one-ton, dual-wheel, diesel pickup truck and a large cab-over camper. This rig provides most of the comfort of a motorhome, though in somewhat more crowded conditions, and it offers almost unlimited flexibility. There is almost no place this rig won't go, gas mileage is generally better than with motorhomes, and, properly rigged, it handles exceptionally well. We used a rig like this for more than 15 years on the Alaska Highway and never regretted buying it. Only recently have we upgraded to a Class A motorhome, mostly because we're spending more and more time on the road in the lower 48 states and need the extra space.

Finally, camping—whether in a motorhome, trailer, pickup camper, or tent—goes a long way toward making an Alaska Highway trip a meaningful experience. Over the years, we've pulled over for the evening in old gravel pits at roadside just because a good-looking fishing stream flowed nearby, and we've stopped in campgrounds in stunningly picturesque places dozens of miles from the nearest motel or lodge. Campers can stop at their leisure, whenever they find something more to explore or just some scenery they want to savor. For most Alaska Highway adventurers, the extra effort required by camping is more than compensated by the additional opportunities it provides along the way.

THE CHEAPEST WAY Tent camping from a small car. Round-trip from Seattle to Fairbanks can be done for about $1,400 worth of gas, food, and campground fees.

THE MOST EXPENSIVE WAY Driving a big, gas-guzzling luxury car; staying in motels, hotels, or lodges; and dining in restaurants. Round-trip from Seattle to Fairbanks could cost as much as $5,000.

THE FASTEST WAY Driving a lightly loaded small car or pickup truck. Sharing the driving duties with a grown daughter, I've made it from Portland, Oregon, to our home near Anchorage in three days this way, averaging 800 miles and 15 hours of driving a day. This is definitely a prescription for a tired butt.

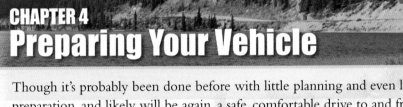

CHAPTER 4
Preparing Your Vehicle

Though it's probably been done before with little planning and even less preparation, and likely will be again, a safe, comfortable drive to and from Alaska requires a little work ahead of time. One should not suddenly decide to go, throw a change of clothing in a bag, back the car down the driveway, and head north. More than anything else, your car, truck, or RV—the chariot that will carry you on this northern adventure—needs some attention before you start. Nothing major should be required, just some fairly routine tasks that can all but ensure a safe and breakdown-free trip.

A quick check of a map of North America will give you some idea of why you want to put some time and perhaps a few dollars into your vehicle before starting out. A round-trip to Alaska from Seattle will easily put 5,000 miles on your vehicle. If you're starting in Florida, double that. And your car, truck, or RV gets to do all the work as well. At least you hope it gets to do all the work. If it breaks down and doesn't do the work you planned for it, you are going to be doing a lot of work in potentially unpleasant environments—like lying in the mud under your car on a rainy day. That's no way to spend even a small part of your vacation.

RUNNING GEAR

The best tires that you can buy will do more for your car on the Alaska Highway than anything else. Good tires can absorb some of the strain imposed by errant driving or less-than-efficient road crews. But, most of all, good tires will provide you with considerable peace of mind in a land where the few tires you might find to buy in an emergency could be frightfully expensive.

Steel-belted radials, ideally with an all-season tread instead of a straight summer tread, are the best way to go in the warm-weather months. The all-season tread might generate slightly more road noise on pavement, but it provides better traction when gravel roads are wet. Full-fledged snow tires and studded tires are unneeded during summer months; studded tires are, in fact, illegal in most areas between May and September. Winter drivers, however, will want studded snow tires on all four wheels and should carry tire chains as well for the really bad spots.

Be sure your spare tire is the equal of the four tires on the ground. There are a couple of reasons for this. If you should tear up one of your tires, you have an equivalent tire available as a replacement. The tire you first find to replace the destroyed one may have to be a compromise of sorts; few places along the highway have complete tire shops with all the various sizes available. The other reason for having a high-quality spare is that you might have to drive a good number of miles after a flat before you can find a place to get a tire fixed or replaced.

The last thing to remember about tires has already been said, but it bears repeating. Make sure the load capacity of your tires is equal to or greater than the actual weight of the loaded vehicle plus its occupants. To do otherwise is to risk catastrophic failure of one or more of your tires at highway speeds.

Equally important are your brakes. If you have the slightest doubt about the stopping ability of your car, take it to a mechanic and have him adjust or repair the brakes.

Particular things to look for are a brake pedal that fades—that is, it tends to take more and more pressure to maintain a given level of stopping power—and a grinding noise whenever you apply pressure to your brakes. If either of these conditions exist, get the brakes checked out.

A Note About Spare Tires

Two or more spares are probably not necessary. Many travelers on the Alaska Highway go to great lengths to carry extra spare tires, tying them to the roof or whatever. In more than 35 trips on the Alaska Highway in 44 years, I can remember only one instance when a traveler needed more than a single spare—my father-in-law's trip north in 1989. That year he had two flats in quick succession on his trailer in an area of road construction.

In the linkage that connects your transmission to the rear axle (assuming you have a rear-wheel-drive car) are two U-joints. These are at the ends of the drive shaft, the long steel shaft running down the center of the underside of your vehicle. If you hear or feel a distinct "clank" or "clunk" when you put the vehicle in gear, your U-joints are probably worn. Replacing them is a simple matter for any competent mechanic.

You can also check the U-joints by firmly grabbing the drive shaft and trying to twist it back and forth. A slight bit of play is normal, but if you have too much play, you'll again hear the clank or clunk sounds.

While you're under the car, look for signs of fluid leaks in three key areas: the rear differential (the bulge in the middle of the rear axle on rear-wheel-drive cars), around the transmission, and under the engine. If you find any evidence of leakage, check it out before you leave. You might also check around the inside of each wheel for evidence of leaking brake fluid.

Take a selection of wrenches underneath the car with you. Place a wrench on every nut and bolt you can reach to ensure that it is tight. In this case, a few minutes prevention is worth many hours of cure if it keeps bolts from wriggling loose as you jounce along gravel roads or roads roughened by frost heaves. Things like this are much easier to fix in your driveway ahead of time than they are somewhere at roadside in northwestern Canada or Alaska.

Well before your trip, test the loading of your vehicle. Place inside the vehicle all of the gear, clothing, and other items you plan to take north, along with all the people who will ride along. If the rear sags significantly under the load, your suspension system will need upgrading. You have several options, including reinforced springs, heavy-duty shocks, and adjustable air shocks. A mechanic can recommend which combination is best for your vehicle. A suspension system inadequate for the load will either fail itself or cause the failure of your tires, even if the tires are adequate for the loaded weight of the vehicle.

When you load your vehicle to test the suspension, take a few minutes to drive it to a truck scale near your home. Weighing a vehicle takes only a moment, and this is the best way to find out if the load-bearing capacity of your tires is equal to the load you plan to carry. Most states maintain weigh stations at regular intervals along major highways. A quick phone call to the state highway department should be sufficient for you to gain permission to have a vehicle weighed. Major trucking companies also have scales to check their vehicles before sending them out on a run. There may be a slight charge for this service, but it's well worth it. I weigh my vehicles at the local landfill, which weighs vehicles as they enter and leave and then charges by the pound for the amount of trash left behind.

ENGINE

Have a complete tune-up done by a competent mechanic before you set out for Alaska. At a minimum, this should consist of a compression check, timing check, spark-plug check/replacement, low- and high-speed idle adjustments, choke adjustment, cap and rotor check/replacement, fan belt check, and a check of all radiator and heater hoses. Modern vehicles need to be checked out on an appropriate engine analyzer to make certain all the computerized components are working properly.

Insider's Tip

Winter drivers should have the anti-freeze in the radiator adjusted so that it's adequate for temperatures of −40°F or colder.

If you are driving north in the winter months, have the mechanic install a circulating heater in the heater-hose system. This allows you to plug the car in at night to keep the engine moderately warm for easier starting in the morning. In the Far North, you'll soon notice that most parking lots have electric boxes by each stall to allow people to plug in their cars.

As part of the tune-up, have the oil and oil filter changed and ask for a complete lube job. Almost certainly you'll need another oil change somewhere in the course of your trip, but the lube job should hold you for the whole distance. For summer driving, most vehicles use 10W-30W or 10W-40W oil; in winter, 5W-30W or 5W-20W. Check the owner's manual for your vehicle to make certain these oils are suitable for your engine.

Along the highway, you may want to change oil more often than the owner's manual for your vehicle recommends. Lots of dust and the heavy loads common to vehicles driving the Alaska Highway are hard on engines. Thus, if the owner's manual recommends changes every 5,000 miles, you should probably change oil every 3,000 miles or so. Fresh oil is cheap insurance for your engine.

Start out with a new air filter as well—again, cheap insurance for the health of your engine.

Once your mechanic has done all these things and totaled up the bill, you need to add a few spare parts to the invoice before you pay him. Carry spare fan belts—many vehicles have two or more. Make sure you have one of each kind. Also buy a couple of cans of oil, a spare oil filter, air filter, radiator hoses, and heater hoses. You probably won't need any of these, except perhaps the oil filter, but if you do need them, there's a lot of security in having them at hand instead of hoping the next gas station along the highway might have the right size. The $50–$75 these extra parts will cost is well worth it. And if you don't need these parts along the way, you've got them available for the next time you tune up your car.

GENERAL ITEMS

Flying gravel kicked up by cars in front of you or by oncoming cars is tough on headlights. Carry at least one spare if yours are the sealed-beam headlamps, which are not very common on contemporary vehicles. Vehicles that have a four-headlight system will need two spares; the low-beam and high-beam lamps are different. Newer vehicles have quartz-halogen bulbs behind clear plastic lenses. Carry at least one spare bulb that fits your car.

Flying gravel chips windshields. Options here are few. Most insurance companies, however, don't hold you to your deductible for replacing a chipped windshield. If your insurance company does, ask for a slightly higher premium to cover broken glass for the duration of your trip. Also, most glass companies have begun repairing windshield chips before they can become a serious problem. A chip that hasn't yet started a major crack in the windshield can usually be repaired for $35 or less, and often your insurance company will pay for it, reasoning quite correctly that it's much cheaper than a windshield replacement.

Over the years, many ingenious devices have been rigged up to keep rocks from striking the windshield. Usually these take the form of a heavy wire screen held in place by a framework of aluminum or wood. Cumbersome in appearance, these do offer some protection, though probably the time and effort required to build them is worth more than the damage they might prevent.

Those driving pickups with campers or Class C motorhomes should fasten some sort of plastic or cardboard over the forward-facing window in the cab-over compartment. The glass in these windows is not the same strength as your windshield and can shatter easily. Duct tape will usually handle the installation with ease.

Flying gravel can also puncture your radiator, though this is fairly unlikely. If you're worried about this, fasten a heavy piece of window screening (not the new nylon material, but the old metal screen) over the outside of your grill. You can tie this in place with stout string, wire ties, or baling wire.

Underneath your vehicle, a few things may need doing for an easier trip. If your gas tank sits aft of the rear wheels, rig some sort of cover over the bottom of it. The easiest way is to loosen the metal straps that hold the tank in place and slide a rubber or flexible-plastic mat between the straps and the tank. Retightening the straps will firmly lock the rubber mat in place. If no straps are around your fuel tank and you feel you need to protect it, clean it off thoroughly and glue a mat over the bottom of the tank. Hardware stores carry a variety of suitable adhesives.

Insider's Tip

If you tow a trailer or other vehicle, mud flaps are a must.

Also underneath your vehicle, check for fuel filters in glass housings. Though not found much anymore, these were once fairly common on motorhomes. Needless to say, gravel kicked up by tires will make short work of any glass container on the underside of a vehicle.

Whether or not you pull a trailer or another vehicle, mud flaps are a good idea. Without them, gravel kicked up by your rear tires will quickly blast the paint off the rear quarter panels. Also, mud flaps reduce the amount of gravel you'll throw behind you into the path of following cars.

If your vehicle does not have outside rear-view mirrors on both sides, install them. These can be rented from a place such as U-Haul if you just want them for this trip and not as a permanent fixture on your car. Safety is the prime concern here; mirrors on both sides give you additional rear visibility. This is particularly important if you load a car so full that you can't see completely through the rear window.

Finally, check your windshield wipers. If the rubber blades have a season or two of use on them, it's best to replace them. These will get a workout on a trip to and from Alaska.

TOOLS

Even if you don't have the faintest idea of how to use tools, carry a basic set sufficient for minor repairs at roadside. If you don't know how to use tools to work on a car, almost certainly someone who stops to lend assistance will.

Here's a short list suitable for most eventualities, along with some odds and ends that belong in a toolbox. If you're so unfamiliar with tools that you don't know what these things are, ask a hardware store clerk for assistance:

- Claw hammer
- 10-inch crescent wrench
- 8-inch crescent wrench
- 3/8-inch drive socket set with ratchet (metric sockets for foreign-built vehicles)
- Set of box/open-end wrenches (metric wrenches for foreign-built vehicles)
- No. 1 and No. 2 common screwdrivers
- No. 1 and No. 2 Phillips screwdrivers
- Standard pliers
- Long-nose pliers
- Channel locks (big, adjustable pliers)
- Vice-grips
- Wire splicing tool
- Assorted wire connectors and terminals (available in kit form with the wire-splicing tool)
- Roll of electrical tape
- Flat file for metal
- Three-quarter ax
- Folding shovel

- Plastic bucket

- Roll of duct tape

- Tube of superglue

- Pair of coveralls

- Flashlight and batteries

- Battery jumper cables

- Roll of baling wire or stout string (60-pound-test or stouter monofilament fishing line is great)

- A pocketknife

Except for the jumper cables, coveralls, ax, shovel, and bucket, these items should fit easily into a fairly small toolbox that you can tuck behind or under your seat. Be sure to keep your tools where you can get to them easily.

Additionally, there are a couple of things provided with your vehicle, notably a jack, jack handle, and lug wrench for changing tires. If you pull a trailer, make certain your jack will fit the trailer and that you have a lug wrench available for the trailer wheels. It almost never fails that the lug nuts on trailers are of a different size than the lug nuts on the tow vehicle.

Motorhome drivers whose rigs are equipped with generators for 110-volt power will find an electric drill and a set of drill bits almost always come in handy. Or carry one of the battery-powered drills with a couple of fully charged batteries. Seems strange, but those who carry power drills almost always have cause to use them, whether for their own needs or while lending assistance at roadside.

A few extra items that you might want to carry along include the following:

- Can of brake fluid

- Bottle of windshield washer fluid

- Rivet gun and assortment of rivets (you'll need a hand drill or power drill to use these)

- Can of WD-40 lubricant or equivalent

- Vehicle tow strap

- Tarp or roll of heavy plastic sheeting

- Assortment of sheet-metal screws, nuts, and bolts

- 50 feet of quarter-inch nylon rope

- Window cleaner and roll of paper towels

Ideally, you'll never need to use any of these tools or spare parts anytime on your trip. Tens of thousands of people drive to Alaska and back each year and have little if any need of making repairs en route. However, there are so many variables involved with a trip of this nature, it's best to be prepared. Being prepared contributes to your confidence and helps solve any problems that might develop.

Here I am fixing the trailer wiring on my motorhome in Clinton, BC, during a trip from Alaska to Seattle.

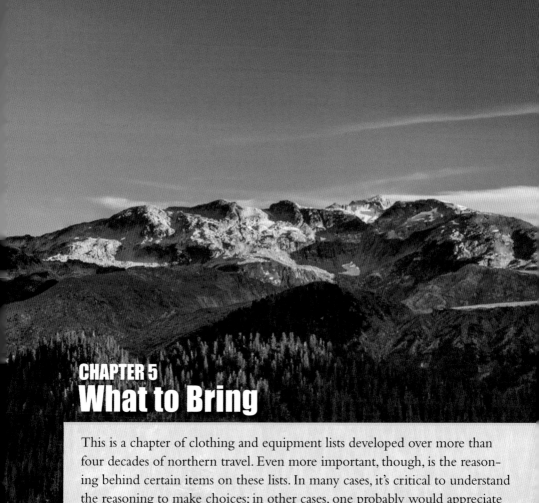

CHAPTER 5
What to Bring

This is a chapter of clothing and equipment lists developed over more than four decades of northern travel. Even more important, though, is the reasoning behind certain items on these lists. In many cases, it's critical to understand the reasoning to make choices; in other cases, one probably would appreciate the reasoning as a means of explanation for something that seems strange.

Nothing here qualifies as an earth-shattering revelation. Probably anyone else could come up with similar lists given sufficient time. And, almost certainly, everyone will want to expand, or even subtract from, these lists to meet his or her own particular needs. But these lists do provide for almost any eventuality, and, if followed, will yield all that anyone needs for a safe, comfortable driving trip to Alaska.

WHAT TO KEEP ON THE SEAT BESIDE YOU

This sometimes seems so obvious it's often overlooked. Then there's much grinding of teeth and swearing the first time a moose or a bear steps out alongside the road and you realize your camera or binoculars are buried somewhere in the trunk. Animals are not likely to wait patiently at roadside while you scramble around searching for things, especially if you have to get out of your car to do it.

- This book: Use it to keep up to date with the kinds of terrain you're traveling through and distances remaining to travel.
- A map
- Binoculars
- Camera
- Notebook and pencil: You never know when you might want to jot down the address of someone you meet—or even make a note of an error in this book so you can later send a testy e-mail to the author. Notebooks are good, too, for keeping track of where you take various pictures. You may also want to keep running totals of your expenses.

Insider's Tip

Never bring an orange tent to the Far North in the summer months. In a land that never darkens, trying to sleep inside an orange tent is like trying to sleep under a searchlight. Stick with darker greens, browns, and blues. You'll sleep lots better.

CAMPING GEAR

Tent Campers

Much of this list will also apply to motorhome/camper/travel trailer campers, though things here are held to more minimal levels in terms of utensils. RVs and their like have more room for that kind of gear.

Tent campers should pay particular attention to packing their camping gear. Most of the camping gear should be loaded last so it's immediately available when you stop to set up camp for the night.

TENT Allow sufficient space inside the tent for each person and some gear storage for that person, about 20 square feet or so per camper. If in doubt about tent space for the number of people in your party, take along another tent.

Tents should be lightweight but strong. And each tent should have a separate, detachable rain fly, a sewn-in floor, and mosquito netting. Big canvas wall tents, long a favorite in northern hunting camps, are unwieldy and far from insect proof. Used in semi-permanent hunting camps in the fall, for which they were designed, they're fine—usually few bugs are around then and you don't have to move the thing every day. Light, strong, weatherproof, and easy to set up and take down are the keys to a good tent for Alaska Highway travel.

When selecting a tent, pick one with stand-up headroom if you can. Lying in a pup tent while trying to wiggle into and out of your clothes gets old in a hurry.

As a final note, practice setting up and taking down your tent several times before you head north. This will pay big dividends if you're in a hurry (maybe it's raining) the first time you try to set it up on the road.

SMALL FLASHLIGHT There's nothing worse than stumbling around inside a dark-colored tent looking for a tiny piece of gear. A small flashlight, one that can be rolled up inside the tent when you break camp so it's always in the tent when you set it up, is handy. Don't forget to pack spare batteries and a spare bulb.

SLEEPING BAGS (one per person) Choices here are many and varied. Those who plan to be on the road only during June, July, and August need bags adequate for temperatures down to about 30°F. Those who will be on the road in May and September should have bags adequate for about 15°F temperatures. Tent campers in any other months of the year should have sleeping bags rated to −30°F or colder.

Bags filled with goose down are lightweight and compressible, as long as they are dry. Down offers absolutely no insulation when wet. However, bags lined with synthetic fibers such as Dupont's Hollofil are great insulators, wet or dry. Relatively light, the major disadvantage is that synthetic-filled bags are not readily compressible and occupy more space when packed away for traveling.

Bulkier and heavier cloth bags are fine, too, for car camping, again as long as they are dry. Don't expect these to be serviceable when wet or in temperatures much below freezing.

PAD OR AIR MATTRESS (one per person) A high-quality air mattress offers the best sleeping support possible for ground beds. But air mattresses are prone to developing leaks. If you choose to go with air mattresses, carry a repair kit and know how to use it. Also, air mattresses require a certain amount of effort each evening to inflate. If uncertain about your lung power, carry a small hand or foot pump—or even a battery-powered pump—to accomplish this task.

Pads come in a variety of materials. Probably the best pads available are part foam, part air mattress. Available in most outdoors stores, these roll up tightly. In camp, you unroll them, open the air valve, and the mattress partially inflates as the foam expands. Once that happens, a couple of breaths from the user fills them firmly.

Other pads include simple pieces of foam encased in a ripstop nylon shell, a dense urethane foam mattress that is very thin and light but offers surprising comfort, and such ingenious devices as a 6- by 2-foot piece of bubble wrap that will suffice for a couple of nights. Whichever way you choose to go, be sure to get full-length pads. Half- or three-quarter-length pads are available for backpackers, but these leave your feet and knees on the cold, hard ground.

For those who want to know how it's done by old-timers in the North, a tanned caribou hide is the answer. Dense, hollow hairs over pliable leather make sleeping in a snowbank a warm experience. Lay the hide out just as any other ground cloth, hair side up. You'll be thoroughly insulated from the ground and increase the comfort rating of your sleeping bag by a factor of 10 degrees or more. Shops in Alaska can sell you a tanned reindeer hide, which is the same thing.

Insider's Tip

Consider taking a pillow along for each person. These can be used by passengers in your vehicle for additional comfort while motoring down the road.

LIGHTWEIGHT DINING FLY This tarp should be packed last so it's the first thing out of your vehicle at camp. Prop it up over a campground picnic table with a couple of old tent poles or a pole from the woods and tie it to trees and bushes with stout cord. You should be able to walk under it from any direction without stooping. Be sure to slope the sides away from the center so rain will run off instead of pooling up on the tarp.

The idea of setting up a dining fly has been with us for decades—it's been in the Boy Scout Handbook for 100 years now—and probably qualifies as one of the best camping techniques around. Yet few people use it. A rain fly over your picnic table provides a dry place for cooking and eating, a place to stand outside of the weather without crawling into your tent, and a dry spot for packing and unpacking your gear. It should be the first thing you put up in camp and the last thing you take down. Tarps sized 12 by 16 feet are about right, with stout grommets sewn in at regular intervals around the outside edge.

Folding Camp Cots

Folding camp cots are generally more trouble than they're worth. They take up considerable space in the car, and sleeping on one is not nearly as warm as sleeping on the ground. If you do choose to use cots, carry a large supply of old newspapers. On cold nights, put several layers of newspapers on the cot before you put your sleeping bag on it; this will keep you surprisingly warm.

GAS LANTERN AND CARRYING CASE Buy a lantern that uses the same fuel as your camp stove, either propane or white gas. That saves having to carry around two different kinds of fuel supplies.

During summer, a lantern has little use as a light source in Alaskan camps—it never really gets dark. However, you'll have some camping in darkness in more southern climes as you head north or return home, so a lantern is a valid investment.

In camp in Alaska, there's an often overlooked function for lanterns—they are perfect devices for drying wet clothing or sleeping bags. Light the lantern, set it on the picnic table (which is under the rain fly), and rig a rack over the lantern to keep objects from actually touching it. The heat given off by the lantern will quickly dry damp clothes and sleeping bags placed on the rack above it.

Carry several extra mantles for your lantern and know how to install them. Any outdoor equipment store should be able to assist you in selecting the proper mantle for your lantern. Also pick up a small funnel for filling the lantern if you have a model that uses a liquid fuel.

CAMP STOVE (two or three burners) Though there's a lot of romance connected to the idea of cooking over an open fire in the north woods, in practice such an activity is a real pain. Smoke-blackened pots have to be scrubbed and scrubbed to get them clean, and few people have the skills necessary to properly regulate the heat from a fire, which leads to either burned or raw food.

By all means, have a campfire if you're able; it's the center of social activity in camp and a means of warmth. But do the bulk of your cooking on a camp stove; it's faster, cleaner, and simpler.

Insider's Tip

In a pinch, you can make a dining fly out of several yards of plastic sheeting that's at least four mils thick, though this will probably be usable only a couple of times before being ready for the trash. I do not, however, recommend sleeping under a lean-to made from clear plastic sheeting. Several bear attacks over the years have occurred when the bears attacked right through the plastic sheeting. The thinking is that bears can't quite understand what they can see through the plastic and thus rip it apart to investigate.

The Secret to Camp Cooking

Keep things simple and use as few dishes and utensils as possible. For example, if your menu calls for hot dogs, don't boil them in a pan of water. Cut a couple of green sticks, scrape the bark off one end, and have a wiener roast over the campfire. Other tips include things such as the pan used just for boiling water; it doesn't need to be washed. Or don't set out a full service of silverware for each meal; set out just those utensils needed or use plastic, disposable flatware. When you take time to think about it, you'll find that you can prepare wholesome meals using few dishes and utensils, all of which saves considerable time at cleanup.

KITCHEN UTENSILS This is a pretty basic list, but it covers most cooking situations likely to occur in camp:

- Two frying pans (with nonstick coating)
- Three pots of varying sizes
- Plastic or nylon spatula
- Wooden spoon
- Table knives (one per person with one spare)
- Forks (one per person with one spare)
- Teaspoons (one per person with two spares)
- Dinner plates (one per person with two spares for serving plates)—Use paper plates whenever possible for ease of cleanup.
- Bowls (one per person with two spares)—Again, paper products will make cleanup easier.
- Cups (one per person with one spare)—Tupperware offers a fine set of cups for campers and a good set of bowls with lids that double as small plates.
- Can opener
- Assorted kitchen knives

- Tongs for handling hot food
- Large fork and large spoon for cooking
- Two plastic tubs for doing dishes (about 18 inches square and 8 inches deep)—These tubs are also great containers for your kitchen utensils.
- Aluminum coffeepot—Even if you don't drink coffee or use instant coffee while camping, this is great for heating water for any hot drink.
- Containers for spices (salt, pepper, and whatever else you like)— Tupperware makes sets of these that are convenient, indestructible, and have lids to keep out moisture.
- Pot holders for handling pans
- Washrag for dishes

Kitchen extras, if you want to get fancy:

- Dutch oven for baking—It takes a certain amount of practice to get things right with coals from your fire, but once you've figured it out you can produce hot rolls, biscuits, pies, and any number of other goodies.
- Fireplace popcorn popper
- Corkscrew (for those romantics who want to share a bottle of wine around the fire)
- Portable charcoal broiler (with charcoal and charcoal lighter) or gas grill for barbecues—Several models fold into small packages for traveling.
- Colander (for draining pasta)
- Large griddle that fits over two burners on camp stove (great for hotcakes)

Kitchen disposables:

- Paper towels
- Aluminum foil
- Wooden matches
- Hand soap
- Dish soap
- SOS/Brillo pads or other pot scrubbers
- Garbage bags

Motorhomes/Campers/Travel Trailers

Obviously, tents, dining flies, sleeping pads, lanterns, and the like are unneeded here. And, depending on the rig, it's possible to leave sleeping bags behind as well and go with regular bedding. Other than those items, the above lists are valid in RVs as well as tents. However, the extra space and creature comforts available in these rigs offer added possibilities. Here are just a few items in that category.

ELECTRICAL APPLIANCES If your rig has a generator or if you expect to spend most nights in private campgrounds with electrical hookups, many of the devices in your kitchen at home will serve you well on a trip to Alaska. The biggest problem may be storage space, thus you may have to set a few priorities:

Insider's Tip
We've found that a camp stove is a valued addition to our RV supplies. Sometimes when the weather is great outdoors, you don't want to be cooped up inside to cook. And when we fry the fish we catch outdoors, the odor doesn't permeate our bedding.

- Toaster
- Blender
- Food processor
- Microwave oven (most rigs are equipped with these when they are built)
- Coffeemaker
- Electric griddle

For the refrigerator/freezer:

- Ice trays
- Plastic containers for mixed juices and other liquids

Extra utensils:

- Ice cream scoop
- Grater for cheese and vegetables
- Mounted paper towel rack
- Assorted baking pans
- Roasting pan
- Additional pots and pans of your choice

General Camping Gear for all Situations

- Three-quarter ax

- Folding shovel

- Plastic bucket

- Firewood saw

- Pocketknife for each member of the party old enough to use it safely. Avoid big sheath knives—a big knife on your belt signals greenhorn status. These knives have no real function other than decoration.

- Folding camp chairs (optional)

- Insect repellent

- Potable water

CLOTHING

Personal clothing—the jeans, socks, shirts, underwear, and whatever you wear from day to day—won't be subject to a list. Usually, sufficient changes of clothes good for five to seven days will suffice. About once a week, plan on devoting half a day or so to doing laundry. Most private campgrounds offer laundry facilities, and virtually all of the towns in the North have some sort of facility for doing laundry.

Shirts should be a mix of long- and short-sleeved. Shorts, in lieu of long pants, are optional, though be certain your week's worth of clothing does include several pairs of long pants.

For women, dresses or skirts are strictly optional in the North. You might want to include one for a fancier evening on the town in Anchorage or perhaps for church, but otherwise pants are acceptable in virtually every situation you're likely to encounter in northwestern Canada and Alaska.

For traveling in the colder months, wool is still the preferred material for pants and shirts, though some synthetics are making inroads here. Long underwear is a must as well. Besides routine personal clothing, here's a list of the other things you'll probably need.

RAINGEAR On a driving trip to Alaska, you can all but guarantee at least a couple of wet days. Raingear is thus a necessity. This can take two forms: either a full suit of raingear (pants and hooded jacket) or a hooded rain poncho that hangs almost to the ground. A trip to Alaska is an outdoor vacation, and raingear allows you to move around in the weather in relative comfort. Purchase raingear one size larger than you normally buy so you can wear it over a warm jacket. Temperatures are usually pretty cool when it rains in the North. GORE-TEX

Old hands in the North universally agree that you should dress in layers for dealing with the cold.

rainsuits are increasingly popular here. They're generally much more comfortable to wear than the heavier oil cloth or rubberized materials.

GLOVES/MITTENS Summer travelers will appreciate a lightweight pair of gloves. Winter travelers should carry heavily insulated mittens, even gauntlets.

WARM VEST OR JACKET Each traveler will need one or both of these. Summer temperatures in Alaska can range from just above freezing to 90°F or more. A jacket is a must. Winter travelers should have parkas.

CAP A baseball-type cap will usually suffice in the summer months. For spring, fall, and winter travel, stocking caps are best. Many travelers appreciate the stocking caps during cool, rainy summer days too.

FOOTWEAR Gym shoes or other comfortable shoes are adequate for most day-to-day uses in camp and on the road. Those planning to do more extensive day hikes or even add some backpacking to their trips will appreciate a hardier pair of hiking boots. Smooth-bottomed leather shoes are relatively functionless along the Alaska Highway. At a minimum, shoes should have dense foam rubber soles, molded rubber soles with some sort of tread pattern or, for hiking boots, lug soles made of Vibram or similar material. When selecting footwear for your trip, start with the realization that sometime on your trip you're going to get your feet wet and probably muddy. *Waterproof* and *washable* are the two key words to remember when selecting footwear.

SOCKS In addition to the socks you wear from day to day, pack a pair or two of heavy wool socks for each member of the party. Few things are more uncomfortable than cold feet, and wool socks will keep feet reasonably warm even when wet.

FISHING GEAR

A large variety of opportunities exists for fisher-men along the Alaska Highway and within Alaska. Along the highway, the primary species available are lake trout (to 30 pounds or more), northern pike (to 25 pounds), Dolly Varden (to about 4 pounds), and arctic grayling (to about 4 pounds).

In Alaska, these four species are also available along with five species of Pacific salmon (pinks [humpies], 3–10 pounds; sockeye [reds], 5–15 pounds; silvers [cohos], 8–20 pounds; chums [dog salmon], 10–25 pounds; and kings [chinooks], 15–90 pounds), rainbow trout (a few ounces to 25 pounds or more), Pacific halibut (10–400 pounds), and other saltwater fish, primarily different species of rockfish.

Trying to carry enough gear to cover all these situations is mind-boggling. However, you can narrow it down and allow yourself to cover most eventualities.

Spin- or Bait-Cast Fishing

Here's what you'll need:

- **A medium-weight rod** with reel capable of holding 150 yards or more of 15- to 20-pound test line. This rig will handle most situations for salmon, northern pike, and lake trout.

- **A lightweight rod** with reel holding up to 100 yards of 4- or 6-pound test line. This rod's for grayling, rainbows, and Dolly Varden.

- **Lures:** Popular lures for northern fishing include the following: Pixies—pounded silver spoons with a colorful plastic insert. Preferred insert colors are green and pink. Mepps spinners—the zero-size plain silver Mepps is probably the greatest grayling lure ever devised; the Mepps with a fluorescent green blade, size 1 or 2, seems to inspire a death wish in both rainbow and lake trout. Other Mepps spinners in a variety of colors and patterns up to the very largest will take every fish available in Alaska or northern Canada. Assorted spoons of varying sizes—red-and-white and black-and-white seem to be preferred color combinations. Large spoons are particularly effective for northern pike but will also work for salmon and lake trout. Rainbows and grayling will hit small spoons. Vibrax spinners are similar to Mepps spinners, but the lure body makes a buzzing sound when dragged through the water. Various sizes will catch all fish listed. Preferred colors seem to be plain silver or a silver blade with a blue body. Rapalla jigs—great for lake trout. Large sizes will take halibut.

Fishing for lake trout from the Tagish River bridge south of Whitehorse.

- **Baits:** More fish in Alaska fall to baits than lures. These are readily available in Alaska; there's no need to carry your own. Whole or cut-plug herring is available at most tackle stores in coastal areas. Troll or mooch for salmon and lake trout. Jig for halibut. Commercial salmon roe is available, but fresh roe from a salmon caught yourself is better. Usually big globs of it rigged on a treble hook bounced along the bottom will produce salmon in streams or big Dolly Varden. If you want to use fresh roe from a salmon you catch, you'll have to cure it before it will stay on the hook. Kits to cure salmon roe are available in most tackle stores and even in some grocery stores. Single salmon eggs are commercially available in jars from most tackle stores. Best for rainbows in lakes: Pat-ske's Balls o' Fire seem to be the most popular.

- Assortment of lead weights up to and including large 2-ounce weights for trolling
- Spare fishing line
- Varying sizes of swivels
- Long-nosed pliers
- Landing net (particularly needed if fishing from a boat)
- Club for subduing large fish
- Filet knife
- Flashers for trolling
- Folding gaff (needed for large fish caught from a boat)
- Steel leaders for northern pike
- Hip boots or chest waders
- Tackle box or other equipment container

Fly-Fishing

Other than rods, lures, flashers, lead weights, and steel leaders, most of the tackle listed under spin- and bait-casting will be needed here. Fly fishermen should also remember that big fish are caught primarily near stream bottoms. With the exception of grayling, fish deep for best success. Here are the additional items you'll need:

- **Rod designed for #8 or #9 line:** It should have plenty of backbone. Reel should carry fly line with a 10-foot, fast-sinking tip and 50 yards or more of 20-pound test or heavier backing. This is for salmon, northern pike, and big rainbows.

- **Rod designed for #5 or #6 line:** Use floating line. Backing is optional. This is for grayling and most trout fishing.

- **Flies:** Grayling is a fly fisherman's dream come true. Grayling will hit almost any small fly tied on a #10 hook or smaller, fished wet or dry. The most popular flies are winged black gnats and mosquitoes or a bit of pink and white chenille known locally as a "Salcha pink." Use a short leader, 4–6 feet long. To catch rainbows, use muddlers and woolly worms. Also try an egg-sucking leech and various egg patterns, the latter usually pink with a red eye. Northern pike like big, bright streamers in red-and-yellow or red-and-white. Rig the 12-inch shock tip of 40-pound leader material at the end of an 8- to 10 foot, 12-pound-test leader before tying on a fly. A pike's teeth will make short work of light line. Salmon also like big, bright streamers usually fished just off the bottom. Also popular is a fly called the Alaska MaryAnn. You may have to inquire locally in Alaska to find these. Try McAfee's Fly Shop (750 W. Dimond Blvd. in Anchorage, 907-344-1617) for MaryAnns and almost any other fly used in Alaska.

Boat Fishing

You'll need a few additional items if you plan to fish from a boat:

- **Life jackets (one per person):** Wear one at all times on the water. The water in most northern lakes and all Alaskan coastal regions is very cold. If you fall in, you likely will become quickly incapacitated and unable to swim.

- **Depth finder (also called fish finders):** Depending on the weather, fish will hold at different depths. These sonar devices will allow you to find them much faster.

- **Down riggers:** These are particularly effective when fishing in salt water for salmon or in deep lakes for lake trout.

- **Motor:** Get one suitable for extended slow trolling. Troll backward in calm water conditions if your motor won't run slow enough to troll effectively.

- **Large cooler:** Many Alaskans strap a large plastic garbage can in place near the transom to hold the fish they expect to catch. Fill one half full with crushed ice before starting out.

CAMERA EQUIPMENT

In the past 20 years, digital cameras have completely altered the photography land-scape. Very few people use film anymore, and with good reason: digital photogra-phy and digital darkrooms offer so many more options, allowing almost anyone to produce professional-quality pictures.

The most ubiquitous camera these days is built into a mobile phone; we use our phones to take billions of pictures every year. And it's possible to travel the Alaska Highway and take a large collection of nice pictures with your phone. I find this fairly limiting, however, and carry digital single-lens reflex cameras with a number of interchangeable lenses. Currently, my collection of lenses ranges from 16mm to 500mm, or very wide angle to extreme telephoto.

Digital photography, however, does require additional equipment to get the most out of it. You will need a means to store the digital files created by your camera, whether a computer or any one of a number of handy devices available in photo stores. After shooting pictures all day long, I never rest at night until my photos are taken from the card in the camera and stored on two different hard drives con-nected to my computer. Also, the Cloud offers tremendous opportunities for stor-ing anything digital, but you may not always have an internet connection at stopping places along the Alaska Highway.

Programs for properly processing your digital photographs will require a computer. Adobe Photoshop is considered the industry standard, but it's fairly expensive. Photo-shop Elements, also by Adobe, with many of the same features is adequate for most needs and costs only about $100. Another option that may suffice for many is Adobe Lightroom, which was primarily designed as a means of organizing and cataloging images, but has an ever-growing list of processing functions available.

The key thing to remember when thinking of photos on an Alaska Highway trip is the sheer variety of situations. You'll want to capture images of stunning scenic vistas as well as close-ups of bears and other wildlife. And while a wide-angle lens works well for scenic shots, it's not such a good idea when dealing with bears.

Finally, the most sophisticated camera equipment in the world produces few pic-tures if not used. If you're uncomfortable with single-lens-reflex cameras and the assortment of interchangeable lenses available, stick with the smaller cameras you normally use or your phone.

For those who prefer the high-tech world available to camera buffs, here are my recommendations:

CAMERA Carry one or two camera bodies of your favorite type. If you carry two, they should both have the same lens mounts so you don't have to carry two sets of lenses.

LENSES Take a 20mm wide-angle lens, which is great for working close up, such as when out fishing in a small boat; a 50mm "normal" lens should be fairly fast lens, f1.2 or f1.4 to provide more options when the light is weak; and a 35-105mm or 35-135mm zoom lens—if you dislike zooms, a series of lenses covering these ranges should be carried. The new generations of zoom lenses, however, pretty much mute the old arguments about zooms not being sharp enough; telephotos of 200mm or larger (optional)—these are primarily for those interested in photographing wildlife. They will require a tripod for best results, and these lenses tend to get fairly heavy if you have to carry them any distance.

TRIPOD Use one whenever possible. A tripod all but eliminates camera shake and almost always yields better pictures.

You may also want to carry the following items:

- Electronic flash
- Spare batteries for camera and flash
- UV or skylight filter on all lenses
- Polarizing filter
- Lens tissue
- Carrying bag for equipment

Digital Photography

CAMERAS The cost of a digital camera is usually in direct proportion to the number of pixels it produces on every image; the more pixels, the sharper the image. If prints of about 5 inches by 7 inches in size are satisfactory, all you need is 1.5–2 megapixels. If you want occasional 8-by-10-inch prints or wish to crop your photos extensively for smaller prints, you probably need something closer to 4 megapixels. Professional-quality work will require 6 megapixels or more.

STORAGE MEDIUM Most digital cameras these days use either a compact flash card, an SD card, or a memory stick to store images. Each of these devices is, in effect, your film, and each can be reused more or less indefinitely so long as you make time to download images regularly to your computer and clear the card for reuse. Cards and memory sticks are available in various sizes. I normally carry two

Insider's Tip

Digital cameras are notorious for "eating" batteries. Carry plenty of spares, or if yours uses a recharge-able battery, buy and carry a second battery with you.

256K compact flash cards for my smaller camera. Each card will hold about 100 high-resolution images taken with a 5-megapixel camera. Only once, frantically shooting pictures in every direction while in the middle of a herd of buffalo in Yellowstone National Park, did I ever worry about not having enough storage space. For my professional-level single-lens-reflex digital cameras, I use 8-gigabyte cards that allow about 300 of the highest-resolution images my camera is capable of taking. I carry at least three of these cards.

Midnight Sun, Dawson Dome

COMPUTER WITH CD BURNER AND A SUPPLY OF BLANK CDS Digital photos will quickly fill up the largest hard disk. After downloading the pictures from your storage medium, burn the files onto CDs or DVDs. (If you're shooting lots of digital video, you will need a DVD burner on your computer along with a supply of blank DVDs.) And don't forget the necessary cables and/or a card reader to connect your camera to your computer. Always make sure you back up your digital photo files every day.

FILE SIZE Most digital cameras give you the option of shooting pictures at various resolutions. For example, with my camera my 256K memory card will hold more than 600 low-resolution photos or, as noted above, about 100 high-resolution photos. Generally, it is best to shoot photos using the higher resolutions, particularly if you want to make prints from your pictures. Photos meant to be viewed only on a computer can be low resolution. But remember that you can downgrade a high-resolution photo for ease of use on a computer, but it is much more difficult to upgrade a low-resolution photo to make a better print.

Author's Note on Camera Gear

As a magazine editor years ago, I made part of my living taking photographs, often on very short notice. My ready bag contained only what I considered essential equipment —I really don't like lugging around a lot of gear. It held a Nikon FE2 camera body, a 20mm lens, a 50mm lens, and a 35-135mm zoom, along with an electronic flash. That plus 20 rolls of film and the filters listed here kept me instantly ready for any situation I had to face. Altogether, it weighed less than 10 pounds. On extended trips, I added a second Nikon camera body equipped with a 35-105mm zoom lens and additional film. This equipment plus a pocket-size Rollei 35 that I carried everywhere has never failed me. In the few instances a longer telephoto lens would have been handy, I simply used my feet to get closer. All of the older photographs in this book were taken with just the equipment in my ready bag. And, incidentally, the Rollei 35 that I carried in my pocket for so many years probably produced more pictures for publication than my Nikons for the simple reason that it was always in my pocket and available.

In the digital age, I now carry a Nikon D300S with a 16-85mm zoom lens on the camera and a 70-300mm zoom lens in the pocket of my vest. I travel with fewer pieces of gear but have much greater capability.

MISCELLANEOUS

These items don't necessarily fit in any category already discussed, but they represent several other necessities and good ideas.

DAY PACK Bring along a small one that can be wadded up and stuck in an odd corner. It's handy for carrying a lunch if you're exploring a trail or walking down the shore of a lake.

FIRST AID KIT An absolute necessity, as it's often a long way between medical facilities in the North.

SEWING KIT You never know when you might need to sew on a button or mend a sock.

TOILETRIES Everybody has his or her own favorites in this department, so a list is unneeded. It's a good idea to carry more than one towel per person, as these have many uses. Electrical devices such as hair dryers, curling irons, and electric shavers will work in Canada. Electrical power in Canada is delivered at 110 volts, just as in the United States.

ENTERTAINMENT A few odds and ends to support various hobbies or favorite leisure activities are nice to have along—to kill time on rainy days or for relaxation. Here are a few ideas: cribbage board; deck(s) of playing cards; sewing, knitting, or crochet projects; a favorite book or novel; travel games such as checkers or backgammon.

Packing

Mention has already been made about where to pack and carry certain items. In general, remember that the first thing you need should be the last thing packed; thus, the last thing you need should be the first thing packed.

It's also a good idea to use duffel bags instead of suitcases. Soft-sided containers are easier to put away in most cases. And, if you want to take advantage of some fly-in fishing trips while traveling, most pilots will insist on duffel bags for your gear. A wide variety of sizes are available, with some that open only at the narrow end and others that offer full-length zippers. Place a piece of adhesive tape on each bag and write on the tape the contents of that bag to save opening several bags searching for just one item.

When loading your vehicle, it's usually a good idea to put heavy items as far forward and as low as possible, particularly if you're driving a passenger car. This tends to shift more weight to the front wheels and results in a more stable ride. Also, pay attention to the weight you load to the right or left sides of a vehicle. Putting all the heavy items on one side may make your car or truck lean uncomfortably.

Kluane Lake Picnic

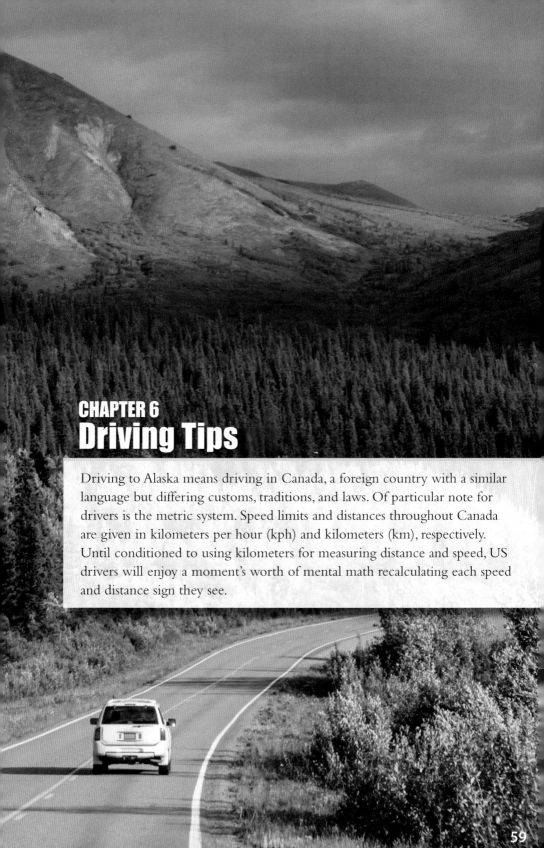

CHAPTER 6
Driving Tips

Driving to Alaska means driving in Canada, a foreign country with a similar language but differing customs, traditions, and laws. Of particular note for drivers is the metric system. Speed limits and distances throughout Canada are given in kilometers per hour (kph) and kilometers (km), respectively. Until conditioned to using kilometers for measuring distance and speed, US drivers will enjoy a moment's worth of mental math recalculating each speed and distance sign they see.

The road system in Canada differs in one major respect as well: no network of interstate highways laces the country together. Multilane, limited–access highways do exist, mostly near major cities, but these are relatively few.

The plus side, however, is that most of the Canadian roads leading to the start of the Alaska Highway are among the best-engineered and best-maintained roads in North America. Because of this, driving in Canada is an absolute delight. Only when you enter remote areas in northwestern Canada are roads less than excellent, and this is not for any lack of trying on the part of the Canadians. It's just that wilderness roads are frightfully expensive to build and maintain. Even these, however, are being continually upgraded.

Maintenance and road-repair crews will be highly visible almost everywhere in Canada during the summer months. Because Canada is a northern country with severe winters, extensive road maintenance and construction can only be performed in the warmer months. Delays occur for lengthy sections undergoing repair or rebuilding during the summer. Expect and plan for the delays—figure one or two delays of up to 30 minutes for each driving day.

Watch Out for Permafrost

In Alaska and northwestern Canada, for many folks there is an unexpected hazard— permafrost. Permafrost is permanently frozen ground underlying the surface of the land. It is constantly shifting, wreaking havoc with things such as highways. Often you can find ice (frozen ground) by digging a shallow hole, even in July or August. In places, that frozen ground is hundreds, even thousands, of feet thick.

Permafrost usually shows up in unexpected dips or bulges in the surface of paved roads. Hitting these at high speed can sometimes tear the suspension right out of a vehicle. Even the best-engineered and newest roads in Alaska and northern Canada can develop permafrost heaves within a few weeks. Road maintenance crews try their hardest to post signs warning of the worst of these, but there are so many in some years that it's hard for them to keep up.

When driving almost any road in Alaska or near the end of the Canadian portion of the road, watch the solid white line marking the road shoulder to your right, if one is provided. If it appears to squiggle up ahead, you are approaching an area of active permafrost heaving. Slow down.

In reality, getting to the start of the Alaska Highway is little different from driving on roads around your hometown. Once past Dawson Creek or entering the Cassiar Cutoff northbound at New Hazelton, British Columbia, things require a little more attention.

KPH/MPH Conversion Tables and Examples

Eighty percent of the Alaska Highway is in Canada, and Canada operates under the metric system. Distances are in kilometers; speed limits are in kilometers per hour.

The following speed conversions are accurate to within 1 or 2 mph:

10 kph = 6 mph	65 kph = 39 mph
20 kph = 12 mph	70 kph = 42 mph
25 kph = 15 mph	75 kph = 45 mph
30 kph = 18 mph	80 kph = 48 mph
35 kph = 21 mph	85 kph = 51 mph
40 kph = 24 mph	90 kph = 56 mph
45 kph = 27 mph	95 kph = 58 mph
50 kph = 30 mph	100 kph = 60 mph
55 kph = 33 mph	105 kph = 63 mph
60 kph = 36 mph	110 kph = 66 mph

The most-frequent speed-limit sign on two-lane rural roads is 90 kph, roughly equivalent to the 55 mph speed limit in the United States.

Distances convert on a similar pattern.

1 kilometer = 0.6 miles

100 kilometers = 60 miles

150 kilometers = 90 miles

200 kilometers = 120 miles

300 kilometers = 180 miles

If in doubt about converting any distance or speed, here's a simple solution: Multiply any figure given in kilometers by six, then drop the last digit of your answer for an approximate distance in miles. Examples:

243 km x 6 = 1,458

Drop the 8 and you have approximately 145 miles.

622 km x 6 = 3,732

Drop the 2 and you have approximately 373 miles.

92 kph x 6 = 552

Drop the 2 and you have 55 mph.

On the Alaska Highway, the first 300 miles or so from Dawson Creek to Fort Nelson are pretty much like the rest of Canada's major highways. Over the years, as more and more people have moved to this area, it's gradually been built up. There are no gravel stretches along here, and the road is high-grade asphalt.

Past Fort Nelson and on the Cassiar Cutoff, things get a little more remote, hence a little more exciting. Virtually the only long stretches of gravel road you'll find en route to Alaska these days are on the Cassiar. Any gravel encountered on the actual Alaska Highway will most likely be a patched area or a construction zone. The Campbell Highway running north and west out of Watson Lake, covered in a later chapter, is almost all gravel, but few travelers venture onto this road.

The pavement north from Fort Nelson won't necessarily be of the same quality as paved stretches already traveled. Often the pavement is made of crushed rock and oil compressed into a pavement-like surface by the vehicles driving over it, not asphalt laid down by paving machines. While this certainly makes for a solid, dependable road and one that is more easily repaired, it does offer some additional problems. This crushed-rock-and-oil pavement is known as chip seal.

Chip seal can be extremely slippery when wet. Slow down in the rain. Curves are not as likely to be banked adequately, and lower speed limits are posted for winding stretches. Heed these. Road shoulders are likely to be narrow or occasionally nonexistent and probably fairly soft when wet. Avoid slipping over to the road shoulders at highway speeds. Conversely, if forced to stop, pull as far to the side as possible. Try to avoid stopping in areas where cars coming from either direction cannot see you in plenty of time to either slow down or drive around you.

> **Insider's Tip**
>
> In Alaska, it is against the law not to pull over when five or more vehicles become stacked up behind you. It's also just good manners to do so, even when not required by law.

On the rare stretches of gravel road, high speed gets you into trouble, whether the road is wet or dry. Gravel roads create more friction, thus you increase fuel consumption when trying to maintain highway speeds. Loose gravel acts almost like ball bearings under your tires as well. It's much easier to get into a skid on gravel roads.

When wet, northern gravel roads act as if they have been greased. In Canada, a wetting agent is applied to most gravel roads to hold down the dust during warm, dry periods. This increases the slickness of the road during periods of rain. Slow down, way down.

Wet gravel roads also mean mud, and lots of it. Avoid tailgating—the car in front of you will quickly cover you with brown goo, which will harden to the consistency of concrete when the sun comes out. Watch out for oncoming vehicles, big trucks in particular. These can instantly throw enough water and mud on your vehicle to temporarily blind you. Keep your windshield wipers going constantly and make certain you have an adequate supply of fluid in your windshield washing system.

Dust, even though it is partially controlled by wetting agents, can be unbelievable during dry periods or where road crews are spreading rock for new chip seal. Again, avoid tailgating and watch carefully for dust clouds thrown up by oncoming vehicles. Under certain conditions, it's wise to slow almost to a stop and pull as far to the right as possible when a dust cloud threatens to engulf you. Losing all visibility, as often happens for a few seconds, when you're traveling 50 mph (80 kph) can be extremely hazardous.

Insider's Tip

Absolutely the worst tires available for highway-speed driving on gravel roads are the oversize, wider-than-normal, high-flotation tires favored by off-road enthusiasts. These tires tend to float on gravel and can make vehicle control marginal at speeds of 50 mph (80 kph) or faster. Use the narrowest tires that offer adequate strength for your loaded vehicle.

Watch your rear-view mirror carefully at all times. Many long stretches of the Alaska Highway and side roads offer limited opportunities for passing. If traffic starts stacking up behind you, pull over at the first opportunity so those vehicles can get around.

Plan for frequent stops. Driving on narrow, winding roads, in heavy dust, or on rain-slick highways takes a lot of concentration. You'll be much safer if you take some time to relax and refresh yourself at frequent intervals.

Once on the Alaska Highway system, don't be overly ambitious in your daily driving goals. About 300 miles (500 km) a day allows plenty of time to stop and check out the scenery or wildlife and does not commit you to a frantic "I have to get there" pace. The traveling chapters in this book are broken down into segments of about 300 miles per day for this reason.

When planning your trip, allow plenty of flexibility in your schedule. It would be a shame, for example, to allow just a lunch stop near a lake and then find out that the lake trout were really biting. Be able to take a day out of your schedule now and then to sample the fishing or hike a trail you didn't expect to find. Your trip will be much more meaningful for doing so.

When on the Alaska Highway, its side roads, or on alternate routes, drive with your headlights on at all times. It's the law on portions of the road in Yukon, Canada, and it makes sense.

Broken down into basics, these five simple rules will go far to make your trip safe and comfortable:

Insider's Tip

When you stop for gas and to clean your windshield, take a moment to wipe off your headlights and tail-lights as well. These can be covered with mud just as easily as any other part of your vehicle.

• Slow down, particularly on gravel roads.

• Allow plenty of time.

• Drive with headlights on at all times.

• Plan a flexible travel schedule.

• Be a courteous driver.

In reality, nothing on this short list is more than plain common sense. Most people driving to and from Alaska ultimately recognize these simple truisms. You'll be ahead of the game if you start out with them in mind. A safe, rewarding trip to and from Alaska is best achieved if you heed three simple words: take your time.

CHAPTER 7
Dealing with Fuel Costs

Consider tiny Point Roberts, Washington. This small town on the Canadian border in western Washington has some of the highest per-gallon gasoline costs in the United States. But the main economic engine driving the town's economy is the large number of Canadians from the Vancouver, British Columbia, area who duck across the border to fill up their cars, pickups, and SUVs. To help serve this market, in Point Roberts you can buy gas either by the gallon for US dollars or by the liter for Canadian dollars.

In other words, no matter how bad we think the cost of gasoline might be in the United States, it's always worse in Canada—anywhere in Canada, not just the remote areas along the Alaska Highway. This was certainly true in 2016. Gasoline prices in Canada varied for the most part a couple of cents per liter from the southern end of the country to the northern end—at least in the prices we paid for fuel. It was certainly possible to have paid a lot more, but there are still a few tricks you can use to make things a little less costly. Some of these tricks test your shopping skills, and some of them relate to your driving skills.

MAXIMIZE YOUR MILEAGE

Before getting into where and how to buy fuel en route to Alaska, take a good look at your vehicle. You can do some pretty simple things to extend your mileage and thus get the biggest bang for your fuel-purchase buck.

ENGINE An engine tuned up for maximum efficiency is the first step, and a surprising number of people ignore this. It doesn't cost much, it extends the life of your vehicle, and it just makes sense. Why spend money buying extra gasoline or diesel fuel to feed an engine that is not working at peak efficiency? Make sure your vehicle is tuned up and running right before you head north. This alone will pay for itself in fuel savings.

TIRES Once your vehicle is tuned up and before you hit the road, check the air pressure in all of the tires, both on the vehicle you are driving and on anything you are towing. Inflate each tire to the manufacturer's recommended maximum inflation. This information is molded into the sidewall of the tire, usually as part of a statement that says something like, MAX LOAD SINGLE 2120KG (4675 LBS) AT 760KPA (110 PSI) or MAX LOAD DUAL 2000KG (4410 LBS) AT 760KPA (110 PSI). Those are the words from the tires on my motorhome. Basically that tells me to inflate my tires to 110 pounds per square inch of air pressure if I want the maximum pressure. The reason you inflate to maximum is to reduce rolling friction, which means your engine doesn't work as hard.

Be sure the tires are cold when you inflate them. As you drive, heat builds up in the tires and actually increases the air pressure. Thus 110 pounds of air in a warm tire will be considerably less after the vehicle sits overnight. Tires are designed to be filled when they are cold. As long as they are kept within the specified limits, they will handle the increased pressure that comes from driving down the road.

Your tires are probably different from mine, so check what's molded into the sidewall before you inflate them to maximum. Few tires require 110 psi of air pressure.

Inflating your tires to maximum will probably make the vehicle ride just slightly rougher because the tires won't be as soft and as able to absorb some of the bumps. The difference is negligible, in my opinion. The results, though, are actually measurable at the gas pump. This one thing alone kicked up the mileage in my motorhome about a tenth of a mile per gallon. That doesn't sound like much at first, but I drive a lot of miles in my motorhome, and for every 1,000 gallons of diesel I put in the tank, that equates to 100 free miles of fuel.

LIGHTEN THE LOAD Go through your vehicle ruthlessly and unload any excess items. In other words, don't take along anything you don't need. Almost every one of us tends to carry way too much stuff on an Alaska Highway adventure, and every bit of weight that you haul will bring your fuel mileage down. The lighter the load, the farther you can go on a gallon of gas. The results on your gas mileage may be hard to measure but will add up considerably over time and distance.

Some of the things I found going through my motorhome might help illustrate this point. For example, we really did not need service for eight of heavy plates, cups, bowls, and saucers. Our motorhome can entertain six, feed four, and sleep two, so anything beyond four dinner plates, plus a spare to use for serving, is overkill. Applying this thought to the whole set of dishes saved us almost 15 pounds.

Our motorhome came with a built-in cutting board. Why were we carrying two others? Three more pounds were off-loaded right there.

Did we really need two campground directories and two road atlases? No. Another six pounds lighter.

Did we really need to carry 100 gallons of water with us everywhere we went? By cutting back to a half-full water tank, we saved about 300 pounds. Starting out with an empty gray water tank whenever possible also saved us 100–200 pounds, depending on how much we used it the night before. Exceptions include when you expect to be camping without hookups for several days, but for the most part we found that we rarely needed more than half a tank of water.

Some people cutting back on weight will also refrain from topping off their fuel tanks, relying instead on the ability to stop every couple of hours and add a few gallons. I don't particularly care for that idea on the Alaska Highway. I tend to fill up completely every time I stop for fuel in order to take advantage of price (when possible) and recognizing that it can be a long way between gas stations in the far north.

By now you get the idea. We could probably cut back more than 1,000 pounds in our rig if we work at it. My wife is finally getting through to me that I probably don't need four sets of irons and every other golf club ever created. If I give in to her on this one, we'll probably save another 40 or 50 pounds.

LEARN HOW YOUR VEHICLE HANDLES By this I don't mean knowing how the various controls work. You need to experiment some to find out just how your vehicle handles different driving situations. For example, my motorhome as typically loaded gets better fuel mileage at 60 mph than it does at 55 mph. That's because at 55 mph the transmission will just barely get into overdrive and will have no momentum to keep it there if I run into a slight upgrade or a headwind. At 60 mph, on the other hand, the transmission will not shift down until the speed falls off by at least 3 miles per hour, which means it can handle modest wind gusts and small grades. By keeping the rig in overdrive, the fuel mileage increases.

Of course, if I turn off the overdrive, the reverse is true. Mileage will be better at 55 than at 60, though both will be worse than the mileage with the overdrive engaged. And there are some situations in the mountains and towing heavy loads where it is best to turn off the overdrive. Check your vehicle owner's manual for recommendations in this regard.

Every vehicle has quirks like this one. The only way to figure them out is to operate the vehicle at different speeds and under different conditions and keep careful records of your mileage. As you do, you'll soon begin to see patterns emerge.

DRIVING HABITS How you drive can greatly affect your gas mileage. For instance, have you ever watched a long-haul trucker approach a stoplight at a crawl so he never comes to a complete stop before the light changes from red to green? By not having to come to a complete stop, he saves a few drops of fuel at every stoplight, something that adds up over time, and it's a technique that will work for you as well.

On the other end of the scale are people like a certain one of my unnamed relatives. I routinely chide him for driving like the brake and the gas pedals have only two positions, on and off. His jackrabbit starts and sudden stops qualify as probably the least fuel-efficient way to drive. He even does this when pulling his travel trailer.

Many people use cruise control to keep things smooth and steady, and for the most part this works great. There are situations, however, where cruise control can actually lower your gas mileage, and the Alaska Highway is filled with them.

When you are using cruise control, an electronic signal tells your engine to deliver more or less power as needed to maintain the speed you have selected. Where you get in trouble with mileage, particularly with larger, heavier rigs, is climbing a hill. In trying to keep you at speed, the cruise control signal for more power will cause the transmission to shift into a lower gear, and in cases of steep hills maybe two or even three gears lower. In an effort to maintain speed, the cruise control will then cause your engine to operate at maximum power, just like you putting your foot to the floorboard. A slightly slower speed in a higher gear will save you a lot of gas on

> Smooth *and* steady *are generally the operative words for the best mileage when you drive, whatever kind of rig you own.*

hills like these. Doing so, though, will require shutting off the cruise control and using the accelerator to select the appropriate amount of power.

In the hills along the Alaska Highway, if I leave the cruise control on, my engine will routinely wind up to almost maximum rpms when trying to maintain speed on various hills. By taking manual control of the throttle, I can usually bring the rpms down, though it means I will climb the hill at a slower speed. Do this a couple of hundred times a day and I guarantee you will raise your gas mileage.

PERFORMANCE PACKAGES Believe it or not, some of these really work. My first motorhome was gasoline powered and, as it came from the factory, it generally delivered just under 7 mpg. After considerable thought and research, I paid about $1,400 to have a performance package put on the engine, which yielded about 50 more horsepower and almost another 100 foot pounds of torque. My gas mileage immediately increased to more than 8 mpg. With the increase in gas mileage, this package paid for itself in about 12,000 miles, about a quarter of it on the Alaska Highway.

How exactly does this work? Basically it's the increased horsepower that does the trick. Prior to gaining the extra horsepower, the slightest headwind or upgrade would cause my rig to shift into a lower gear to maintain speed. The extra horsepower keeps me in overdrive, which offers the best gas mileage at highway speeds.

This extra power is most noticeable on hills. When using cruise control, I describe upgrades in terms of one-gear, two-gear, and three-gear hills, referring to the number of times the transmission shifts down to try and maintain speed. With the extra power, I rarely see a three-gear hill anymore, and it takes a lot steeper hill to cause the transmission to shift down one or two gears.

Before you purchase a performance package, spend some time in RV parks talking to people who have used the various brands on rigs similar to yours. And it's not necessary to go whole hog. The $1,400 I spent was only part of a total package that would have retailed for around $3,000 to have the whole thing installed. I put on only those things I was certain would contribute most to an increase in gas mileage.

THE COST OF GAS

If you drive to Alaska, at least 2,000 miles of the trip will be in Canada. During 2016, most Canadian gas stations were selling unleaded regular for about $1.099 (Canadian currency) per liter. The conversion rate at the time was about 25 percent, which means the Canadian dollar was worth only about $0.75 in US currency. Thus the actual price per liter came in around $0.82 in US funds.

Certain areas you might visit on your trip—Dawson City, Yukon, for example—will charge considerably more. Typically gas there goes for 25–30 cents more a liter than in other areas, which will push your costs to well over $4 (US currency) for one gallon of fuel based on the currency conversion rate in 2016. Another community with what I feel are unrealistically high fuel costs is Fort Nelson, British Columbia. Fuel costs there are typically 20 cents more a liter than in Whitehorse, Yukon, another 600 miles up the Alaska Highway. In 2016, gas in Fort Nelson was $1.299 per liter. When I passed through Whitehorse two days later, I purchased gas for $1.099.

If you drive a large rig that often takes 200 liters or more at a fill-up, you can see the difference just a few cents per liter will make in your wallet. The trick is finding the stations with the best prices for gas and planning your fuel stops accordingly.

Calculating where to get the best gas prices along the Alaska Highway used to be pretty simple—fill up in the larger towns and avoid the small mom-and-pop stations in outlying areas. Not so anymore. The best deal we have found for fuel for the past several years along the Alaska Highway is at Contact Creek, a two-pump, log-cabin filling station about 40 miles south of Watson Lake. The owner generally sells his gas for 2–5 cents a liter cheaper than any we could find in Watson Lake.

The most expensive fuel we found in larger towns in 2016, oddly enough, was at Fort Nelson, a town connected to the

Remote gas station

Canadian Rail system and easily accessible via road, transportation options that should have kept fuel prices fairly low. Thus, it's often hard to predict where you'll find the best deals for fuel. However, the following list offers some solid recommendations about when to purchase fuel and when to avoid purchasing it, if possible.

- Northbound: Put in all the fuel you can hold at Dawson Creek at the start of the Alaska Highway or at New Hazelton at the start of the Cassiar Highway. We found a good price for fuel at the Farmington Store, about 15 miles up the road from Dawson Creek.

- Southbound: Fill in Tok before you leave Alaska and enter Canada, no matter how high the price seems. It will still be cheaper than any gas you buy in Canada. Border City Lodge just inside Alaska from Canada once had fuel at a good price, but I found in 2016 that they had raised their prices such that gas cost more there than it did in Canada after applying the currency conversion rate. I no longer stop there like I used to.

- In built-up areas with more than one gas station, avoid those stations that do not have the price posted so it is visible from the road. In our experience, the stations that don't post their prices charge the most.

- Don't stop at the first gas station you see if you are in a built-up area. Look things over carefully before making your choice.

- Do not buy gas at Junction 37 Services, 13 miles north of Watson Lake where the Cassiar Highway joins the Alaska Highway. The price here is almost always a nickel or more per liter higher than you'll pay in Watson Lake. And gas in Watson Lake is almost always two cents or more expensive than gas at Contact Creek, 40 miles farther down the road. If you're northbound at Junction 37 Services, another 50 miles or so will bring you to Rancheria, which generally sells gas for several cents less per liter.

- For the past few years, the cheapest gas in Whitehorse and Fort Nelson has been at Fas Gas stations.

- In Alaska, avoid refueling at Glennallen. This road junction, a little more than halfway between Anchorage and Tok on the Glenn Highway, charges almost the highest price for gas anywhere on the Alaska road system.

- Avoid filling up in the built-up area near the entrance to Denali National Park. The gas here will make even Glennallen's prices look cheap.

- One last trick is to fill up in the morning when temperatures are cool. Gasoline and diesel tend to expand slightly as the day warms, and what was 100 gallons of fuel the afternoon before may be only 98 gallons in the morning.

CHAPTER 8
Choosing a Route

Just getting to the start of the Alaska Highway will be an adventure for most people. There are dozens of possibilities. In the following pages, suggested and alternate routings are presented for people starting from anywhere in the United States or Canada. All lead to a single town in northern British Columbia, Dawson Creek, Milepost 0 of the Alaska Highway.

In this chapter the United States and Canada are broken down into four distinct regions: the West Coast (California, Oregon, Washington, and British Columbia); the Rocky Mountain states together with the western plains (the latter including Texas, Oklahoma, Kansas, Nebraska, South Dakota, North Dakota, Alberta, and Saskatchewan); the Midwest (essentially the Mississippi Valley states, Manitoba, and western Ontario); and the East (everything from Florida to Quebec, including Canada's maritime provinces).

Sample routing is provided from a major US city in each of these regions, as well as an alternate route for those desiring some options. Primary routes were chosen by the simple expedient of selecting the shortest driving distance from the sample city to Dawson Creek. To vary your trip, consider using one route northbound and the other for your return.

Mileages are rounded to the nearest 50. Trips to and from Dawson Creek are figured at about 450 miles a day, which should prove a comfortable figure on the better roads stretching across the built-up parts of North America.

Those who don't live in the cities featured will have to adjust their own travel times and distances based on their individual situations. For example, the West Coast trip as defined here starts in San Francisco. If you live in Los Angeles, add an extra day and 380 miles (one way) to the figures presented as part of the sample trip.

For ease in finding a suggested route most appropriate to your home, this chapter is broken into four sections based on the regions described above. Choose the one most appropriate for where you live.

WEST COAST PRIMARY ROUTE

Travelers heading for Alaska from the West Coast have available the most obvious routing to Dawson Creek, British Columbia. Just head north.

Mount St. Helens near Interstate 5 in Washington

West Coast Primary Route

San Francisco, California, to Dawson Creek, British Columbia

TIME REQUIRED: 4 days (without side trips)

MILEAGE: 1,650 miles (2,750 kilometers)

OVERNIGHT STOPS: Grants Pass, Oregon

Seattle, Washington

100 Mile House, British Columbia

Dawson Creek, British Columbia

POSSIBLE SIDE TRIPS EN ROUTE *(and minimum additional time required):*

Crater Lake National Park, Oregon *(one day)*

Columbia River Gorge National Scenic Area *(one day)*

Mount St. Helens National Volcanic Monument *(half day)*

Olympic National Park *(two days)*

Mount Rainier National Park, Washington *(one day)*

Vancouver Island, British Columbia *(two days)*

ROUTING:

• *San Francisco to Grants Pass:*

I-80, San Francisco to Sacramento

I-5 Sacramento to Grants Pass

• *Grants Pass to Seattle:* I-5

• *Seattle to 100 Mile House:*

I-5 to Canada 1 (at or near Vancouver)

Canada 1 to Cache Creek, British Columbia

Canada 97, Cache Creek to 100 Mile House

• *100 Mile House to Dawson Creek:* Canada 97

But what you have along the way is nothing short of spectacular. Using the primary routing north from San Francisco, start by heading east on Interstate 80 to Sacramento, California, where you intersect the major north-south route in the West Coast states—Interstate 5. Moving north on I-5, travelers enter the Siskiyou and Cascade mountains, Mount Shasta being the most obvious peak in north-central California. Northbound from Sacramento, the major California cities encountered are Redding, Weed, and Yreka. Weed is where the primary and alternate routes recommended here diverge.

Mostly the terrain is mountainous; as you approach the Oregon border, the Cascades are to the right and the Siskiyou Mountains are to the left. Once in Oregon, the major cities prior to Grants Pass are Ashland and Medford. Ashland is the home of the University of Southern Oregon, a small liberal arts school of excellent reputation.

Ashland hosts a thriving Shakespearean theater in the summer months. The theater is outdoors, just as in Shakespeare's time, but this one sits on a bluff above Lithia Park, a small jewel of a park laced with pleasant pathways. If you have time, a night of Shakespeare followed by a lingering walk in Lithia Park combine for an unforgettable evening.

Travelers desiring to add Crater Lake National Park to their itineraries turn east on OR 62 in Medford. It takes about an hour and a half to drive to the park from Medford.

Moving on to Grants Pass, you'll find a modest-size city on the banks of Oregon's Rogue River, surrounded by forested mountains. Full facilities are available for travelers, and the pace in Grants Pass is pretty laid-back, allowing for plenty of relaxation if you select this as an overnight stop.

Leaving Grants Pass, it's a comfortable one-day drive to Seattle, all of it on Interstate 5. From Grants Pass to Roseburg, the mountainous terrain continues. Leaving Roseburg you drop into Oregon's Willamette Valley. This long, broad valley hosts Oregon's finest farms. The climate is relatively mild all year long, and rainfall is more than adequate for almost any crop.

Major cities in the Willamette Valley include Eugene and Salem (Oregon's capital). Neither is particularly large; both offer full facilities for travelers at reasonable prices.

Leaving Oregon's breadbasket, you approach Portland and the surrounding towns that have been absorbed as bedroom communities for the city. An obviously western city, Portland and its suburbs sprawl across miles of low rolling hills. Sixty or so miles to the east, Mount Hood, Oregon's highest peak, rises above the city.

Insider's Tip

The easiest route past Portland is to take the Interstate 205 exit near Tualatin and drive around the east side of the city. I-205 intercepts I-5 again just north of Vancouver, Washington. The traffic is usually much gentler on I-205 than it is on I-5 in downtown Portland. This route, too, should be avoided during rush hour.

Interstate 5 continues through Portland, across the Columbia River. The city continues north of the river, but here it is known as Vancouver, Washington. If at all possible, avoid workday rush hours when traveling through the Portland–Vancouver area. Freeways are jammed during those times.

North of Vancouver, Mount St. Helens, the volcano that erupted in 1980 and was slightly active in late 2004 and again in 2006, is to your right (east). The mountain is not nearly as tall now as before the eruption, and the jagged edge of its crater is clearly visible from the highway. Even today, Mount St. Helens occasionally spews small amounts of steam and ash into the air, so there exists the possibility of witnessing a minor eruption as you drive past. If you want a closer look, it's about a 50-mile drive east from I-5; take WA 504 at Exit 48.

Heading for Seattle, you'll pass first through Olympia, Washington's capital, located near the southern edge of Puget Sound. I-5 meanders through several tricky curves passing through Olympia, so be on the alert.

Approaching Olympia, Mount Rainier is to the right. Several options for driving to Mount Rainier National Park are available prior to reaching Olympia or between Olympia and Seattle. Allow a minimum of a full day if you wish to add this side trip to your journey north.

One could argue that Seattle actually starts when you approach the city limits of Tacoma, Washington's third-largest city and officially about 40 miles south of Seattle. Over the years the two cities have grown to the point that they form a long, slender metropolitan area strung out along the eastern shore of Puget Sound. All told, you'll have about 60 miles of city freeway driving from the southern edge of Tacoma to the northern parts of Seattle. It, too, can be extremely crowded during workday rush hours.

Insider's Tip

I-405 offers an alternative route around the east side of Seattle if you wish to avoid Seattle's downtown areas. It's usually best to avoid Seattle's interstates from 7 to 9 a.m. and from 3:30 to 7 p.m.

Sneak Route

You can shave about 50 miles off your trip north if you turn east on WA 542 in Bellingham and then follow it to WA 9, which leads north to Sumas. Cross the border at Sumas and intercept Canada 1 just north of town. Most longtime Alaskans who regularly drive back and forth use this route. Another good reason for using this route is the I-5 border crossing at Blaine, Washington, is normally quite congested, and delays in processing through customs can often be an hour or more.

Leaving Seattle, northbound to Alaska, the excitement begins to mount. This is the day you cross over into Canada and begin edging away from the more crowded parts of the North American continent. Ahead are the Canadian Rockies of British Columbia. As you travel farther and farther north, the cities and towns become smaller and farther apart.

Interstate 5 continues to the Canadian border, then becomes Canada 99 from the border into Vancouver. Should you not wish to enter Vancouver itself, take advantage of the first available access route to Canada 1. Turn east on Canada 1.

The last city of significant size prior to reaching Canada is Bellingham, Washington. Bellingham is the southern terminus of the Alaska Marine Highway, a system of oceangoing ferries with stateroom accommodations for passengers and space for vehicles. Many travelers opt to drive their vehicles on the ferry either coming or going to Alaska. Up until 2002, the northern terminus of the ferry system was Haines, Alaska, about 150 miles from the Alaska Highway, altogether about 600 miles from Fairbanks. However, with the commissioning of a new ferry, the *M/V Kennicott,* there is now twice-monthly service during the summer months from Bellingham to a south-central Alaska port near Anchorage. Chapter 15 of this book provides a detailed look at the ferry system and includes information on reservations.

Canada 1, an east-west route just north of the US–Canada border, is also referred to as the Trans-Canada Highway. More than 3,000 miles long, it is the major artery connecting eastern Canada to western Canada. When you intercept this highway east of Vancouver, it actually leads you north to the town of Cache Creek. At Cache Creek, Canada 1 turns eastward to Banff National Park, and Alaska-bound travelers continue north on Canada 97.

However, before intercepting Canada 97, the 120 miles of Canada 1 from Hope to Cache Creek provide some of the most spectacular scenery of the entire trip—the Fraser River Canyon.

Leaving Hope, the river is to the east. Thirty-three miles farther, the road crosses the river and clings to the east side of the canyon. Appropriately, the river crossing is made near Hell's Gate, at least partially descriptive of this raging, frothing river roaring out of the mountains. The road follows the canyon for nearly 75 miles. The vistas are awe-inspiring. Numerous tunnels lace the route. The road is first-rate, and almost all uphill sections provide broad passing lanes.

Pulling out of the canyon, Canada 1 follows the Thompson River into Cache Creek. Fishermen can find all sorts of excuses for spending time in or around the Thompson River, among them: steelhead to 30 pounds in the spring, king and silver salmon in the summer and fall, and rainbow trout and Dolly Varden almost any time of the year.

Phantom Ship, Crater Lake National Park, Oregon

In and around Cache Creek (population about 1,300) are an assortment of public and private campgrounds, fishing opportunities, and open country. If you need groceries for an RV or other odds and ends, Cache Creek is a fairly good place to shop for them.

From Cache Creek, it's about 70 miles to 100 Mile House, a slightly larger town of about 1,900 folks. For those ready to stop for the night, there are plenty of campgrounds, restaurants, motels, and other travelers' services, as well as good fishing in the immediate area. The history of 100 Mile House is colored with fur trappers and later with freight to build Canada's frontier; it was a stop on the old Cariboo Wagon Road. Visitor information is available at the kiosk next to the bird sanctuary in the center of town.

Leaving 100 Mile House, the road heads almost straight north until jogging eastward for the final 75 miles or so into Dawson Creek. Major towns along this stretch are Quesnel, Prince George, and Chetwynd. However, it's the names of the smaller towns along the way that begin to hint at the rich, relatively recent history of the Canadian wilderness. Driving north, you'll pass through Lac La Hache, Bear Lake, Fort McLeod, and McLeod Lake. At McLeod Lake, a turnoff leads a short distance to Mackenzie on the shores of Williston Lake, the largest man-made reservoir on the North American continent. Williston Lake is close to 100 miles long north and south with a 75-mile spur snaking east from the northern part of the lake. Plenty of fish here as well, including rainbows, Dolly Varden, arctic char, and grayling.

Moving north to Chetwynd, Alaska-bound travelers have an option. If you don't wish to visit Dawson Creek, you can turn left in Chetwynd on Canada 29 to Fort St. John on the Alaska Highway. This will cut about 50 miles from your trip, but you do miss Dawson Creek and the opportunity to compare notes with numerous other northbound travelers. Dawson Creek is a natural gathering point for those heading to Alaska and for those just returned. The campgrounds and hotels will be full of trail talk from the Alaska Highway on almost any summer evening.

Dawson Creek's best campgrounds are in and around the junction on the edge of town where you turn left for Alaska or right for the city center. All Dawson Creek–area campgrounds tend to fill up early in summer. If campgrounds close to town are full, continue toward Alaska; several more are within a few miles on the Alaska Highway itself. Be sure to investigate the visitor center in Dawson Creek. Turn right toward the city center at the junction. The visitor center is just a short distance down the street on your left. It has plenty of parking for even the largest RVs.

WEST COAST ALTERNATE ROUTE

Sometimes the most obvious isn't necessarily the best. This alternate route could make a strong argument to that effect.

This route offers much less freeway driving and adds about 150 miles to the trip, but there are some major finds along the way, the kinds of things most people who stick to the obvious will miss. Then, too, the traffic is not nearly as heavy as it is through Portland and Seattle.

Using San Francisco as a starting point, the route is the same to Weed, California, north of Sacramento on I-5. At Weed, turn off on US 97, the road you will follow all the way to the Canadian border. Prior to the completion of I-5 in the early 1960s, US 97 was a major north-south route through Oregon. Now most of the heavy traffic sticks to I-5, particularly the truckers.

After getting on US 97, the first town of any size is Klamath Falls, Oregon, about 75 miles away and less than 20 miles north of the California-Oregon border. Just prior to entering Oregon, CA 161 leads to the east through marshes heavily used by waterfowl. Lots of bald eagles and other birds of prey can often be seen as well. This road provides access to Lava Beds National Monument after it connects to CA 139. Allow an extra day if you want to make this side trip.

Northbound from Klamath Falls (locally called K-Falls) the road parallels Upper Klamath Lake for miles. Just past the lake, about 22 miles from town, is a turnoff on

OR 62, which leads to Crater Lake National Park. This is another one-day side trip well worth taking; Crater Lake is little more than an hour's drive from Klamath Falls. If you visit Crater Lake, take the two-hour boat trip around the inside of the caldera. This is literally a ride through the inside of an ancient volcano, and it is thrilling. Getting to the boats requires a 1.1-mile hike down the inside wall of the caldera at Cleetwood Cove. The hike out is rather heavy exercise, but most who dare find the experience worth the effort.

Face to face with bighorn ram, Banff National Park

West Coast Alternate Route

San Francisco, California, to Dawson Creek, British Columbia

Time Required: 4 days (without side trips)

Mileage: 1,800 miles (3,000 kilometers)

Overnight Stops: Bend, Oregon

Oroville, Washington

Tete Jaune Cache, British Columbia

Dawson Creek, British Columbia

Possible side trips en route *(and minimum additional time required):*

Lava Beds National Monument, California *(one day)*

Crater Lake National Park, Oregon *(one day)*

Columbia River Gorge National Scenic Area *(one day)*

North Cascades National Park, Washington *(one day)*

Banff National Park, Alberta *(two days)*

Jasper National Park, Alberta *(two days)*

Routing:

- *San Francisco to Oroville, Washington:*

  I-80, San Francisco to Sacramento

  I-5, Sacramento to Weed, California

  US 97, Weed to Oroville

- *Oroville to Tete Jaune Cache:*

  US 97 to Canadian Border

  Canada 97 to Kamloops, British Columbia

  Canada 5, Kamloops to Tete Jaune Cache

- *Tete Jaune Cache to Dawson Creek:*

  Canada 16 to Prince George, British Columbia

  Canada 97, Prince George to Dawson Creek

Back on US 97, you travel through the east (dry) side of the Cascade Mountains. Approaching Bend, the Three Sisters are to your left, and Mount Jefferson is somewhat farther north. The forests along the road are semi-arid stands of ponderosa and lodgepole pines and other conifers. Open areas are primarily covered with sagebrush.

North of Bend, the road runs through mostly open country with cattle ranches and sagebrush being the predominant features. Little more than halfway between Bend and the Columbia River is Shaniko, more or less a ghost town these days and worth a short exploration. Talk to the few people who remain to gain a sense of the history behind the abandoned or little-used buildings.

US 97 crosses the Columbia River into Washington at Biggs, and then runs north for about 60 miles to Toppenish. From just beyond Toppenish to a few miles past Ellensburg, US 97 combines with I-82, a pleasant drive past Yakima and through the Yakima River Valley. Past Ellensburg, I-82 becomes I-90, the major route leading west to Seattle from central Washington. Just after connecting to I-90, US 97 turns off northbound, winding into the Wenatchee National Forest. After several hundred miles of driving in the high deserts of eastern Oregon and Washington, it's nice to see trees again.

Insider's Tip

A 110-foot passenger ferry, *The Lady of the Lake*, runs the length of Lake Chelan to the tiny community of Stehekin on the north end of the reservoir. Visiting Stehekin is a real treat; it is one of the very few communities left in the contiguous 48 states unreachable by road. The ferry ride itself, through the narrow gorge filled by the lake, is inspiring as well.

About 55 miles after you turn off I-90, US 97 combines with US 2 and jogs southeast to Wenatchee. The routes separate in Wenatchee with US 97 following the Columbia River. A little less than 40 miles north of Wenatchee is the community of Chelan at the southern edge of Lake Chelan, a long, narrow lake-reservoir leading northwest toward the Lake Chelan National Recreation Area, which adjoins North Cascades National Park.

From Chelan, US 97 continues to the Canadian border just north of Oroville, Washington. En route to the border, at Okanogan, Washington, WA 20 leads west to North Cascades National Park. Allow an extra day if you want to take time to drive through this park.

Insider's Tip

Be sure to sample a bottle or two of the wines produced by local vineyards in the Okanagan Valley. We found a delightful Chablis where we least expected it. The vineyards and local wineries have really developed in the last couple of decades.

After entering Canada, Canada 97 swings through the Okanagan Valley. This valley is Canada's fruit basket, and travelers in July and August will find dozens of roadside stands offering the freshest of the year's crop. Besides the fruit, there are vegetables, but it's the fruit that commands the greatest attention.

This is a scenic stretch of road, winding for miles along the shores of Okanagan Lake, even crossing the lake at one point. There are occasional stretches of four-lane highway as well.

North of Vernon on the eastern side of the lake, drivers have two options—continuing on Canada 97, which turns west for Kamloops, or first driving north to Salmon Arm, and then turning west on Canada 1, which also leads to Kamloops. Both routes offer similar scenery and join just a few miles before entering Kamloops.

At Kamloops, turn north on BC 5. It's about a five-hour drive to Tete Jaune Cache. The closer you get to Tete Jaune Cache, the better the scenery. The mountains of Banff then Jasper National Parks lie to the east, and every mile brings you closer to these magnificent wilderness parks.

Those wishing to visit Jasper National Park will have to turn east at Tete Jaune Cache on Canada 16, also known as the Yellowhead Highway. An optional route would be to start on Canada 1 at Salmon Arm and drive east to Banff National Park. In the park, turn north on Alberta 93 and follow it to Jasper, where it intercepts Canada 16. Turn left to Tete Jaune Cache. If you do use Canada 1 to get to Banff, the drive north from Banff to Jasper on Alberta 93, also known as the Icefield Parkway, is a stunning visual feast through the heart of the Canadian Rockies.

From Tete Jaune Cache, follow the Yellowhead Highway (Canada 16) to Prince George, where it intersects Canada 97, which leads north to Dawson Creek. Prince George is a fairly large town, timber being a primary industry. From here north, the alternate route joins the final leg of the primary route recommended for travelers from the West Coast. Dawson Creek is about 250 miles north of Prince George.

ROCKY MOUNTAIN STATES—WESTERN PLAINS PRIMARY ROUTE

This route parallels the Rocky Mountains to the west until reaching Cheyenne, Wyoming. Heading more or less straight north from Cheyenne, the mountains recede westward and travelers cross the western edge of the Great Plains. To some, driving the plains is boring; to others, however, the endless horizons inspire awe.

Leaving Denver on I-25, the trip is routine freeway driving. Maneuvering around Cheyenne is not at all tricky if you're used to the maze of on- and off-ramps that characterize freeway driving in and around larger cities. Cheyenne, even though it's Wyoming's largest city, just isn't all that big—only about 50,000 people live there.

North of Cheyenne, on US 85, the road wends its way through mostly open country. As you approach the South Dakota border, the road actually parallels it for about 90 miles before crossing—the Black Hills are to the east. The most famous attraction within these hills is Mount Rushmore, where likenesses of four United States presidents have been carved out of a rocky hillside. Travelers desiring to visit Mount Rushmore should turn east on US 16 before crossing the South Dakota border. Combining Mount Rushmore and Badlands National Park makes for a superb two-day excursion in southwestern South Dakota. Lush forests and dense crowds greet visitors to Rushmore in summer. Sixty miles to the east, a desolate, lunar-like landscape and relatively few people await visitors to the Badlands. The contrast is compelling.

Rocky Mountain States–Western Plains Primary Route

Denver, Colorado, to Dawson Creek, British Columbia

Time Required: 4 days (without side trips)

Mileage: 1,800 miles (3,000 kilometers)

Overnight stops: Spearfish, South Dakota

Regina, Saskatchewan

Edmonton, Alberta

Dawson Creek, British Columbia

Possible Side Trips En Route *(and minimum additional time required):*

Badlands National Park, South Dakota *(one day)*

Mount Rushmore National Memorial, South Dakota *(one day)*

Banff National Park, Alberta *(two days)*

Jasper National Park, Alberta *(one day)*

Routing:

• *Denver to Spearfish:*

  I-25, Denver to Cheyenne, Wyoming

  US 85, Cheyenne to Spearfish

• *Spearfish to Regina:*

  US 85, Spearfish to US–Canada border

  Saskatchewan 35, border to Weyburn

  Saskatchewan 39, Weyburn to Corinne

  Saskatchewan 6, Corinne to Regina

• *Regina to Edmonton:*

  Saskatchewan 11, Regina to Saskatoon

  Canada 16, Saskatoon to Edmonton

• *Edmonton to Dawson Creek:*

  Canada 16, Edmonton to Wabamum

  Alberta 43, Wabamum to Grande Prairie

  Alberta/BC 2, Grande Prairie to Dawson Creek

Those who choose not to visit the Badlands or Rushmore will continue north on US 85 to Spearfish, if they wish to keep to this proposed itinerary. Spearfish is fairly small and facilities are available, though limited. Should all options be closed for overnight stays, continue north for another 10 miles to Belle Fourche. Away from the freeway (US 85 crosses I-90 at Spearfish) there should be less demand for available accommodations.

Continuing north, US 85 passes some of the last expanses of natural grasslands left on the Great Plains. Shortly after crossing into North Dakota, the Little Missouri National Grasslands are on the west side of the road for 100 miles or more.

The only North Dakota town of any size encountered on US 85 is Williston, about 70 miles south of the Canadian border. Williston rests on the northwest corner of Lake Sakajawea, a monstrous reservoir created by damming the Missouri River at Pick City, more than 110 miles to the southeast. If you like to fish, this is a great place to try your luck.

From Williston, the road runs straight north almost 60 miles, with hardly a curve to be found. Then there's a slight westward jog to tiny Fortuna, and then north again for 5 miles or so to the US–Canada border. In Canada, the road becomes Saskatchewan 35.

Saskatchewan is Canada's premier prairie province—miles and miles of endless horizons and seemingly boundless wheat fields stretching as far as the eye can see. Roads, too, stretch straight into the horizon and beyond—not much need for curves in this part of the world.

Jog northwest for 45 miles at Weyburn on Saskatchewan 39, and then due north again on Saskatchewan 6 for 24 miles into Regina, Saskatchewan's capital and largest city. Travelers' services are plentiful here, and finding a place to overnight should pose little problem.

Head northwest from Regina on Saskatchewan 11, a multilane highway for the entire 152 miles to Saskatoon. At Saskatoon turn west on Canada 16 (also known as the Yellowhead Highway). Canada 16 leads generally northwest to North Battleford and Lloydminster, the latter where you cross Saskatchewan's western boundary into Alberta. Change your watches from Central Time to Mountain Time at Saskatoon.

From Lloydminster it's about 150 miles to Edmonton, Alberta's capital. Full facilities are available for travelers.

From Edmonton, continue west on Canada 16 for 31 miles to Wabamum. At Wabamum turn north on Alberta 43, a road stretching along about 185 miles of pretty lonely country to Valleyview. Be on the lookout for waterfowl in the ponds, creeks, and rivers at roadside. Alberta's waterways are the breeding ground for great numbers of waterfowl each summer. Drought conditions in the late 1980s lessened their numbers, but in recent years more normal rainfall has brought about something of a revival. Travelers can spot thousands of ducks if they take the time to look.

Edmonton is home to what was once the largest shopping mall in the world. Dedicated shoppers will find hundreds of stores, restaurants, and theaters all under a single roof. The Mall of America near Minneapolis, Minnesota, now holds the distinction of being the world's largest mall.

At Valleyview, really just a road junction, Alberta 43 makes a left turn and continues 65 miles to Grande Prairie. As the name implies, this is flat, or at best slightly rolling country with vast fields under cultivation. Alberta 43 intersects Alberta 2 four miles north of Grande Prairie. Alberta 2, later British Columbia 2, will take you the rest of the way into Dawson Creek, the start of the Alaska Highway.

ROCKY MOUNTAIN STATES–WESTERN PLAINS ALTERNATE ROUTE

In the opinion of many, this routing offers perhaps the grandest scenery of any route leading to Dawson Creek, British Columbia. Travelers follow the Rocky Mountains from Denver deep into Canada. Many of the western hemisphere's premier national parks are either right on the road or just a short side trip away from the route.

From Denver, head north on I-25. In Cheyenne, stay on I-25 through Casper and on to Buffalo, Wyoming. For those wanting to take a side trip to Yellowstone and Grand Teton national parks, access routes lead west from Casper (US 26), Buffalo (US 16), and from just north of Sheridan (US 14). The latter offers probably the most spectacular scenery. In Buffalo, I-25 ends and travelers take I-90 west out of town.

Soon after you enter Montana on I-90, the Custer Battlefields are just east of the highway. A lot of research has been done on these battlefields, and the Park Service historians on duty are able to tell a fascinating story about what actually happened to Custer and his men at the battle of the Little Bighorn. It's well worth a stop.

Insider's Tip

Once in Montana, the lands on both sides of I-90 are part of the Crow Indian Reservation. Indian reservations are private property. Make certain you have permission before you go exploring the lands at roadside.

Stay on I-90 to Billings, Montana. There, turn north on US 87, which gradually makes its way northeast to Great Falls. This is part of Montana's fabled Big Sky Country. Vast horizons seemingly go on forever in all directions. Early mornings, before the heat-induced haze of afternoon sets in, are the best times to appreciate this incredible landscape.

At Great Falls, it's back on the interstate again—I-15 this time. I-15 ends at the Canadian border, little more than 100 miles from Great Falls.

In Canada, the road becomes Alberta 4. Stay on it to Lethbridge. From there, Alberta 3 leads west to Fort Macleod. There, turn north on Alberta 2 to Calgary.

And, if you thought the mountain scenery so far was something special, wait until you depart Calgary on Canada 1, and then turn north on Alberta 93. This road, known as the Icefield Parkway, follows the continental divide north through Banff and Jasper national parks. It is a stunning drive to Jasper, and then west across the continental divide to Tete Jaune Cache on Canada 16, and on to Prince George, British Columbia. This is scenery that numbs the senses. You really haven't seen the Rockies until you've driven Alberta 93 from Banff to Jasper.

At Prince George, turn north on Canada 97 and follow this road to Dawson Creek, as described in the West Coast routes earlier in this chapter.

Rocky Mountain States–Western Plains Alternate Route

Denver, Colorado, to Dawson Creek, British Columbia

Time Required: 5 days (without side trips)

Mileage: 1,850 miles (3,100 kilometers)

Overnight Stops: Buffalo, Wyoming

Great Falls, Montana

Calgary, Alberta

Prince George, British Columbia

Dawson Creek, British Columbia

Possible Side Trips En Route *(and minimum additional time required):*

Yellowstone and Grand Teton National Parks *(two days or more; reservations most likely required to camp in the parks)*

Custer Battlefields *(one day)*

Glacier National Park *(one–two days)*

Calgary Stampede *(one–ten days in mid-July)*

Banff and Jasper National Parks *(one day per park)*

Routing:

• *Denver to Buffalo:* I-25

• *Buffalo to Great Falls:*

  I-90, Buffalo to Billings, Montana

  US 87, Billings to Great Falls

• *Great Falls to Calgary:*

  I-15, Great Falls to US–Canada border

  Alberta 4, border to Lethbridge, Alberta

  Alberta 3, Lethbridge to Fort Macleod, Alberta

  Alberta 2, Fort Macleod to Calgary

• *Calgary to Prince George:*

  Canada 1, Calgary to Lake Louise

  Alberta 93, Lake Louise to Jasper

  Canada 16, Jasper to Prince George

• *Prince George to Dawson Creek:* Canada 97

MIDWEST PRIMARY ROUTE

Probably no greater contrast exists for scenery on any route leading to Dawson Creek than starting in the corn and soybean fields near Chicago and winding up in the north woods in Canada.

Insider's Tip

For 10 days in mid-July, Calgary stages the Calgary Stampede, probably North America's finest rodeo–western party. It's well worth a few days to take part in the fun.

Leaving Chicago on I-90, drivers pass through low, rolling terrain, mostly farmers' fields interspersed with wooded creek bottoms, in northern Illinois, Wisconsin, and on into Minnesota. This is good, easy driving, all on interstate highways. Stay on I-90 to Tomah, Wisconsin, and then change to I-94 for Minneapolis.

As you approach Minneapolis, and later driving through Minnesota, cultivated fields give way more and more to forests, though small rural towns continue to dot the landscape. Travelers wishing to add Voyagers National Park to their itineraries will turn off I-94 in Minneapolis and head north on I-35. Voyagers, a relatively new national park, celebrates the legacy of the Canadian voyageurs who first explored south-central Canada and the north-central states more than 200 years ago. Voyagers National Park is primarily water, a chain of lakes on the US–Canada border in northern Minnesota. Absolutely the best way to experience it is to rent a houseboat from one of the concessionaires near the park and spend several days lazily motoring from one anchorage to another. The fishing's good, and the scenery wonderful, especially in the fall when the leaves turn.

For those not visiting Voyagers National Park, continue out of Minneapolis on I-94 to Fargo, North Dakota. At Fargo, turn north on I-29. I-29 follows the eastern edge of North Dakota to the US–Canada border. From the border, Manitoba 75 leads north to Winnipeg, the capital and largest city in the province. North of Winnipeg are some of the largest freshwater lakes in North America: Lake Winnipeg, more than 250 miles long; Lake Manitoba, 120 miles long; and Lake Winnipegosis, about 150 miles long.

Insider's Tip

Beaches and boat-launching facilities are available, particularly on Lake Winnipeg about 35 miles north of Winnipeg.

From Winnipeg, head west on Canada 1 to Regina, Saskatchewan. Much of this route is multilane highway, and it's a comfortable drive. Saskatchewan is considered one of Canada's prairie provinces, and as you head westward, more and more wheat fields can be seen filling the horizon in all directions.

Midwest Primary Route

Chicago, Illinois, to Dawson Creek, British Columbia

Time Required: 5 days (without side trips)

Mileage: 2,050 miles (3,400 kilometers)

Overnight Stops: Minneapolis, Minnesota

Winnipeg, Manitoba

Saskatoon, Saskatchewan

Edmonton, Alberta

Dawson Creek, British Columbia

Possible Side Trips En Route *(and minimum additional time required):*

Voyagers National Park, Minnesota *(two–three days)*

Banff and Jasper National Parks, Alberta *(two days)*

Routing:

* *Chicago to Minneapolis:*

  I-90, Chicago to Tomah, Wisconsin

  I-94, Tomah to Minneapolis

* *Minneapolis to Winnipeg:*

  I-94, Minneapolis to Fargo, North Dakota

  I-29, Fargo to US–Canada border

  Manitoba 75, border to Winnipeg

* *Winnipeg to Saskatoon, Saskatchewan:*

  Canada 1, Winnipeg to Regina, Saskatchewan

  Saskatchewan 11, Regina to Saskatoon

* *Saskatoon to Edmonton:* Canada 16

* *Edmonton to Dawson Creek:*

  Canada 16, Edmonton to Wabamum

  Alberta 43, Wabamum to Grande Prairie

  Alberta/BC 2, Grande Prairie to Dawson Creek

At Regina, turn northwest on Saskatchewan 11, another multilane highway leading to Saskatoon. In Saskatoon, those who wish to detour through Banff and Jasper national parks should turn west on Manitoba 7, which becomes Alberta 9 at the Manitoba–Alberta border. Alberta 9 continues to Calgary; from there, follow Canada 1, and then Alberta 93 to Banff and Jasper national parks. Routing through the parks and on into Dawson Creek is described in the Rocky Mountain States– Western Plains section of this chapter.

From Saskatoon, Canada 16 leads on to Edmonton, Alberta. Routing from Edmonton to Dawson Creek has already been described in the Rocky Mountain States–Western Plains primary route earlier in this chapter.

MIDWEST ALTERNATE ROUTE

Two obvious choices confront travelers going west from Chicago before heading north: I-80 and I-90. I-90 is actually a little shorter and offers a few extras along the way.

As before, leave Chicago on I-90. Instead of turning off on I-94 at Tomah, Wisconsin, continue west on I-90 to Sioux Falls, South Dakota's largest city. Plenty of travelers' services are available here.

I-90 continues almost straight across South Dakota to the Wyoming border. However, before entering Wyoming, both Badlands National Park and Mount Rushmore National Memorial are just to the south of the freeway. Spending the night in or near Badlands allows travelers to drive through the park and then through Rushmore all in a single day. Both parks are worth the time to visit.

Badlands National Park is essentially a desert. It can be exceedingly hot with little shade to provide relief from the sun. Carry plenty of water and sunscreen.

From the region around Badlands and Rushmore, continue west to Buffalo, Wyoming. From here, the route north to Dawson Creek is the same as described under the alternate route for the Rocky Mountain States earlier in this chapter.

Athabasca River, Jasper National Park

Midwest Alternate Route

Chicago, Illinois, to Dawson Creek, British Columbia

Time Required: 6 days (without side trips)

Mileage: 2,600 miles (4,350 kilometers)

Overnight Stops:

Sioux Falls, South Dakota

Buffalo, Wyoming

Great Falls, Montana

Calgary, Alberta

Prince George, British Columbia

Dawson Creek, British Columbia

Possible Side Trips En Route *(and minimum additional time required):*

Badlands National Park/Mount Rushmore, South Dakota *(two days)*

Yellowstone National Park, Wyoming *(two days)*

Glacier National Park, Montana *(one day)*

Routing:

- *Chicago to Sioux Falls:* I-90
- *Sioux Falls to Buffalo:* I-90
- *Buffalo to Great Falls:*

  I-90, Buffalo to Billings, Montana

  US 87, Billings to Great Falls
- *Great Falls to Calgary, Alberta:*

  I-15, Great Falls to US–Canada border

  Alberta 4, border to Lethbridge, Alberta

  Alberta 3, Lethbridge to Fort Macleod

  Alberta 2, Fort Macleod to Calgary
- *Calgary to Prince George:*

  Canada 1, Calgary to Banff

  Alberta 93, Banff to Jasper

  Canada 16, Jasper to Prince George
- *Prince George to Dawson Creek:* Canada 97

EAST COAST PRIMARY ROUTE

Obviously, when starting from the East Coast, travelers have a lengthy trek just getting to the start of the Alaska Highway at Dawson Creek. But by using this primary route, there's a much greater opportunity to sample Canada's generous hospitality.

Northbound from New York City, I-87 gets you on your way in a hurry. Within a few hours you'll be driving past the Adirondacks, with Lake Champlain to your right. And, the biggest plus, as you get farther north in New York, you'll leave behind the congestion and big-city hustle and bustle. For the next several weeks on your way to and from Alaska, the driving should be much more relaxed, with a couple of obvious exceptions, such as driving through Montreal.

Crossing into Canada just north of Champlain, New York, I-87 becomes Canada's I-15, which takes you into Montreal. In Montreal you'll have to do some big-city freeway maneuvering until you exit the west side of town on I-40. Stay on I-40 through Ottawa until it ends in about 15 miles. From there, take Ontario 17 westward to Sault Ste. Marie, which sits just across a narrow neck of water from Sault Ste. Marie, Michigan. This waterway, with locks for Great Lakes shipping, joins Lake Superior to Lake Huron. Those wishing to spend a few hours or a few days exploring Michigan's remote Upper Peninsula would cross back into the United States on the bridge at Sault Ste. Marie.

Continuing on Ontario 17, the road skirts the north shore of Lake Superior for several hundred miles to Thunder Bay. At Thunder Bay, a visit to Isle Royale National Park can be arranged by detouring south on Ontario 61 to Grand Portage, Minnesota. Boat service to Isle Royale is available from Grand Portage. Isle Royale offers the first real taste of northern wilderness for those who want to devote a day or two to exploring. More or less in its natural

It was at Isle Royale that L. David Mech developed much of his information leading to the balance of nature theory back in the late 1950s and early 1960s.

state, Isle Royale has offered a relatively undisturbed laboratory for biologists to study the interaction between wolves and moose.

Leaving Thunder Bay, continue westbound on Ontario 17. At Kenora, about 20 miles from the Manitoba border, the road crosses a narrow arm of Lake of the Woods, a large lake partly in Ontario and partly in Minnesota. Fishermen won't have to try real hard to find excuses to hang around this lake for a few days.

Once in Manitoba, Ontario 17 officially becomes Canada 1, the Trans-Canada Highway. Though it might not be flagged as Canada 1 east of Manitoba, Ontario 17 is actually the eastern extension of the highway.

From the Manitoba border, it's about 60 miles to Winnipeg. From Winnipeg, continue west and north as outlined in the primary route for the Midwest found earlier in this chapter.

East Coast Primary Route

New York City, New York, to Dawson Creek, British Columbia

Time Required: 7 days (without side trips)

Mileage: 2,900 miles (4,850 kilometers)

Overnight Stops: Ottawa, Ontario

Sault Ste. Marie, Ontario

Thunder Bay, Ontario

Winnipeg, Manitoba

Saskatoon, Saskatchewan

Edmonton, Alberta

Dawson Creek, British Columbia

Possible Side Trips En Route *(and minimum additional time required)*:

Michigan's Upper Peninsula *(two days)*

Isle Royale National Park, Lake Superior *(one day)*

Banff and Jasper National Parks, Alberta *(two days)*

Routing:

- *New York City to Ottawa:*

   I-87, NYC to US–Canada border

   I-15 (Canada), border to Montreal

   I-40 (Canada), Montreal to Ottawa

- *Ottawa to Sault Ste. Marie:* Quebec 17 (Canada 1)

- *Sault Ste. Marie to Thunder Bay:* Quebec 17

- *Thunder Bay to Winnipeg:*

   Quebec 17, Thunder Bay to Manitoba border

   Canada 1, border to Winnipeg;

- *Winnipeg to Saskatoon:*

   Canada 1, Winnipeg to Regina, Saskatchewan

   Saskatchewan 11, Regina to Saskatoon

- *Saskatoon to Edmonton:* Canada 16

- *Edmonton to Dawson Creek:*

   Canada 16, Edmonton to Wabamum

   Alberta 43, Wabamum to Grande Prairie

   Alberta/BC 2, Grande Prairie to Dawson Creek

EAST COAST ALTERNATE ROUTE

This route offers the option of taking part of the most-traveled east–west route in the United States, Interstate 80, which stretches from New York City to San Francisco.

Basically, all you do is drive west out of New York City on I-80, and stay on that highway until you reach Chicago, some 800 miles away. Assuming you actually start in the city, you'll cross northern New Jersey, central Pennsylvania, northern Ohio, and northern Indiana. When you leave Indiana, you enter Chicago.

Most of I-80 is a toll road in Ohio and Indiana. As well, the same road is both I-80 and I-90 in those two states. After coming together in Cleveland, the two interstates don't separate again until Chicago.

Cities along the route include Cleveland, Toledo, South Bend, and Gary. All figure prominently in industry around the Great Lakes. With the exception of South Bend, all these inland cities have ports for oceangoing ships, which reach the Great Lakes via the St. Lawrence Seaway.

In Chicago, you have the option of taking either of the routes described in the Midwest section of this chapter. The alternate route described for the Midwest was used to compute the mileage listed for this alternate routing from New York City to Dawson Creek.

Milepost 0, the start of the Alaska Highway, in downtown Dawson Creek, BC

East Coast Alternate Route

New York City, New York, to Dawson Creek, British Columbia

Time Required: 8 days (without side trips)

Mileage: 3,400 miles (5,650 kilometers)

Overnight Stops: Akron, Ohio

Chicago, Illinois

Sioux Falls, South Dakota

Buffalo, Wyoming

Great Falls, Montana

Calgary, Alberta

Prince George, British Columbia

Dawson Creek, British Columbia

Possible Side Trips En Route *(and minimum additional time required)*:

Badlands National Park, South Dakota *(one day)*

Mount Rushmore National Memorial, South Dakota *(one day)*

Yellowstone National Park, Wyoming *(one day)*

Glacier National Park, Montana *(one day)*

Banff and Jasper National Parks, Alberta *(two days)*

Routing:

- *New York City to Akron:* I-80
- *Akron to Chicago:* I-80
- *Chicago to Sioux Falls:* I-90
- *Sioux Falls to Buffalo:* I-90
- *Buffalo to Great Falls:*
  I-90, Buffalo to Billings, Montana
  US 87, Billings to Great Falls
- *Great Falls to Calgary:*
  I-15, Great Falls to US–Canada border
  Alberta 4, border to Lethbridge
  Alberta 3, Lethbridge to Fort Macleod
  Alberta 2, Fort Macleod to Calgary
- *Calgary to Prince George:*
  Canada 1, Calgary to Banff
  Alberta 93, Banff to Jasper
  Canada 16, Jasper to Prince George
- *Prince George to Dawson Creek:* Canada 97

CHAPTER 9
North to Alaska

Getting to Dawson Creek, British Columbia, is, in itself, more adventure than many drivers experience in a lifetime. However, driving north to Alaska on the Alaska Highway, which begins in Dawson Creek, is the expedition that lures people this far in the first place. Here begins the last great driving adventure remaining in North America.

This chapter is laid out in five sections, each section representing a comfortable day's drive of about 300 miles. All told, it's slightly more than 1,500 miles from Dawson Creek to Fairbanks, Alaska. Each section will provide a chart with pertinent driving information, condensed for ready reference. On each of these information charts are blanks for you to write in your starting mileage, to aid you in keeping track of distances driven and distances remaining to go. Distances given for services are in miles (with kilometers in parentheses) from the departure point for that section of the trip. If you're following along in the book as you drive, you might want to zero out the trip odometer on your speedometer before you start each section.

Along the route in Canada, kilometer posts are placed at 5-kilometer intervals. Some of these get knocked down every year, so don't be upset if some are missing. In Alaska, these become mileposts at 1-mile intervals. Periodically, whenever the road intersects with the original Alcan, you may see a special marker with an inscription reading something like "Historic Mile Marker 483." This particular marker is in the Muncho Lake overlook on the north side of the lake.

A Note on Campgrounds

Public campgrounds are run by government agencies and have few amenities available beyond gravel parking sites and (sometimes) grassy spots for tents along with picnic tables and outhouses. Private campgrounds usually offer some hookups for RVs, as well as dump stations, showers, and laundry facilities. Public campgrounds will cost about $15–$20 (Canadian) per night; private about $25–$40 (Canadian) with an occasional high-priced exception. The highest-priced RV park I've found along the Alaska Highway is at Northern Rockies Lodge on the northwest end of Muncho Lake—$50 or more a night for water and 20-amp power hookups (no sewer hookups available).

As far as making campground reservations, it's rarely necessary along the Alaska Highway. In 44 years on the Alaska Highway, I've been turned away by a full campground only one time—Liard River Hot Springs—which is exceedingly popular with locals and tourists alike. I would, however, make a few exceptions to the reservation rule. Holiday weekends in Canada—such as Canada Day, July 1; Civic Holiday, August 1; and Labor Day, first Monday in September—can result in very crowded conditions at some of the more popular campgrounds. I would consider reservations, if available, for the first weekend of each of the summer months.

SECTION ONE: Dawson Creek, British Columbia, to Fort Nelson, British Columbia

With about 75,000 people in the immediate area, Dawson Creek is the last town of this size until you reach Fairbanks, which has a similar area-wide population. The Fort St. John area, less than 50 miles away on the Alaska Highway, is about 80 percent the size of Dawson Creek and its environs, but after that, only Whitehorse, Yukon, offers an area population of any size—about 18,000 people. In other words, you'll pass the homes of more people in the first 50 miles of the Alaska Highway than you will on the entire 1,475 miles from Fort St. John to Fairbanks.

During the summer, Dawson Creek hums with activity. Obviously, it's the gathering point for the 100,000 or more vehicles headed to Alaska each year. Also, there is considerable farming, oil and natural gas production, and lumbering in the immediate area.

Approaching Dawson Creek from the south on BC 97, as many travelers do, all you need to do is turn left at the stop sign to continue on BC 97. Turning right will lead to the downtown area, the visitor center, and the monument marking Mile 0 of the Alaska Highway. The Alaska Highway is actually BC 97 all the way to Watson Lake, Yukon, where it becomes Yukon 1. Numeric signs for 97 and printed signs for the Alaska Highway will guide you north—both mean the same thing throughout the rest of British Columbia.

> ### Insider's Tip
>
> Those driving live-aboard RVs should fill their propane tanks in Dawson Creek. Sitting on top of some of the largest natural gas fields in North America, Dawson Creek's propane is usually pretty cheap.

Those desiring to spend the night in Dawson Creek should plan to arrive fairly early in the day. Campgrounds and hotels fill quickly within or near the city. An average of more than 1,000 vehicles daily pass through Dawson Creek en route to Alaska or other destinations along the Alaska Highway during the summer months. Just as many pass through on return trips. Things will tend to spread out a bit as you get farther down the road, but at Dawson Creek, everybody tends to gather at least once.

Look closely at the other northbound vehicles in the campgrounds in Dawson Creek or at the hotels. Odds are good that you'll see these people again on your way north. A pleasant afternoon and evening in Dawson Creek are good times to make acquaintances that can often turn into long-lasting friendships. The fact that most visitors in Dawson Creek have the same goal strongly suggests shared inter-ests. Many travelers, in fact, team up with newfound friends to make the drive north together.

Dawson Creek, British Columbia, to Fort Nelson, British Columbia; 283 miles (472 km)

Our Starting Mileage:

Driving Time: About 5 hours without stopping

Towns En Route *(all offering most travelers' services):*

Fort St. John, 47 miles (76 kilometers)

Wonowon, 101 miles (162 kilometers)

Pink Mountain, 141 miles (226 kilometers)

Fort Nelson, 283 miles (472 kilometers)

Gas Available *(besides towns listed above):*

Farmington, 17 miles (30 kilometers)

Taylor, 35 miles (53 kilometers)

Shepherd's Inn, 72 miles (115 kilometers)

Sasquatch Crossing, 143 miles (238 kilometers)

Sikanni Chief, 159 miles (257 kilometers)

Buckinghorse River Lodge, 176 miles (300 kilometers)

Campground *(Provincial parks are public campgrounds; most towns listed above have private campgrounds as well.):*

Farmington Fairways, 10 miles (16 kilometers)

Kiskatinaw Provincial Park, 17 miles (30 kilometers)

Peace Island RV Park, 35 miles (58 kilometers)

Beatton Provincial Park, 50 miles (80 kilometers)

Charlie Lake Rotary RV Park, 52 miles (86 kilometers)

Charley Lake Provincial Park, 54 miles (90 kilometers)

Shepherd's Inn, 72 miles (115 kilometers)

Pink Mountain, 140 miles (235 kilometers)

Sasquatch Crossing, 143 miles (238 kilometers)

Sikanni Chief, 159 miles (257 kilometers)

Buckinghorse River Provincial Park, 173 miles (279 kilometers)

NaaChe RV Park, 230 miles (390 kilometers)

Andy Bailey Lake Regional Park, 266 miles (431 kilometers)

Hotels/Motels/Lodges *(Besides these, all towns listed above have overnight lodging available.):*

Shepherd's Inn, 72 miles (115 kilometers)

Sasquatch Crossing, 143 miles (238 kilometers)

Buckinghorse River Lodge, 176 miles (300 kilometers)

Neighbors' Inn, 229 miles (388 kilometers)

(continued on next page)

Major Terrain Features:
Mostly low, rolling hills along this stretch
Farmland gradually gives way to forests
Major rivers crossed: Peace and Sikanni
Wildlife: Black bears, grizzly bears, white-tailed deer, moose, raptors
Fishing Available: Northern pike, whitefish, grayling, perch, occasionally rainbow trout

Heading northwest out of town, things at first don't seem much different from the several hundred miles of Canada you drove through prior to reaching Dawson Creek. If anything, it might seem slightly more crowded. That's because the part of British Columbia between Dawson Creek and Fort St. John is the population center in the northern part of the province. Traffic will be relatively heavy except late at night or early in the morning.

Traveling either late or early is not without advantages. This far north, days are long. Sunsets are late—10 p.m. or later—during the summer, and sunrise is early—like 4:30 a.m.—so daylight is rarely a factor. And you'll markedly increase your odds of seeing wildlife if you drive the roads at these times. The major liability would be for those traveling late at night; you may have to hunt for a campground or hotel with lodging space. Those traveling early in the day can stop in mid-afternoon, when space is available almost everywhere.

The major terrain feature in the first hour's driving out of Dawson Creek is the Peace River, one of the largest and most impressive waterways in the Canadian north. The wild country of British Columbia and Alberta drained by this stream is often known as Peace River Country. You'll cross the river about 35 miles out of Dawson Creek. The approaches to both sides of the river are pretty steep, so be prepared to gear down.

The river offers clear water with plentiful populations of northern pike, rainbows, and grayling. A boat-launching ramp is available.

About 12 miles beyond the Peace River Bridge is Fort St. John, the last town of significant size prior to reaching Fort Nelson, 235 miles farther on. Fort St. John also offers reasonable prices for motor fuel and for propane, though both will likely be priced slightly higher here than in Dawson Creek. A wide range of hotels, motels, campgrounds, and restaurants are available in Fort St. John.

Trappers and Tourists

May 20, 1972, about 50 miles southeast of Fort Nelson: It was my third flat tire of the day. Luckily, there was a small gas station just a few miles ahead where I could get the punctured tire fixed to use as a spare for the miles ahead.

As I pulled in, I smelled something burning. A beat-up 1959 Ford sedan sat alongside the service station, faint wisps of smoke curling out from under the back. Before I could open the door of my station wagon, the most grizzled old guy I'd ever seen leaned in my open window. I recoiled from his bad breath and then listened to his tale of woe.

"Northbound? Can you take us to Fort Nelson?" He pointed to his equally grizzled partner.

I started to stammer, not knowing whether or not to be scared, and he cut me off with an explanation. "We're comin' out to sell our fur and burnt out the rear end in our car. Nearest Ford dealer's in Fort Nelson. We need a lift to town to get parts."

I couldn't help but like the old coot. I hesitated just long enough to tell him about getting a tire patched, and said I'd take them the 50 miles to Fort Nelson as soon as that was done.

While the gas station owner patched the tire, I looked inside the broken-down car, scraping not just a little grime off the window to do so. The back seat was filled with raw furs: beaver, what looked to be martin, and a wolverine hide or two, most of it in a hopeless jumble.

Tire fixed and gassed up, I made room in the front seat for the three of us, and off we went. Turns out they were trappers who kept an old car by the road for annual trips to town to sell furs, whoop it up a little, and buy supplies for the new season. Depending on the price of furs in a given year, the length of their stay in town, Fort Nelson, could last most of the summer. "We always buy our grubstake before we spend the other money," the second man assured me.

Luckily it was a warm day and we could drive comfortably with the windows open. We had gone but a few miles when each pulled a flask from an inside pocket, which demonstrated the only disagreement between them during the entire trip. One had a fiery whiskey, the other a very seductive but potent rum.

"Care for a snort?" one of the men asked. I did. I sampled each a couple of times in an hour and a half while they regaled me with tales of the winter of 1948–49 when it was ungodly cold, at least 70 below for days on end, or so they said. Then there was lots of speculation about how much money this year's catch would bring, the price of liquor in Fort Nelson, and whatever else that was important in their world.

As we reached the outskirts of town, I saw a sign for a Ford dealer some distance ahead and asked if that's where they wanted to go. Looking outside, the one closest to the window spotted a tavern and pointed to it. "Jes' let us out there," he said. "We'll work our way up the road." I stopped, we shook hands for the third or fourth time, they went inside, and I headed down the road shaking my head. I never did learn their names, and I counted three more bars between them and the Ford dealer.

A couple of hours later, nearing the summit of the Rocky Mountains, I came through a hairpin curve and had to brake quickly to avoid hitting a pickup truck with a camper broken down in the middle of the road. The truck had a flat tire, a bad one that bent the wheel. The license plate had been issued in Louisiana.

The driver, an older fellow, was under the truck cussing in the finest Cajun style. His jack wasn't strong enough to lift the truck and camper combined. His wife was in the camper fixing dinner. I pulled out a hydraulic jack and helped him change the tire. That earned me an invitation to supper—still in the middle of the road. There wasn't much traffic in those days. While we ate, I learned that they had recently retired as bakers in Shreveport, Louisiana, and were on their way north to spend the summer in Alaska, a lifelong dream.

We exchanged names and addresses. For the next several years, they regularly sent me a cake and a card at Christmas.

Those are just four people met in a single day along the Alaska Highway. Admittedly, things have changed since then. Though traffic isn't heavy yet by lower 48 standards, it's too heavy now to spend an hour sitting in the middle of the road changing a tire and eating dinner. And there are still trappers in the wilderness bordering the highway, though I doubt the two guys I hauled to Fort Nelson are still alive. If they are, they're in their 90s. And there are more people living and working along the highway these days. The last time I was in Fort Nelson, I couldn't even find the Ford dealer, much less the tavern where I let off my trapper friends.

Yet these are still special people, special people who live in a special place. When you break down along the Alaska Highway, the first car along will usually stop to help—if it's not another tourist or a long-haul trucker. Most of the tourists and the truckers these days are in too big of a hurry to get somewhere, and perhaps fearful that stopping to help along the Alaska Highway offers the same hazards that stopping at roadside in the lower 48 states can bring. Significantly, though, most of the tourists eventually get into the mood of stopping to help by the time they're several hundred miles up the road. That's just the way things are done up here.

These days, the real adventure of the Alaska Highway begins after you pass Fort St. John. Up to Fort St. John, facilities have kept pace with growing populations over the last several decades. Travelers don't really begin to touch the Alaska Highway wilderness until they pass Fort St. John. For many longtime Alaska Highway travelers, the real wilderness adventure doesn't even start until you're past Fort Nelson, the second day of this suggested itinerary. However, there are many unspoiled vistas and beautiful spots between Fort St. John and Fort Nelson.

Insider's Tip

Years ago the best advice about refueling was to choose gas stations in the larger towns along the Alaska Highway. That is no longer the case. Since 2006 the best deal for fuel we found was at a wide spot in the road known as Contact Creek, about 40 miles southeast of Watson Lake. Gas prices in the larger towns were, for the most part, the same from one end of the Canadian portion of the Alaska Highway to the other, the exception being Fort Nelson, where gas was always 15–20 cents a liter higher than the other large towns.

In and around Dawson Creek and the first 50 miles or so of the Alaska Highway, visitors in late July will see acres of brilliant yellow flowers in cultivated fields. This is canola, also known as rapeseed, used in the production of vegetable oil. The other common crop is hay.

Besides the visual impact of farmers' fields, the odor of natural gas will often be present in the early miles of the Alaska Highway. This doesn't mean you have a leak in your propane system. Several natural gas refining plants are scattered along the road system, and the smell can carry quite a distance. Fort St. John, for instance, almost owes its existence to the large number of natural gas facilities in or near the town.

By the time you've gone a hundred miles or so, the farms pretty much give way to forests, mostly small spruce and birch. No really big trees are evident from the road, but the forests of small trees can be quite dense. This pattern will repeat itself often as you go north. Larger trees are generally only found in coastal parts of Alaska and British Columbia or deep in protected stream valleys.

Unless you're up very early in the morning when deer might be moving about, the wildlife you're likely to see in the farming areas are various birds of prey, including eagles, hawks, and, with luck, a falcon or two. Occasionally, a snowshoe hare and, perhaps, a fox might show up.

Once you move into forested areas, black bears are much more numerous, though generally shy and retiring. Often the best place to see a bear is at the local landfill. The best time of year to see a bear at roadside is late May or early June, when the dandelions beside the road have flowered. Bears love dining on the dense patches of yellow flowers.

Campgrounds may have bears about, as well, particularly bears with a taste for raiding garbage cans. Away from refuse disposal sites, peer intently into the underbrush along creek bottoms from your vehicle; you might be rewarded with a glimpse of a black bear. Don't expect these bears to deliberately make themselves visible in open areas. Tracks in the soft mud of stream banks are often the only positive sign that black bears are in the area.

Your chances of seeing moose will increase after you leave the farming areas behind. Very early or very late in the day are the best times to see moose. Look closely in areas with good browse—low-growing alders and other bushes. Areas that burned in wildfires a few years earlier also offer good browse for moose and other ungulates. Moose tend to stay close to areas offering plenty of food.

One of the original bridges from the construction of the Alaska Highway crossed the Sikanni River a few hundred yards downstream of today's modern bridge. Unfortunately, vandals burned the old bridge down, and this bit of history has been lost forever.

Farther on, a pleasant part of the Prophet River region is the provincial park of the same name. Follow the signs and turn left off the highway and drive about half a mile on a gravel road. This access road crosses the original Alaska Highway (no longer in use, but still visible) and an airstrip. There's an excellent chance of seeing black bears near here.

Approaching Fort Nelson, you roll across the Muskwa River bridge on the edge of town. The Muskwa River at this point represents the lowest elevation above sea level on the entire Alaska Highway, about 1,000 feet. The bridge itself is an impressive span, built in 1970 to replace the old one, which was in danger of washing out during breakup every year. The Muskwa River can rapidly rise 20 feet or more during periods of heavy rain or snow melt. You can see evidence of these flood conditions if you look down from the bridge to the river shoreline.

Insider's Tip

When making a fire in camp, take a moment and try to count the growth rings in a small log cut up for your campfire. Although northern trees are very small in diameter, they are often very old. Rings will be so closely spaced in some trees that they are often impossible to count without a magnifying glass. Growing seasons are short in the North Country, thus each annual ring is very thin. The farther north you go, the thinner the growth rings on trees.

Hot Dogs and Beer

I like Canadians, which is something that should already be apparent. To me, they are the most special part of an Alaska Highway adventure. Because of that, I find the best times to travel the highway are mid-May or September, just before and just after the summer's onslaught of tourists. Roadside businesses aren't so busy then, and the people running them have time to talk. The road is less crowded as well.

Pulling into Fort St. John one May evening demonstrates what I mean. It was an unseasonably hot day, I was traveling alone, and it had been a long, dry afternoon. By about 9 p.m., I was ready for a beer, a meal, a shower, and sleep, in that order. I stopped at the first motel I saw.

The woman behind the counter was in her 30s; four or five kids of varying ages played in the yard out front. I filled out the form, she handed me a room key, and I asked about a place for dinner. Her eyes lit up a little, she apologized that there was no restaurant close to the motel, and then she asked me if I wanted a beer. "Absolutely."

She opened a small refrigerator behind the counter, pulled out two frosty bottles of good Canadian beer and said that should be enough to hold me until dinner. I started to pay for it and she stopped me. "We don't have our liquor license yet."

As for dinner, she said her husband would be home from work soon, and they were going to have a hot dog roast out front. I was told to join them.

I did join them, eating hot dogs and potato chips and sampling more of that good beer until well past midnight. We watched the sun go down and talked throughout the lingering twilight that ultimately evolved into sunrise. I slept quite late the next morning, well past checkout time, and was sent on my way with a friendly wave from the whole family. At times being the only guest in a motel can be a wonderful experience.

The motel is still there, though I haven't stopped for years. It's the first one on your left as you approach Fort St. John from the south.

This was not an isolated incident. Some years later, again driving north, this time with my wife and two young children, we pulled into a gas station at Teslin, Yukon Territory. Again, a warm day, and we were pushing to get a few miles behind us.

I pumped a thirsty pickup truck full of gas and paid the owner. After a little snarling from me, everybody climbed back in the truck, the kids less than eagerly, and I started the engine. Just as I was putting it in gear, out came the owner carrying four ice cream cones, one for each of us. Handing them through the window, he wished us a great trip and mumbled something about the ice cream being free because of the fill-up.

We would stop there on almost every Alaska Highway trip. The place, on the north side of Teslin, was called Halstad's, the name of the family that owned it. While their kids were growing up it was a family business in every sense of the word. Mom got up at 3 a.m. every summer morning to bake the doughnuts and pastries she was famous for. Dad sold gas and worked on the campgrounds and the rental boats. The kids were everywhere, helping out as needed.

Unfortunately, it's no longer there. The last time we visited, I was told they were probably going to close because the kids were grown and Dad wanted to go gold mining. The building has since been torn down, and the grounds are overgrown with wildflowers and weeds.

The largest private campground within the city limits of Fort Nelson is on the left side at the far end of town if you are northbound. It offers numerous amenities and has a restaurant on the premises.

Make plans to visit the Fort Nelson Heritage Museum, next to the West End Campground. This is a dandy facility offering a good look at the region's history and major events, such as the construction of the Alaska Highway in 1942.

Fort Nelson
Heritage Museum

SECTION TWO: Fort Nelson, British Columbia, to Watson Lake, Yukon

Though the Muskwa River bridge on the southeastern edge of Fort Nelson is the lowest elevation above sea level on the Alaska Highway, within 100 miles of leaving Fort Nelson, travelers will cross the highest point above sea level along the route. Fort Nelson lies on the eastern edge of the Rocky Mountains.

Insider's Tip

For years in previous editions of this book I warned readers about filling their RV water tanks in Fort Nelson because the water tasted so bad. In 2015, the head of the visitor center chewed me out in an e-mail and said the problem had been fixed and that I should fix the comment in my book. I tasted the water in 2016 and agree—it is much, much better.

About 3,500 people live in the town, with a total of perhaps 5,500 living in the town and the immediate area. The site of the present city is the fifth site of the actual town, as it was moved several times in its history to avoid flooding and other calamities.

In its early days, Fort Nelson existed primarily to service the fur trade. It was named for Lord Nelson, the British admiral who was victorious at Trafalgar. As recently as 80 years ago, Fort Nelson was still a frontier town without electrical power, telephones, or running water. Today, the city is fully modernized. Its primary industry is forestry. The railroad reached Fort Nelson in 1971. This is the last community along the Alaska Highway to have railroad service available that connects to the major lines serving North America. Fairbanks, it's true, is served by the Alaska Railroad, but that line only runs south to Anchorage and Seward. The Alaska Railroad does not connect to the continent-wide network of railroads that have grown up since the 19th century. Fort Nelson is literally the end of the line insofar as railroads are concerned.

Change for the railroads may be in the works, however. Alaskan and northern Canadian politicians are starting to seriously consider extending the railroad north from Fort Nelson to connect with the Alaska Railroad near Fairbanks. This is a construction project that most Alaskans consider long overdue.

Leaving Fort Nelson, northwest bound, travelers embark on the most beautiful stretch of the Alaska Highway, and the stretch that normally offers the most bountiful opportunities to observe wildlife. In fact, it's almost possible to guarantee wildlife on this stretch of the road, unlike all of the other segments described in this chapter.

The Rockies are nothing if not rugged. Quickly travelers will begin twisting their way up the mountains, through thickly forested areas with glimpses of ragged granite peaks. This is not a stretch of road to plan on driving fast. Grades approach 8 percent in some areas, and hairpin curves, both climbing into and descending from the mountains, are numerous.

Also, services are fewer and farther apart along this stretch of road. Though there are a good number of lodges and gas stations, these tend to be concentrated in and around Muncho Lake, about halfway between Fort Nelson and Watson Lake. The positive aspects of this, however, are the provincial parks (public campgrounds) that sit alongside the road. Some of these are in absolutely stunning locations.

If time permits, this stretch of road is a good one to break down into two days instead of one. Those considering doing so should plan to stop either near Summit or Muncho Lakes or perhaps Liard River Hot Springs.

Fishermen will want to stop and sample the Tetsa River along this part of the road. Good Dolly Varden and grayling fishing is available, and the fish are pretty good size. Try small flies (black gnats probably being tops for grayling) or small silver spinners. Salmon eggs will also entice fish. A good place to try is Tetsa River Provincial Park, about 63 miles from Fort Nelson. Campsites in this park are right on the river and offer great access for fishermen. Be sure you have a current British Columbia fishing license.

About 88 miles from Fort Nelson, the Alaska Highway enters Stone Mountain Provincial Park. It winds through the park for about 10 miles, past the abandoned settlement of Summit and over the crest of the Rockies. Starting here and for the next 50 miles or so comes the almost-certain guarantee of seeing wildlife.

Stone sheep, which inhabit the peaks of the northern Rockies, come down to lick minerals from the surface of the road. For most of the summer, mostly ewes and lambs—called nursery bands—are visible at roadside. Travelers in spring, right after breakup, or in the fall have a much better chance of seeing the big full-curl rams at roadside. Rams quickly head for the high country once summer begins in earnest.

Be prepared to stop. These sheep aren't likely to be too excited by the presence of your vehicle or any other vehicles. Often, you will be able to drive within a few feet of these animals to snap a picture or two out of the car window. In fact, you can probably get closer to the animals in your car than you can on foot. In past years whenever I've stepped out of the car to take a picture, the sheep have immediately gotten nervous and begun to move away from the road and into the rocks.

Stone sheep ram on Alaska Highway

Fort Nelson, British Columbia, to Watson Lake, Yukon; 330 miles (550 km)

Our Starting Mileage:

Driving Time: 8–10 hours

Towns En Route (all offering most travelers' services):

Toad River, 123 miles (205 kilometers)

Muncho Lake, 152 miles (253 kilometers)

Liard River, 193 miles (321 kilometers)

Watson Lake, 330 miles (550 kilometers)

Gas Available (besides towns listed above):

Tetsa River Services, 74 miles (123 kilometers)

Rocky Mountain Lodge, 95 miles (158 kilometers)

Toad River Lodge, 123 miles (205 kilometers)

Double "G" Service, 153 miles (255 kilometers)

Northern Rockies Lodge, 156 miles (260 kilometers)

Coal River Lodge, 230 miles (383 kilometers)

Fireside, 240 miles (400 kilometers)

Contact Creek Lodge, 286 miles (477 kilometers)

Campgrounds (Provincial parks are public campgrounds; most towns listed above have private campgrounds as well.):

Tetsa River Provincial Park, 63 miles (105 kilometers)

Tetsa River Services, 74 miles (123 kilometers)

Summit Lake Provincial Park, 90 miles (150 kilometers)

Toad River Lodge, 123 miles (205 kilometers)

Stone Mountain Safaris Lodge, 127 miles (210 kilometers)

Strawberry Flats, Muncho Lake, 154 miles (257 kilometers)

Northern Rockies Lodge, 156 miles (260 kilometers)

MacDonald Campground, Muncho Lake, 159 miles (265 kilometers)

Liard Hot Springs Lodge, 191 miles (320 kilometers)

Liard River Hotsprings Provincial Park, 194 miles (324 kilometers)

Coal River Lodge and RV, 230 miles (390 kilometers)

Fireside, 238 miles (403 kilometers)

Hotels/Motels/Lodges (Besides these, all towns listed above have overnight lodging available.):

Rocky Mountain Lodge, 95 miles (158 kilometers)

Toad River Lodge, 121 miles (202 kilometers)

Double "G" Service, 153 miles (255 kilometers)

Northern Rockies Lodge, 156 miles (260 kilometers)

Liard Hot Springs Lodge, 191 miles (320 kilometers)

Coal River Lodge and RV, 230 miles (390 kilometers)

Fireside, 238 miles (403 kilometers)

Major Terrain Features:

The Rocky Mountains

Mountainous, mostly forested

Steep grades, hairpin curves

Major rivers crossed: Liard and Coal

Wildlife: Moose, black bears, Stone sheep, white-tailed deer, caribou, grizzly bears, buffalo

Fishing Available: Lake trout, grayling, northern pike, whitefish, Dolly Varden

Black Bears

Some 50 miles or so from Fort Nelson, as the road climbs toward the summit of the Rockies, is the part of the highway most likely to offer sightings of both black and grizzly bears. My wife and I have seen as many as 20 black bears in less than 30 miles along this part of the road. However, in 2004, the black bears just seemed to disappear. I found out why while taking a walk one evening while we were camped at Steamboat (no longer open) that year, about 50 miles from Fort Nelson.

This campground used to be right on the edge of where we would see the black bears. From camp, I decided to walk a mile or so uphill, and then turn around and walk back to camp. About 15 minutes later, rounding a curve in the road, I had just decided to turn around at a road sign I could see several hundred yards ahead when the hair on the back of my neck started to rise. I stopped and looked more closely at the terrain ahead. Not 100 yards away a large grizzly bear stood on a rise looking down on me. Muttering something like, "You go your way and I'll go mine," I turned around and forced myself to walk slowly and evenly back toward camp—to run might cause a chasing instinct in the bear. A quick glance over my shoulder showed the grizzly, too, had turned and was headed back into the trees, much to my relief.

Almost certainly when this grizzly took up residence in the area, he either chased the local black bears out of the area or killed them outright. Thus there are fewer bears in this stretch of road than in the past, but if you do see one, it will likely be a big one.

The best places to be alert for sheep are where steep, jagged rock outcroppings—which mean safety for the sheep—come very close to the road. Most often these are cuts made in rocky areas to make room for the road. If you spook the sheep for any reason, they almost always run into the rocks, where few people or predators can follow. And remember to drive carefully in sheep country. Numerous blind corners and small rises can have sheep on the other side. Caribou are also seen frequently along this stretch of highway.

While you're in sheep country, several of the prettiest campgrounds in British Columbia are at roadside. Summit Lake Provincial Park and the two campgrounds within Muncho Lake Provincial Park are unsurpassed for scenery. And you'll find fishing opportunities for lake trout at both Summit and Muncho Lakes, though some sort of boat is probably necessary.

Insider's Tip

Big fish almost always hold near the bottom in northern streams, the one notable exception being grayling. Fly fishermen will almost always catch larger fish by fishing wet flies instead of dry, particularly for trout and Dolly Varden.

Because this area is mountainous, campers, fishermen, and boaters should watch the weather carefully. Sudden winds and squalls can arise with little warning, becoming almost instantly dangerous. Always leave yourself an option in case of sudden changes in the weather. Also, please note that snow is possible during any month of the year in the Rockies. Though infrequent in the summer, it still happens in June, July, and August. In 2016, 30 inches of snow fell at Summit Lake on the Friday before Memorial Day.

Beyond Summit Lake, as you begin easing down the west side of the Rockies, lies Muncho Lake, called by many the prettiest lake along the Alaska Highway. The blue color of this lake in deep areas and the green in shallows must be seen to be believed.

The enhanced color, though, is easily explained. There's considerable copper in the mountains surrounding Muncho Lake. Leached into the lake, it forms a copper oxide, which suspends in the water. Though the amount of copper oxide is relatively small compared to the volume of the lake, there's just enough of it to show up as enhanced color. Take pictures of Muncho Lake—few of your friends will believe your tales of the color.

Die-hard fishermen have been known to salivate at the thought of Muncho Lake. Lake trout to 35 pounds or more swim in its depths. These are natural fish—no stocking programs here. June and July are usually the most popular months for lake trout fishing. You'll probably need a boat and heavy-duty equipment for trolling. Guided fishing trips are available from lodges along the lakeshore.

Muncho Lake is best viewed in the early morning calm of a sunny summer day. By most afternoons, a breeze ruffles the surface, and the reflections of the surrounding mountains are washed away. The road winds along the shore of Muncho Lake for several miles, offering numerous vantage points.

Northern Rockies Lodge, near the north end of Muncho Lake, offers a superb RV park–campground on the lakeshore. However, it's also the highest-priced RV park along the entire Alaska Highway. The prettiest sites on the lakeshore, which are also the highest-priced sites, have only 20-amp power and no sewer hookups. Boondocking at one of the two provincial parks along the lakeshore for $15 or so is a much better deal financially, and the views are just as good.

About 30 miles past Muncho Lake is the most popular public campground on the Alaska Highway, Liard (locally pronounced "leerd") River Hotsprings Provincial Park. The government of British Columbia has provided bathhouses and a boardwalk to the pool a short distance from the campsites. There used to be a second pool higher on the mountain, but it was frequently closed because of grizzly bear sightings. In 1997, a sow grizzly with cubs attacked and killed a couple of tourists walking the trail to the upper pool. The trail to the upper pool was permanently closed after that, and some years later the facilities at the upper pool were removed. Because there are so many people in and around the lower pool, you should not have to worry about being bothered by bears. The upper pool, when it was in use, was often a fairly lonely place.

This campground fills up early on most summer days from mid-June to early August, so if you want a campsite, plan for an early afternoon arrival. Late-season travelers and early spring visitors will also find this park available, a relative rarity for provincial parks in this part of British Columbia. Jumping in the hot springs pool on a crisp winter day is a special experience.

Liard Hotsprings also offers a great chance for seeing moose. Usually there are a couple hanging around near the boardwalk that crosses the warm-water swamp en route to the lower pool. Late in the evening or early in the morning are the best times to see these big ungulates.

If the park is full, there is a private campground on the other side of the road near the park entrance. I don't particularly care for this RV park. Both my wife and I have noted in the past that this particular facility is unkempt, even dirty. If we find the provincial park full, we continue on and look for another place to spend the night.

Muncho Lake, BC

Little less than 20 miles past Liard Hotsprings, the road crosses the Swift River. Just past the bridge, a small green sign next to a narrow gravel road on the right reads, SMITH RIVER FALLS 2KM. There's no warning and really no place to park. But a turnout another few miles down the road offers the chance to unhook a dinghy or a tow vehicle and return to this narrow gravel road, which leads to one of the most beautiful sites in upper British Columbia. Smith River Falls is one of the best-kept secrets along the highway. Not only is there excellent grayling fishing in the pool below the falls, but it is a spectacular sight.

Despite the road being better than average along here, there are two fairly dangerous sections of highway prior to reaching Watson Lake. These are all the more dangerous because drivers have relaxed a bit after passing through the continuous grades and curves over the Rocky Mountains. The first of these is a 4.5-mile stretch about 50 miles past Liard River. The second is of lesser length about 10 miles farther on. Both are well marked.

Another road hazard between Liard Hotsprings and Watson Lake are buffalo, or American bison if you prefer. It is not at all uncommon to see hundreds of the big lumbering beasts alongside or on the road. Slow down—hitting a buffalo could easily destroy your vehicle.

Smith River Falls

Approaching Watson Lake, be on the lookout for Contact Creek Lodge, really just a small, two-pump filling station with a tiny café on the left. For years now, the owners here have offered one of the best prices for gas and diesel along the Alaska Highway. This is a much better place to fill up than Watson Lake, some 40 miles farther on.

About 28 miles prior to reaching Watson Lake, the road crosses the Hyland River, another of those spots fishermen may show an uncanny interest in. There's good fishing here for rainbows, Dolly Varden, and grayling.

Approaching Watson Lake, Yukon, drivers will actually zigzag back and forth across the British Columbia–Yukon border three times after passing through Fireside, though the border may not be marked at every crossing. Between these crossings, once again in British Columbia, is a settlement called Lower Post. No travelers' services are available here. A short gravel road leads to the site, originally a Hudson's Bay Company trading post. Now there's a British Columbia Forest Service field office installed in Lower Post, but little else.

Best of all, once you enter Yukon Territory, the actual road itself becomes much improved. Other than short stretches repaired each season, this good road pretty much continues for more than 400 miles, until well past Whitehorse.

My favorite RV park in Watson Lake is the Downtown R.V. Park in the center of town. There's Wi-Fi available, endless hot water in clean showers, and an RV wash station. While the full hookup sites are close together, the park is situated within easy walking distance of a grocery store, restaurants, and a department store. A slightly longer walk will take you to the Sign Post Forest where, since 1942, people have been posting signs from their hometowns.

Insider's Tip

For short periods twice a year, lake trout are available to shore-bound anglers on almost any large northern lake. In May, as the ice starts to go out, try casting in the limited open water close to shore, particularly near the inlets of small streams. After a long winter under the ice, lakers are hungry and can often be taken near the surface at the edge of the ice with light tackle. In late September, just before freeze-up, lakers can again be found close to shore when they seek out gravel areas in shallower places on the lake bottom to deposit and fertilize their eggs. Check the regulations carefully, though, before fishing. Because lake trout populations are highly susceptible to overfishing, British Columbia is considering an outright ban on fishing during the spawning season and tightly regulates size and bag limit restrictions in lakes where fishing for lakers is still allowed.

SECTION THREE: Watson Lake, Yukon, to Whitehorse, Yukon

If you're headed up the Alaska Highway and staying close to this book as you go, you've probably raised your eyebrows a time or two. Various longtime businesses along the Alaska Highway list as locations mileages from Dawson Creek, but those mileages don't coincide with anything given here, or at least don't come within 20 miles or so of what's given here.

Well, both this book and those businesses are right. When the older businesses were built, the Alaska Highway was a longer road. Thus a gas station put up at say mile 550 some 25 years ago might actually be at mile 535 today. Ever since the Alaska Highway was built, but especially in the past 30 years, engineers and road crews have been hard at work straightening the twisting path selected by the first surveyors. Thus, every year the Alaska Highway gets a little shorter.

Watson Lake, Yukon, to Whitehorse, Yukon; 271 miles (452 km)

Our Starting Mileage:

Driving Time: 7–8 hours

Towns En Route *(all offering most travelers' services)*:

Teslin, 163 miles (272 kilometers)

Whitehorse, 271 miles (452 kilometers)

Gas Available *(besides in Teslin, above)*:

Junction 37 Services, 13 miles (22 kilometers)

Nugget City, 14 miles (23 kilometers)

Rancheria, 74 miles (123 kilometers)

Continental Divide Lodge, 86 miles (144 kilometers)

Swift River, 97 miles (162 kilometers)

Johnson's Crossing, 196 miles (327 kilometers)

Jake's Corner, 224 miles (373 kilometers)

Klondike Highway 2 Junction, 261 miles (435 kilometers)

Campgrounds:

Watson Lake Campground, 3 miles (5 kilometers)

Upper Liard River Village, 7 miles (11 kilometers)

Junction 37 Services, 13 miles (22 kilometers)

Baby Nugget RV Park, 14 miles (23 kilometers)

Big Creek Yukon Campground, 39 miles (66 kilometers)

Rancheria (RV park), 74 miles (123 kilometers)

Rancheria Falls Recreation Site, 82 miles (137 kilometers)

Continental Divide Lodge, 86 miles (144 kilometers)

Dawson Peaks Resort and RV Park, 157 miles (261 kilometers)

Teslin Lake Campground, 172 miles (287 kilometers)

Johnson's Crossing, 197 miles (330 kilometers)

Squanga Lake Campground, 208 miles (347 kilometers)

Lakeview Resort and Marina, 237 miles (395 kilometers)

Marsh Lake, 247 miles (412 kilometers)

Caribou RV Park, 261 miles (435 kilometers)

Wolf Creek Campground, 264 miles (440 kilometers)

Pioneer Trailer Park, 268 miles (447 kilometers)

Hotels/Motels/Lodges *(besides those available in Teslin)*:

Upper Liard River Village, 7 miles (11 kilometers)

Junction 37 Services, 13 miles (22 kilometers)

Nugget City, 14 miles (23 kilometers)

Rancheria Hotel-Motel, 74 miles (123 kilometers)

Continental Divide Lodge, 86 miles (144 kilometers)

Hotels/Motels/Lodges (continued):

Dawson Peaks Resort and RV Park, 157 miles (261 kilometers)

Johnson's Crossing, 197 miles (330 kilometers)

Lakeview Resort and Marina, 237 miles (395 kilometers)

Inn on the Lake, 242 miles (404 kilometers)

Major Terrain Features:

Mostly low rolling hills

Alternating partly open and forested

Major rivers crossed: Upper Liard, Teslin, Yukon

Wildlife: Black bears, moose, caribou (occasionally), grizzlies (rarely)

Fishing Available: Lake trout, northern pike, grayling

Take Whitehorse as an example. Officially, Whitehorse has been at mile 918 (from Dawson Creek) ever since the road was built. However, the road has been rerouted to bypass Whitehorse, and, as already noted, has been considerably shortened. The turnoff for downtown Whitehorse is now just 884 miles from Dawson Creek. That's a difference of 34 miles.

At Watson Lake, the difference between the official mileage and the reality is 22 miles. Watson Lake these days is actually 613 miles from Dawson Creek, but it's still listed as being at mile 635.

Locating a business or a home by its mileage from a known point is fairly common throughout the North. And, because there are relatively few roads outside the towns, it's a convenient practice. As you drive along rural roads, you'll regularly see mailboxes listing mileages as an address or signs on lodges and gas stations listing a mileage. That the mileages are actually shorter than the official addresses is simply a sign of progress. Don't let these distances confuse you. Just remember that the actual distance these days is almost always less than the mileage a longtime highway business gives in its name or even in its official address.

To get an even better idea of how tortuous and twisted the original route was, visit the Alaska Highway Interpretive Centre before leaving Watson Lake. It's right alongside the highway with the Sign Post Forest, the latter all but impossible to miss as you drive past. In the Centre, a 40-minute movie details the building of the road, and various displays highlight different aspects of the construction. After you've seen the movie, walk outside into the Sign Post Forest, the Alaska Highway's oldest, and perhaps only, tradition. (See the sidebar on page 122.)

Once your visit to the Interpretive Centre and Sign Post Forest is over and you head northwest out of Watson Lake, you'll quickly realize that the wilderness is growing ever closer. Just compare the condensed information chart for this section with the same chart in previous sections. In this entire day's suggested drive, there's only one other town between Watson Lake and Whitehorse—Teslin. And, when you get to Teslin, you'll quickly see that it's a pretty small town. From here north to Fairbanks, all those spare parts for your vehicle suggested in earlier chapters will hold greater meaning. Though gas stations come along at fairly frequent intervals, the odds of these remotely located businesses having exactly the right size fan belt or other minor item are small.

Shortly after leaving Watson Lake, you'll come to the junction of the Cassiar Highway. The Cassiar is a north-south road that connects British Columbia's Yellowhead Highway 16 with the Alaska Highway. It's an alternate route for either northbound or southbound travelers. It is covered in more detail in Chapter 13 of this book.

Except for a couple of lodges and a public campground or two, the Alaska Highway is pretty much unpopulated for most of the 160 miles to Teslin. The terrain is mostly boreal forest with small creeks and rivers crossing the route or running alongside the road. Most of the clear streams offer opportunities for grayling fishing.

The scenery along this stretch of road is far from boring, but it does strike some travelers as repetitive. More than one first-timer on the Alaska Highway has been heard to remark, "Don't you ever run out of mountains?" or words to that effect.

Indeed, there are a lot of mountains. Though still more or less a part of the Rockies, most of the groups of mountains in this area have additional names, such as the Cassiar Mountains to the left and the Pelly Mountains to the right as you're northbound. You actually leave the Rockies as you approach Teslin. From Teslin on, the mountains to your left are extensions of the Coast Range, the ragged spine that

Nisutlin Bay, Teslin Lake, Yukon

marks the boundary between southeastern Alaska and Canada. Were you to carry things to extremes, it could be argued that the Coast Range is the extension of the Cascade Mountains of Washington and Oregon.

Teslin Lake, with the community of Teslin about midway along its eastern shore, is the first of three major lakes along this portion of the Alaska Highway that are partly in Yukon and partly in British Columbia. If you choose to fish the Teslin,

Insider's Tip

Fishing guides are available in and around Teslin if you want to try out this first of the three big lakes.

Atlin, or Tagish Lakes, be certain to check the fishing regulations carefully. While a British Columbia or a Yukon license can be used in any part of Teslin and Tagish Lakes, at Atlin you'll have to have a license appropriate to whichever province you are in. Confusing, I know, but the fishing is worth it.

All three lakes are roughly 100 miles long and 2–5 miles wide. All offer excellent lake trout, northern pike, and grayling fishing, though it helps to have a guide the first time you go looking for fish in these massive bodies of water.

Coming into Teslin, drivers cross the Nisutlin Bay bridge, the longest over-water span on the Alaska Highway, which crosses an arm of Teslin Lake. Teslin itself is home to about 350 people. Some 2,200 feet above sea level and this far north, Teslin offers a pretty cool climate, even in summer. The average date for the last spring frost is in mid-June. Fall frosts start the latter half of August, so Teslin averages little more than 60 consecutive frost-free days each summer. All travelers' services are available in or near Teslin, but choices are fairly limited.

Leaving Teslin, the road follows the lakeshore to Johnson's Crossing at the north end of the lake. A bridge crosses the Teslin River, which flows out of the lake. It's 32 miles from Teslin to Johnson's Crossing, which gives you some idea of just how big this lake really is.

After Johnson's Crossing, it's 28 more miles to Jake's Corner, a road junction offering a couple of options for travelers. Jake's Corner is not an official name. The name of the gas station and café at the junction is JAKE'S CRYSTAL PALACE, according to the sign. However, the spot has locally been known as Jake's Corner for decades.

Insider's Tip

Avoid buying gas at the Cassiar Junction, 13 miles past Watson Lake. The owners of this gas station (Junction 37 Services) think they have a captive audience at the start/finish of the Cassiar Highway and charge significantly more than gas stations in Watson Lake or those farther up the Alaska Highway. Gas is normally about a nickel or more higher per liter here than in Watson Lake. Better yet, head another 60 miles or so up the road to Rancheria and pay a penny less for gas than in Watson Lake.

Sign Post Forest

Back in 1942, a homesick soldier stationed in Watson Lake put up a sign for his hometown. Ever since, travelers to Alaska have been carting along road signs pirated from local highways to hang at the same location. Today, thousands upon thousands of signs

from all over the world decorate a "forest" of poles put in place to hold as many as possible. By all means bring along a sign of your own from your hometown to put up. Just about anything will do—a street sign, a WELCOME TO . . . sign, an old license plate, or a sign for some local attraction. Most popular seem to be signs frequently seen at city limits, that is to say a sign with the name of a town and a number indicating either elevation or population.

The best part of Sign Post Forest is putting up a sign one year and then returning several years later to try and find it again. As you walk through the sign forest, you'll almost certainly come across people trying to do just that. The adjacent visitor center maintains a log of signs and locations for help in locating specific signs.

The Alaska Highway continues straight ahead to Whitehorse from Jake's. If you turn left on the Atlin Road, there's another junction just a short distance away. Atlin Road continues to the left at this junction; the road straight ahead leads to Tagish and Carcross. A separate part of this section details the Atlin Road trip (see pages 124–125).

The road leading to Tagish and Carcross offers an alternative route to Whitehorse from Jake's Corner. It leads first to Tagish, little more than a campground and a collection of summer homes at the bridge over the Tagish River. The Tagish River is a short, slow-flowing stream joining Tagish Lake to the south with Marsh Lake to the north. A public campground sits next to the road on the east side of the bridge.

Fishermen should note that this bridge produces some of the finest catches of lake trout in Yukon Territory in late June and July. Fish from 5 to 20 pounds are regularly taken by locals and vacationers fishing with bait from the fishwalk thoughtfully built onto the north side of the bridge. Use fresh-frozen herring, sometimes available at the small marina near the bridge, for bait. What locals call herring is really cisco, a small freshwater fish that spawns in the Tagish River. In years past you could jig for these from the bridge for your bait. However, now a special permit is required to jig or use a net for cisco, so you'll have to find someone willing to sell you a couple for bait. Frozen bait herring (often available in outdoors stores) will work just fine if you can't find any cisco.

Those with a boat will find excellent trolling for lakers in both Marsh and Tagish Lakes, as well as pockets of northern pike and grayling. If you like to fish, this is a great place to spend a few days.

Back in 1978, my son, Eric, caught his first fish from the Tagish River bridge—sort of. He was 5 at the time, and I had paid about $7 for one of those cheap rod, reel, and line starter kits. The whole family, including grandparents, hiked out on the bridge, baited up, and dropped their lines into the water. Sure enough, the first fish to bite took Eric's bait.

Eyes wide with excitement, he reeled forward and backward, shouting all the while. Then the fish flopped on the water's surface just below his feet. He took one look at that 7-pound lake trout, screamed, threw his rod into the air, and lit out for camp at a dead run. Grandma went after the boy. Mom grabbed the fishing rod and finished reeling in the fish. Dad's still laughing.

If you elect to continue on the Alaska Highway from Jake's Corner, it's about 48 more miles to the turnoff for downtown Whitehorse. You will drive along the north shore of Marsh Lake and cross the headwater of the Yukon River as it flows out of Marsh Lake. This, the most famous of the North's great rivers, flows almost 2,000 miles through Yukon

Eric Dalby pulled this lake trout out of Marsh Lake late on a June evening.

Territory and Alaska to its outlet in the Bering Sea on Alaska's west coast. The Yukon was the great transportation artery that served the Klondike Gold Rush at the end of the 19th century and other gold rushes in the early 20th century in Alaska. Several of the stern-wheelers that carried people and supplies have been restored over the years and can be seen in Whitehorse, Dawson, and Fairbanks. Though stern-wheelers no longer ply its waters, the Yukon still qualifies as a major transportation artery in the North.

Prior to reaching the turnoff for downtown Whitehorse, the road intersects Klondike Highway 2, which leads south to Carcross and Skagway, Alaska. This is another great side trip and should be considered by anyone interested in the gold-rush history of the North. Skagway was the starting point for argonauts rushing to the Klondike goldfields near Dawson. Would-be miners sailed to Skagway, hiked over the treacherous Chilkoot Trail to Lake Bennett, and built boats to float through Bennett, Tagish, and Marsh Lakes into the Yukon River.

From the junction with Klondike 2, it's about 11 miles to the turnoff for downtown Whitehorse. If you choose to go downtown, the road actually makes sort of a loop through the city and rejoins the Alaska Highway on the other side of town. Those who elect not to visit downtown Whitehorse will have about 3 miles on the Alaska Highway to where the other end of the loop turns off for downtown. Mileage measurements for the next section of this chapter will be made from this second access road (westernmost) to Whitehorse.

The Atlin Road

From Jake's Corner, a narrow gravel road leads 58 miles south to Atlin, British Columbia, a town often called Canada's Little Switzerland. This is, I believe, the most beautiful setting anywhere in northwestern Canada.

The drive takes less than two hours if you elect to do it nonstop. However, there are a couple of places worth visiting along the way.

The first of these is Snafu Lake Campground, about 16 miles south of the Alaska Highway. Canoeists and kayakers will thoroughly enjoy this chain of small lakes connected by narrow sloughs. Fishermen will find hungry pike at almost every turn, and wildlife enthusiasts will have a chance to see grizzly bears and moose along the shores of the various lakes. Some years back, my son experienced the thrill of watching a grizzly chase a moose through shallow water and along the lakeshore. When last seen going over a hill, the moose was winning.

Two miles beyond the Snafu Lake turnoff, there's an old abandoned trapper's cabin at the right side of the road. This is great for investigating how trappers built small log cabins to house themselves over a long winter. It's small by almost any standard, with low ceilings. Walk inside and try to imagine spending several months alone in this tiny shelter.

From just beyond the cabin, the road follows the shore of Atlin Lake all the way to Atlin. Snow-capped mountains are visible in every direction from Atlin, the lake is a sparkling blue jewel, and the setting is all but unbelievable. The town itself looks like something out of the Old West.

From Atlin, drivers can venture east through active gold mining country for about 12 miles to Surprise Lake. The more adventurous can continue into the hills above Surprise Lake, though this road isn't recommended for large motorhomes or trailers.

Pine Creek, Surprise Lake's outlet stream, is crossed twice, the last time within site of the lake. There's excellent fishing for grayling right at the second bridge.

Also from Atlin, drivers can venture south for an additional 16 miles on Warm Bay Road. There are several fairly primitive campgrounds along this road, which parallels the lakeshore.

Though this side trip can be done in a day, you'll feel cheated if you do. Better to allow two days and plan to overnight in one of the campgrounds or the hotel in Atlin.

For more information on overnight accommodations and attractions, contact the Atlin Mountain Inn at 250-651-7546 or visit atlinmountaininn.com.

Sunset at Atlin Lake

Skagway, Alaska: A Step Back into Alaska's Past

Klondike Highway 2 runs 99 miles from its Alaska Highway junction to Skagway, Alaska, in part alongside the White Pass and Yukon Railway.

The railroad closed in the 1970s when the road was completed into Skagway. In 1988 it reopened to carry tourists on short day trips from Skagway to Lake Bennett and back. This short train trip is one of the most popular shore excursions available to cruise ship passengers whose vessels dock in Skagway (an average of three to four ships a day during the summer).

Klondike 2 runs due south, passing at least one unique terrain feature before reaching Carcross—a small desert of sand dunes about 32 miles south of the junction.

From there the road proceeds 66 miles south, across White Pass in the Coast Range to Skagway. The scenery is spectacular. Windy Arm of Tagish Lake and then Tutshi Lake are to the left; craggy peaks fill the skyline in all directions. Watch closely for Rocky Mountain goats on the rugged ridges.

At the summit of White Pass, you enter Alaska. The road descends quickly into Skagway with steep grades and hairpin curves. Watch for US Customs on your right. All vehicles entering from Canada must stop. Canadian Customs is open 9 a.m.–9 p.m., and US Customs 8 a.m.–8 p.m. These take into account the time zone change at the border. When it's 8 a.m. in Skagway, it's 9 a.m. just across the border in Canada.

Much of Skagway is now a National Historic Park, as is the Chilkoot Trail, which begins a few miles out of town near the abandoned townsite of Dyea. False-front wooden buildings, some dating back to the gold rush, still characterize the town. By all means drive out to Dyea and hike at least a few hundred yards on the Chilkoot Trail. You'll almost certainly meet some hikers who plan to hike to Lake Bennett, a rather arduous climb.

The best time to visit Skagway is on the 4th of July. The party lasts all day and includes events for young and old alike. The parade along Broadway is large by the standards of the size of the town, the various games held during the day are right out of small-town America, and the American Legion is standing on the corner selling corn on the cob.

Northbound travelers can also drive aboard an Alaska Marine Highway ferry in Skagway for a short cruise to Haines. From Haines, they can venture north to rejoin the Alaska Highway at Haines Junction, Yukon Territory. It's a pleasant variation for the trip north.

For additional information on Skagway, check out the Skagway Convention and Visitors Bureau website at skagway.org.

SECTION FOUR: Whitehorse, Yukon, to Beaver Creek, Yukon

Whitehorse is a town that bears investigating. First and foremost are the restaurants; there are some great ones in Whitehorse, several offering food with a distinctly European flair. There is also, to the horror of some parents, a McDonald's, that peripatetic sign of contemporary civilization. If the kids insist, buy them their favorite gut bomb at McDonald's, and then make them wait patiently while you sample the much better fare available in dining rooms in downtown hotels.

The centerpiece of Whitehorse is a riverfront park holding the rebuilt stern-wheeler *SS Klondike II* and a barge similar to the type the river steamer used to push back and forth between Whitehorse and Dawson. Parks Canada completely refurbished the *Klondike II* in the late 1970s and early 1980s. As much as is possible, the ship today looks just as it did on its maiden voyage nearly 80 years ago. Tours are conducted through the boat at half-hour intervals, seven days a week. Each tour lasts about an hour and takes visitors through the entire boat, from the engine room to the bridge. The *Klondike II* was last in active service in the 1950s.

Insider's Tip

Campers planning to overnight in Whitehorse should consider staying at The Caribou RV Park, just a mile or so before the junction with Klondike 2 leading to Skagway. The private campground offers full hookups for RVs, grassy sites for tents, tepees for rent, and has nice laundry and shower facilities. It's a great place to unwind and divest yourself of some trail dust. This has been a favorite stop of ours since the 1970s. Also on site is the Wolf's Den restaurant, specializing in German food. Try the Yaegerschnitzel.

The park holding the boat also hosts Canada's biggest summer event, Canada Day on July 1. Similar to the US celebration of Independence Day on July 4, Canada Day brings out the finest Whitehorse has to offer. Parades, events, and entertainment combine for a daylong festival. The local Royal Canadian Mounted Police even break out their legendary red uniforms for this event.

Although Whitehorse offers a great Canada Day celebration, don't forget that Canada Day is a nationwide event. Even the smallest towns throughout northwestern Canada will be hosting some sort of festivity to celebrate July 1. Don't be shy about participating.

Take advantage of your time in Whitehorse to check your vehicle over carefully. You've come several thousand miles by this point, some of it on less-than-perfect roads. It's time to take a good look underneath for loose bolts, to change the oil if appropriate, and to closely examine your tires. There are still quite a few miles to Fairbanks and its full range of car-care services. Some of those miles are pretty lonely ones.

Whitehorse, Yukon, to Beaver Creek, Yukon; 282 miles (470 km)

Our Starting Mileage

Driving Time: 7–8 hours

Towns En Route:

(all offering most travelers' services)

Haines Junction, 98 miles (163 kilometers)

Destruction Bay, 165 miles (275 kilometers)

Burwash Landing, 175 miles (292 kilometers)

Beaver Creek, 282 miles (470 kilometers)

Gas Available *(besides towns listed above):*

Porter Creek, 3 miles (5 kilometers)

Otter Falls Cutoff, 76 miles (127 kilometers)

Destruction Bay, 165 miles (275 kilometers)

Note: While gas is available in or near the towns listed, it is not available in many other places. Significantly, there is no gas available for 108 miles when leaving Burwash Landing. This is now the longest stretch of the Alaska Highway with no gas available.

Campgrounds *(Towns listed above have private campgrounds as well.):*

Kusawa Lake Campground, 40 miles (67 kilometers)

Otter Falls Cutoff, 76 miles (127 kilometers)

Pine Lake Campground, 94 miles (157 kilometers)

Cottonwood RV Park, 148 miles (247 kilometers)

Congdon Creek Campground, 153 miles (255 kilometers)

Lake Creek Campground, 232 miles (387 kilometers)

Discover Yukon Lodging/White River RV Park, 248 miles (415 kilometers)

Snag Junction Campground, 268 miles (447 kilometers)

Hotels/Motels/Lodges *(Towns listed previously have overnight lodging available.):*

Wolf Ridge B&B Log Cabin Rentals, 18 miles (30 kilometers)

Major Terrain Feature:

Mostly open, lightly forested country to Haines Junction (large, old forest fire burns visible)

Wrangell–St. Elias Mountains to left, Haines Junction to Burwash Landing

Low rolling hills with muskeg, Burwash Landing to Alaska border

Major rivers crossed: Takhini, Donjek, Koidern, White

Wildlife: Moose, black bears, eagles, elk, Dall sheep, caribou (occasionally), and grizzlies

Fishing Available: Lake trout, northern pike, and grayling

Fill up your gas tank before heading out of Whitehorse. One of the longest stretches of Alaska Highway without gas available is most of the 76 miles from Whitehorse to Otter Falls Cutoff.

Takhini Hot Springs Resort

Campers who stay in the Whitehorse area for more than a day should investigate Takhini Hot Springs Resort just outside of town. Drive west on the Alaska Highway to where Klondike 2 turns north for Dawson. Follow the signs a few miles north on this road to the turnoff for Takhini. More than 100 campsites, a restaurant, and a hot-springs pool make this one of the North's more pleasant places to spend a few days. Kids, especially, will love it.

Leaving Whitehorse, it's a comfortable 90-minute drive to Haines Junction, all of it on good wide road. There are no dangerous grades or blind, hairpin curves. The only population concentration of any sort is the Indian village of Champagne, which is a short distance south of the road, and no services are available there.

History buffs will find one of the original highway bridges still standing along this stretch of road. At the Aishihik River, 78 miles from Whitehorse, the original bridge can be seen to the right from the road. The old bridge, rebuilt in 1942 for the construction of the Alaska Highway, has stood at this site since about 1920.

Insider's Tip

Combining Canada Day in Whitehorse and Independence Day in Skagway makes for a great interlude in early July. In fact, several residents of both Skagway and Whitehorse take in both celebrations every year. Only 100 miles separate these two towns, so the logistics are pretty simple. Be advised, though, campgrounds and hotels are jammed for these two events.

Originally it was used to move freight and passengers across the Aishihik River to Silver City on the shores of Kluane ("kloo-aw-nee") Lake. A turnoff just prior to the bridge in use today leads to the old bridge, which can no longer support vehicles.

As you approach Haines Junction, the Wrangell–St. Elias Mountains will be ahead. This range is on the border of Yukon Territory and Alaska where Alaska's Panhandle joins the mainland mass of the state. Mount St. Elias, which peaks 18,008 feet above sea level, straddles the US–Canada border and is the second-highest peak in both Canada and Alaska.

At Haines Junction, the Alaska Highway turns off to the right. If you drive straight through town, you will, 150 miles or so later, find yourself in Haines, Alaska. Turn right at the junction if Fairbanks is your goal.

Haines Junction is the headquarters of Canada's Kluane National Park, which encompasses most of the Canadian portion of the Wrangell–St. Elias Mountains.

On the Alaska side, Wrangell–St. Elias National Park, the largest national park in the United States, abuts Kluane National Park at the US–Canada border.

Insider's Tip

Kluane National Park and Yukon Government Information Centre offer interpretive displays and a slide show. The center is open daily 9 a.m.–9 p.m. in the summer. It's well worth the time to stop.

Driving out of Haines Junction, Kluane National Park will be continually on your left until past Kluane Lake at Burwash Landing, some 75 miles farther on. As you approach the lake, the scenery becomes more impressive with each mile you drive. If the weather's clear, you'll be able to see glaciers on distant mountainsides. Various marked turnouts allow ample opportunity to marvel at the vastness of the Wrangell–St. Elias Mountains.

Approaching the southeastern edge of Kluane Lake, a lengthy bridge leads across one of the rivers feeding the lake. The mountain visible straight ahead as you cross the bridge is Sheep Mountain. Dall sheep, the only pure white mountain sheep in North America, are frequently visible on the slopes of Sheep Mountain. Northbound travelers in May will almost certainly see bands of sheep all over the mountainside. Later in the summer, luck becomes a factor in whether or not you will see Dall sheep from the road.

Across the bridge, at the base of Sheep Mountain, a Parks Canada station provides information on the park. This is primarily a wilderness park; there are no roads into it. If you wish to experience Kluane National Park, you're going to have to get out of your car and do some hiking.

Dall sheep

Within a half mile of the Sheep Mountain visitor center is a sign commemorating Soldier's Summit. This is the point where the southbound builders met the northbound builders in 1942. A small ceremony held here on November 20, 1942, marked the official opening of the Alaska Highway.

The next few miles as you drive along the lakeshore offer a visual feast at any time of the year. Steep mountains rise from the road's edge on your left, and a stunningly beautiful lake fills your vision to the right.

As the road moves away from the lake, travelers pass first through Destruction Bay, and then 10 miles farther on, Burwash Landing. At Burwash Landing, the Kluane Museum of Natural History is an excellent stop and a bit of a surprise. Not many travelers expect to find a museum of this quality in such a remote area. It's small but quite fascinating and offers stunning wildlife dioramas. There's a small admission fee for each adult.

From Burwash Landing to the Alaska border, the road is paved, after a fashion. Unfortunately, it was a better road when it was gravel. Pavement is almost impossible to maintain in this region of heavy permafrost—permanently frozen ground. The next 140 miles offer probably the slowest driving on the entire Alaska Highway because of dips and bulges in the road surface. There's little that can be done other than to slow down and tough it out. Drivers of big motorhomes and vehicles towing large trailers should be particularly careful along this part of the road. Some of these frost heaves can literally tear the suspension out of a vehicle going too fast.

Insider's Tip

Hikers in Kluane National Park should stay in groups of two or more. This mountain wilderness is grizzly bear country, as my cousin, Torbin Himmelstrup (from Denmark), and I can well attest. Talking and laughing during a 1979 hike, we entered an expansive patch of alder on a mountainside. Seconds later a grizzly bear exploded out of the far side. Grizzlies are rarely a danger to people traveling in groups; most grizzly attacks are directed at people traveling alone.

Kluane Museum of Natural History, Burwash Landing, Yukon

The countryside along here is typical of permafrost regions. The surface is mostly muskeg, sort of half swamp and half ground—tough to walk across. Trees are mostly stunted spruce. Big trees are a rarity in permafrost areas; tree root systems spread out near the surface instead of penetrating deep into the earth because of the frozen soil. Because their hold on the ground is tenuous, high winds uproot them easily.

By the time you've bounced yourself around on the permafrost heaves from Burwash Landing, Beaver Creek almost seems an oasis, though it's the kind of place not many people would have given a second glance just a few days before. Those desiring hotel accommodations should arrive early. Bus tours use Beaver Creek as an overnight stop, and many of the rooms in town are pre-booked. Campers will find a campground in the middle of town. A pleasant site, though not really a great one for tent campers, this campground was designed for RVs. Tent campers should plan to stay at Snag Junction Campground about 13 miles southeast of town.

Southbound travelers will have to process through Canadian Customs at Beaver Creek, a procedure that has become slightly more complicated for Americans since September 11, 2001. Prior to then, a driver's license was about all you needed. But now, all Americans entering Canada are required to show a passport.

SECTION 5: Beaver Creek, Yukon, to Fairbanks, Alaska

On this leg of the trip you'll quickly note a kind of trade-off. First of all, the road is markedly improved once you enter Alaska, a real treat after the last 150 miles of driving in Yukon Territory.

On the debit side of the ledger, however, the public campgrounds in Alaska are not nearly as well maintained as the public campgrounds in Yukon or the provincial parks in British Columbia. With isolated exceptions, this holds true for the entire state. But this distinction is relative. Alaska's public campgrounds are reasonably well maintained; they just don't quite come up to the level that you may have grown accustomed to in Canada.

Burwash Grizzly

Long-Term Friends

In 1979 a chance stop at the Squanga Lake Campground, about 50 miles south of Whitehorse, led to a long lasting family friendship, thanks to our dog, a perky miniature dachshund we called Pretzel.

We had picked this spot as a place to meet my wife's parents on their drive to Alaska—a favorite fishing hole was nearby. We set up a tent to give the kids a place to nap and settled back to wait. A few minutes later, a Canadian family came over and introduced themselves.

Joe and Sheighla Pollock had been talking about getting a dog, and Sheighla really liked Pretzel. We showed off the dog, chatted for awhile, and they invited us to stop in White-horse for a slice of the apple pie Sheighla was planning to bake after their weekend was over. We sort of agreed, not knowing for certain which day we would be in Whitehorse, and left it at that. A few minutes later, Jennifer's folks pulled in and we left for Tagish Lake to set up camp and fish for lake trout.

In a grocery store in Whitehorse four or five days later, we bumped into Sheighla buying apples, the invitation was repeated, and we headed over to their place.

Joe was then the Yukon Territory engineer for Parks Canada, and he was deeply involved in rebuilding the *SS Klondike II,* a stern-wheeler that had plied the Yukon River several decades earlier. The boat is now the centerpiece of a riverfront park in Whitehorse.

After the pie, nothing less than an insider's tour of the boat would do, and we spent the afternoon crawling all over the boat as Joe pointed out everything involved with its construction. It was an unbeatable experience, and one that I later turned into a couple of magazine articles. Over the years, we've shared many visits back and forth over the Alaska-Canada border, and all of us look forward to getting together whenever our schedules allow.

Distances in Alaska are measured in miles, just as in the rest of the United States. In lieu of kilometer posts at 5-kilometer intervals along the road as in Canada, there will now be mileposts at 1-mile intervals. Again, some of these get knocked down, so don't be distressed if some are missing.

Insider's Tip

A major exception to my suggestion about not bothering to fish near highway bridges is Koidern River Bridge #2, about 33 miles before reaching Beaver Creek. One of the North's most perfect grayling holes is on the upstream side of the bridge, and there is a graveled turnout that leads almost right to it. Keep a couple for supper if you like, but catch-and-release fishing is the order of the day here, as grayling do not freeze well.

Beaver Creek, Yukon, to Fairbanks, Alaska; 317 miles (530 km)

Our Starting Mileage:

Driving Time: About 8 hours

Towns En Route:

Tok, Alaska, 110 miles (181 kilometers)

Delta Junction, 220 miles (362 kilometers)

North Pole, 304 miles (508 kilometers)

Fairbanks, 317 miles (530 kilometers)

Gas Available *(besides towns listed above)*:

Border City Lodge (just across Alaska border), 21 miles (35 kilometers)

Scotty Creek Services, 24 miles (40 kilometers)

Naabia Niign, 61 miles (103 kilometers)

Dot Lake, 159 miles (265 kilometers)

Silver Fox Roadhouse, 202 miles (337 kilometers)

Richardson Roadhouse, 248 miles (414 kilometers)

Salcha River Lodge, 275 miles (460 kilometers)

Salcha, 283 miles (472 kilometers)

Campgrounds *(Towns listed above have private campgrounds as well.)*:

Border City RV Park, 23 miles (38 kilometers)

Deadman Lake State Campground, 47 miles (79 kilometers)

Lakeview State Campground, 55 miles (83 kilometers)

Naabia Niign, 61 miles (103 kilometers)

Tok River State Recreation Site, 107 miles (180 kilometers)

Tundra Lodge and RV Park, 111 miles (185 kilometers)

Moon Lake Wayside, 130 miles (212 kilometers)

Cathedral Creek B&B and RV Park, 134 miles (224 kilometers)

Mountain House Lodge, 210 miles (350 kilometers)

Delta State Campground, 221 miles (370 kilometers)

Smith's Green Acres RV Park and Campground, 222 miles (370 kilometers)

Quartz Lake Recreation Area, 232 miles (386 kilometers)

Birch State Recreation Site, 259 miles (432 kilometers)

Lazy Moose RV Park, 269 miles (446 kilometers)

Salcha River State Recreation Site, 274 miles (457 kilometers)

Harding Lake State Recreation Area, 276 miles (460 kilometers)

Chena Lakes Recreation Area, 301 miles (511 kilometers)

Hotels/Motels/Lodges *(Besides these, all towns listed above have overnight lodging available.)*:

Border City Lodge, 23 miles (38 kilometers)

Scotty Creek Services, 24 miles (40 kilometers)

... Continued

Hotels/Motels/Lodges (continued):
Cathedral Creek B&B and RV Park, 134 miles (224 kilometers)
Silver Fox Roadhouse, 202 miles (337 kilometers)
Mountain House Lodge, 210 miles (350 kilometers)
Salcha River Lodge, 275 miles (460 kilometers)
Salchaket Homestead, 276 miles (462 kilometers)
Major Terrain Features:
Low, rolling hills, mostly forested
Mountains to south
Major river crossed: Tanana
Wildlife: Moose, black bears, eagles, buffalo
Fishing Available: Grayling, northern pike, rainbows (stocked), salmon

With the exception of gasoline, most travelers' services will be more expensive in Alaska than in Canada. By the time you reach Alaska, gasoline for anything less than $4 a gallon will seem like a bargain.

Road construction projects are treated differently in Alaska too. Undoubtedly you will have passed considerable road work in the 2,000 or more miles already driven in Canada, roadwork usually done in fairly short stretches with minimal traffic delay problems. In Alaska, however, it's nothing for road crews to completely tear up a 30- to 40-mile section of road and spend two or three years rebuilding it. Thus traffic delays for road construction in Alaska will likely be longer, and the routes through construction zones more rugged. As in Canada, road crews may be in operation 24 hours a day during the summer months. Construction seasons are pretty short in the Far North.

Leaving Beaver Creek, the road leads about 19 miles to the US–Canada border. This is another stretch where it pays to slow down and take your time because of permafrost heaves in the roadway. Scenery-wise there isn't much; mostly muskeg and scraggly black spruce line the route.

At the border, a turnout with a large sign is to the left. Most travelers stop here for a short celebration of their trek. If you do stop, take a moment to walk down to the actual border and look north and south. A 20-foot-wide swath cut through the trees marks the border. It stretches beyond the horizon in both directions. The actual border is well marked on the Canadian side of the turnout with a post and a line on the ground.

Just past the border, all vehicles and people entering the United States from Canada must pass through US Customs. Passports are now required for entry into Canada and for reentry into the United States. You may also need to show your vehicle registration. Questions pertaining to the value of goods purchased in Canada will likely be asked. For most travelers, processing customs takes a few minutes at most.

If you are southbound, Canadian Customs officials will ask American citizens for a passport to go along with your photo ID. This requirement was put in place in January 2008 and is not likely to change.

From the border, it's about 90 miles to Tok, the first community of any size right on the highway. En route, however, you will pass a turnoff for Northway, an Indian village about 7 miles south of the road. About 350 people reside in or near Northway. Winter travelers should be aware that the region around Northway is often the coldest place in Alaska.

Northway sits within the 950,000-acre Tetlin National Wildlife Refuge, which was established in 1980. This refuge offers a high density of nesting waterfowl in the summer along with year-round populations of moose, grizzlies, black bears, wolves, coyotes, and red fox. For more information about visiting the refuge, visit fws.gov /refuge/tetlin or call 907-883-5312.

Fishing opportunities are fairly sparse along the first hundred miles or so in Alaska. Deadman Lake State Campground does offer fishermen the chance to catch northern pike averaging a couple feet long, but these are real skinny fish, locally referred to as snakes.

Tok bills itself as the "Sled Dog Capital of Alaska." There are daily demonstrations in town for summer visitors, and those who desire to obtain a husky or malamute will find plenty of dogs to consider in Tok. Call the Tok Information Center at 907-883-5667 or visit tokalaska.info. com for information on Tok-area activities.

Our favorite RV park in Tok is the Sourdough Campsite a few miles south of town on the Glenn Highway leading to Anchorage. An on-site restaurant offers up an excellent sourdough hot-cake breakfast to get you going in the morning.

From Tok, it's little more than 100 miles to Delta Junction. About 35 miles prior to reaching Delta, there's a real possibility of seeing buffalo at road-side. These big animals are the descendants of a transplant of a few animals made in the 1920s. The herd has since grown large enough to allow a modest hunting season each fall. Permits to hunt buffalo are highly sought after by Alaskan hunters.

One of the attractions for buffalo is farms. In the 1970s, Alaska made an effort to start a large commercial farming operation, primarily barley, near Delta Junction. Commercially, the venture proved less than successful, though some of the farms on lands leased from the state are still in operation. Mostly these farms are alongside roads leading off the highway to the north.

As folks in Delta Junction will quickly tell you, their town is the official end of the Alaska Highway. When the road was built in 1942, a road already existed from Delta Junction to Fairbanks, the final leg of the Richardson Highway connecting Valdez to Fairbanks. In both Delta and Fairbanks are markers commemorating the end of the Alaska Highway. But because few folks target Delta Junction as the termination of their Alaska Highway experience, this book will use Fairbanks as the ultimate destination for travelers. A milepost marking Delta Junction as the end of the Alaska Highway is installed in front of the visitor center.

As its name implies, Delta Junction is a road junction. The Alaska Highway/Richardson Highway continues straight ahead through town; the Richardson Highway leading south to Valdez is to the left.

Just outside of Delta, the Trans Alaska Pipeline crosses the Tanana River next to the highway bridge. This is probably the best view of the pipeline anywhere in the state, and there are turnouts on both sides of the bridge for those desiring a longer look. About 400,000 barrels (18 million gallons) of North Slope oil flow daily through the pipeline to the tanker terminal in Valdez. Taxes on oil provide more than 80 percent or more of the state budget. Because of the oil, there is no state income tax or statewide sales tax in Alaska. Any sales taxes charged are local taxes imposed by a city or borough.

Insider's Tip

King salmon fishermen should use medium- to heavy-duty spinning or casting rods with a minimum of 200 yards of 20-pound-test or heavier line on their reels. Best bait for kings is a glob of salmon roe bounced along the stream bottom. Obtain a current Alaska fishing license and check stream regulations carefully. Fishermen are often limited to artificial lures only.

The turnout prior to the Tanana River bridge is for Big Delta State Historical Park, featuring a completely rebuilt roadhouse. Rika's Roadhouse, as it's known, was established in 1910 as an overnight stop for travelers on the stage/sled trail from Valdez to Fairbanks. Meals and lodging are available to help visitors savor this small part of Alaska's history.

A few miles past Rika's is a turnoff to the right for Quartz Lake, probably Interior Alaska's favorite fishing hole for stocked rainbow trout. There's a state park on the lake, but it tends to fill up fast, especially on weekends.

In July, Interior fishermen get their first crack at Alaska's legendary king salmon in the Salcha River, about 57 miles from Delta. If the salmon are in, there'll be plenty of cars near the bridge or along the Salcha River Wayside to the right just before crossing the bridge. These fish have migrated half the length of the Yukon River and several hundred miles of the Tanana River before turning into the clear waters of the Salcha River. Fishermen pull salmon of 45–50 pounds from this stream every year; an average king weighs 20–30 pounds. Though this is far from the best

Rika's Roadhouse & Garden, Delta Junction

salmon fishing stream in Alaska, it's the one most Alaska Highway drivers reach first, and "king-salmon fever" is not easily denied. There are chum salmon mixed in with the kings, though these are not nearly as sought after.

From the Salcha River, it's a pleasant 45-minute drive the rest of the way into Fairbanks. Along the way, about 12 miles out of Fairbanks, a large Santa Claus stands at roadside. The name of the surrounding town—North Pole, of course.

In Fairbanks, visitors can relive some of the flavor of past years by riding a modern-day stern-wheeler or whooping it up in the Malamute or Palace saloons. The latter is located in Alaska Pioneer Park, on Airport Way in Fairbanks. This is a theme park dedicated to preserving the gold-rush heritage of Fairbanks.

If you're looking for a campsite, a good bet for drivers of self-contained RVs is the parking lot of the Alaska Pioneer Park. It's centrally located and offers great access to Alaska's original salmon bake restaurant and, of course, to the park. The best bet for tent campers is Chena River Recreation Site near the Chena River bridge on University Avenue, about a mile from Alaska Pioneer Park.

Fairbanks is a fairly modern city with about 60,000 people residing in the immediate area. Two large military bases, Fort Wainwright and Eielson Air Force Base, are just outside of town.

A must-stop for travelers is the University of Alaska Museum. Sitting on a hill above the university, it houses a superb collection of Alaskan artifacts and natural history exhibits. The exhibit most people will remember is a stuffed Alaska brown bear standing more than 9 feet tall, one of the largest bears ever taken in Alaska.

Gold in Fairbanks

Fairbanks was the site of the second big gold rush after the Klondike Gold Rush of 1898. Between these two events were the discoveries at Nome on Alaska's west coast.

An Italian immigrant prospector, Felix Pedro, discovered gold in a stream about 15 miles north of the city in 1902. The city itself was actually established in 1901, when E. T. Barnette was unable to move a stern-wheeler loaded with supplies any farther on the Tanana or Chena rivers, which join together just west of town. As Barnette's contract with the boat's skipper expired, Barnette, his party, and the supplies for a trading post were rather unceremoniously dumped on the riverbank when it became apparent the boat could proceed no farther due to shallow water. Barnette had hoped to get much farther up the river to a point near present-day Delta to take advantage of inside information he had about a trail being built through the region. His seeming misfortune was reversed with Pedro's discovery of gold. The history of early Fairbanks revolves around Barnette's wheeling and dealing for gold claims and real estate manipulation.

Thus Fairbanks was a boomtown, but a boomtown that survived as a transportation hub for Interior Alaska. Its history since the gold rush has been a series of booms and busts, the most recent being the boom that ensued with the building of the Trans Alaska Pipeline in the mid-1970s.

CITY	MILES	KM
EAGLE	379	610
FORT YUKON	124	200
HAINES	653	1053
HOMER	584	942
JUNEAU	622	1000
KETCHIKAN	855	1380

CITY	MILES	KM
SEWARD	484	781
SITKA	678	1090
SKAGWAY	710	1145
TOK	206	332
VALDEZ	364	587

FAIRBANKS
CONVENTION & VISITORS BUREAU

Welcome to
FAIRBANKS

THE GOLDEN HEART CITY

CITY OF FAIRBANKS ALASKA

FAIRBANKS NORTH STAR BOROUGH January 1, 1964

MILE 1523
Dawson Creek to Fairbanks

The Alaska Highway was built in 1942 in 8 months. The Highway stretches 1422 miles from Dawson Creek, British Columbia, to Delta Junction. The Highway was built as a military necessity and followed along a line of existing airfields, winter roads, old Indian trails and rivers. Because most of the early military traffic was bound for Fairbanks, it is often measured to this point. The Fairbanks to Valdez Trail (now the Richardson Highway) began construction in 1899 and was paved in 1957. The Alaska Highway joins the Richardson Highway in Delta Junction and continues to Fairbanks (98 miles).

CHAPTER 10
10 Roadside Favorites

Forty-four years of driving back and forth along the Alaska and Cassiar Highways have provided me and my family with a number of favorite places. Some of these are fishing holes, some are campgrounds, and some are communities.

The places listed here are not necessarily better than other places we've visited along the road. However, for a variety of reasons, these stops along the road have become part of our family's history. We still stop at all of these when time and travel schedules permit, and we still enjoy what each has to offer.

I suppose the biggest problem with this list was cutting it down to 10. Even more than that, prioritizing the list to determine which gets put down as number one, which is number two, and so forth, was a bit of a problem. That being said, here are our top 10 roadside attractions.

1. LIARD RIVER HOTSPRINGS PROVINCIAL PARK   This stop is between Fort Nelson and Watson Lake. Winter or summer, sunny or cloudy, windy or calm, to our minds this is the premier attraction along the Alaska Highway.

If you are headed to Alaska, it comes just after you cross the Rockies, the most beautiful part of the drive and that part of the road offering the most opportunities for viewing wildlife. Kicking back in a natural hot springs pool while you reflect on such a day is pretty awesome.

Normally the biggest problem at Liard is finding space in the campground. Though a large facility, it tends to fill up early on most days from the middle of June to the middle of August—if you're not there by 3 p.m. or so, you can pretty much forget about camping there. There is, however, a day-use area where you can park for a couple of hours to at least enjoy a quick dip in one of the pools.

A broad, well-maintained boardwalk leads about a quarter mile or so to the lower pool. The boardwalk turns into an expansive deck running along a waist-deep pool of warm water. Steps lead into the water.

Men's and women's bathhouses for changing are provided at both the upper and lower pools. There is no real security in these facilities, so leave your valuables locked in your vehicle.

2. TAGISH, YUKON   This area is about 35 miles south of Whitehorse and has been our favorite fishing hole for more than three

Lower pool, Liard River Hotsprings, BC

decades. Lake trout, arctic grayling, and northern pike are all available within a mile of the bridge over the Tagish River.

The Tagish is a short stream, only a couple of miles long, joining Tagish and Marsh Lakes. Historically, those who came over the Chilkoot Trail from Skagway and built boats to float to the Klondike goldfields passed through here, and if you watch carefully from the stream bank in a boat, you can see the old customs station run by the Canadian Mounted Police more than a century ago. It's also possible to find the station by gravel road from the back of the campground.

Tagish River, Yukon

We always camp at the campground on the eastern end of the bridge. From there, a couple minutes' walk puts us on the bridge to fish for lake trout—I've observed lakers up to 26 pounds being caught from this bridge—or to the small marina across the road where we can rent a boat. A slough a mile or so north of the bridge on the west side of Marsh Lake almost always provides some excellent pike fishing, and an outcropping of rocks in the river a half mile or so south of the bridge almost always yields grayling. Lake trout can also be found in both lakes, not just under the bridge.

Tagish Lake can be approached from two directions. Northbound travelers can turn south on the Atlin Road, about 35 miles before getting to Whitehorse. A short distance from the junction, the road splits. Stay left to go to Atlin, British Columbia; stay right to go to Tagish. Southbound travelers can turn south on the road to Skagway just outside of Whitehorse. Turn left on the gravel road just before reaching Carcross and it's about a dozen miles or so to Tagish.

3. WHITEHORSE, YUKON Whenever possible we like to be in Whitehorse for Canada Day on July 1. It is a great party with a parade, various games, good food, and all manner of friendly people. Most of the festivities are centered in the Yukon River waterfront park that holds the rebuilt stern-wheeler *SS Klondike II* and a rebuilt barge of the type it used to push up and down the river.

When we visit Whitehorse with kids, we normally camp at Takhini Hot Springs, located a few miles west of town. The kids will probably like this facility better than the parents—it's not quite as pristine a setting as that surrounding Liard Hotsprings—but there is a large RV park, normally with plenty of spaces available. The pool is a standard concrete-lined hole in the ground. It is emptied and cleaned every night and refilled with fresh hot water from the hot springs for the following day. When traveling without kids, we normally stay at Caribou RV Park on the south side of town.

4. YUKON DISCOVERY LODGING/WHITE RIVER CROSSING RV PARK   In the past few years a new owner has taken over, upgraded the park, and opened it regularly every summer. We love it and generally spend at least one night here. It's situated in one of the most beautiful spots in the Yukon, there's often a community camp-fire in the evening, and there's great fishing for grayling in the immediate area. The grayling in local streams rarely see a lure or a fly and seem almost eager to become part of your dinner.

5. MEZIADIN LAKE PROVINCIAL PARK   This spot is found along the Cassiar Highway. Of all the campgrounds on the various roads leading to Alaska and the numerous side trips off the main roads, this campground along the lakeshore prob-ably boasts the prettiest location of all. The lake is full of hungry rainbows, and a boat ramp allows for the launching of privately owned boats.

White River Crossing, Yukon

The lake is warm enough for a "cool" swim for the brave, and the best beach is in front of the campground. Because the lake and a number of area streams host major runs of spawning salmon each summer, there are a lot of bears in the area, so chances of seeing one are good, either along the roads near the campground or occasionally wandering through the campground looking for loose garbage or some other handout. Keep a clean campsite and remember that it is against the law to feed the bears.

If you're northbound on the Cassiar High-way from its starting point at Kitwanga, British Columbia, Meziadin is almost exactly 100 miles up the road on your left just a few hundred yards before you reach the turnoff for Stewart, British Columbia. Southbound from Watson Lake on the Alaska Highway, Meziadin is about 350 miles from the junction with the Alaska Highway.

6. DESTRUCTION BAY RV LODGE   The restaurant here (open for breakfast and lunch only) makes this a wonderful stop, as does the fellow who runs the operation, Loren Maluorno. He'll talk your ear off if you give him a chance. The best part of stopping here is exploring the shore of Kluane Lake.

7. BIG BEAR RV PARK   This is our favorite place to camp in Alaska. Located in Palmer, only about 40 miles from Anchorage, it's also convenient to Wasilla and Matanuska Glacier. Locally owned, the park puts on salmon feeds on several summer evenings and offers a free sourdough hotcake breakfast at irregular intervals.

8. MUNCHO LAKE PROVINCIAL PARK   Between Fort Nelson and Watson Lake, this, to me and my family, is probably the most beautiful stretch of the Alaska Highway. The drive alongside the shore of the lake is awe-inspiring, and the various critters seen on the roadside will keep you from driving fast. Over the years we have seen countless Stone sheep, caribou, and bears alongside the road. The lake itself is best viewed looking south, early on a calm, sunny morning from a pullout on the northern edge.

9. CONGDON CREEK CAMPGROUND   Alongside Kluane Lake in the Yukon, this is one of the campgrounds along the Alaska Highway that will make you feel like you're truly in the wilderness. It's far enough off the road that you can't hear any of the traffic, an often heavy wind creates 4-foot or larger waves that crash against the shore, and it sits at the foot of a massive mountain range. As an added bonus, both black bears and grizzlies populate the area; you could see one or both if you're lucky. Because of the bears, no tent camping is allowed. You must sleep in a hard-sided camper of some sort if you stay at Congdon Creek.

10. CASSIAR RV PARK   Kitwanga, British Columbia, is where we discovered this one in 2004. At the southern end of the Cassiar Highway (the alternate route that intercepts the Alaska Highway at Watson Lake), this is a wonderful place for southbound travelers to divest themselves of a little trail dust after surviving the rigors of the Cassiar Highway; for those who are northbound, it's a great place to camp as you make final preparations for the trek north on the Cassiar Highway.

Showers are free, there's an RV pressure-wash station, plenty of pull-throughs for big rigs, and all the other amenities that go toward making a first-class RV park are available. The staff is great too.

Besides these 10 that we like best, some of our "also rans" include these favorite stops:

- Snafu Lake, along the Atlin Road. About 20 miles south of Jake's Corner on the road to Atlin.

- Tutshi Lake, along the road from Whitehorse to Skagway. Halfway between Carcross and the Alaska-Canada border.

- Squanga Lake Campground, between Teslin and Whitehorse.

- Teslin Lake Campground, a few miles northwest of Teslin.

- Stone Mountain Provincial Park, across the summit of the Rockies. About 100 miles northwest of Fort Nelson.

- Kluane RV Kampground in Haines Junction. Turn right toward Fairbanks at the junction in town; about a half mile farther on the left.

- Kluane Museum of Natural History in Burwash Landing. Just past Kluane Lake, about 100 miles northwest of Haines Junction.

- Sourdough Campground in Tok, Alaska. Turn off the Alaska Highway toward Anchorage in downtown Tok. It's about 3 miles south of town. Be sure to visit the restaurant for a sourdough hotcake breakfast before leaving in the morning.

- Skagway, Alaska, about 100 miles south of Whitehorse. This was the jumping-off point for those heading for the Klondike goldfields. It's also the birthplace of your author.

- Atlin, British Columbia. Arguably the most beautiful townsite accessible from the Alaska Highway. From Jake's Corner, about 35 miles southeast of Whitehorse, drive south for 60 miles on the Atlin Road. About half the route is gravel surfaced.

Kluane Lake, Yukon

CHAPTER 11
Touring Alaska by Vehicle

A quick glance at a road map makes it abundantly clear that it's impossible to tour all of Alaska in a vehicle. Roads just don't exist to the western reaches of the state and throughout most of the Arctic. Overall, less than one-third of Alaska can be reached by vehicle.

However, the roads that do exist offer scenery the likes of which can be found nowhere else, and these same roads lead to adventures beyond almost anyone's dreams.

This chapter breaks Alaska's road system into three distinct sections. A fourth section of roads within Alaska is covered in Chapter 13 with suggestions for the return trip. As the sections in this chapter are laid out, it would take a minimum of seven days to cover all the trips listed in the Fairbanks area, two or three days for the road system between Fairbanks and Anchorage, and at least two (three or four are better) for the Kenai Peninsula south of Anchorage. These times are minimum figures and leave little additional time for exploring, sampling the fishing, or berry picking.

If you only have a week or so to spend in Alaska, it's probably better to select one—or at most two—of these areas and explore it more thoroughly. The other parts of the state can wait for a return trip. With rare exception, few visitors are satisfied with a single visit to Alaska.

SECTION ONE: Fairbanks-Area Roads

Unless you're headed south to Anchorage or back down the Alaska Highway toward Canada, all of the driving opportunities in this region start on a single road leading north from town, the Steese Highway. On the Steese, it's 4.6 miles to the turnoff for Chena Hot Springs Road and 11 miles to the Elliott Highway turnoff in Fox. From Fox on the Elliott Highway, it's 73 miles to the start of the Dalton Highway.

All of the mileages given are for the actual start of the road described. Thus, if you are driving the Dalton Highway, you must first drive 11 miles to Fox, and then 73 miles on the Elliott Highway to the start of the road. In this example, you have 84 miles to drive from Fairbanks before you can begin the trip on the Dalton Highway.

All of the Dalton Highway, all but the first 28 miles of the Elliott Highway, and most of the Steese Highway are gravel-surfaced roads. Of these four drives available north of Fairbanks, only Chena Hot Springs Road is completely paved. All suggestions offered in earlier chapters about driving on gravel roads are valid here, with the added provisos that these roads are often less traveled and even more remote, particularly the Dalton Highway. The Dalton was built in the mid-1970s and is locally known as the Pipeline Haul Road or, more simply, the Haul Road.

Chena Hot Springs Road

Length: 57 miles (95 kilometers)

Gas Available: Anders Cache, 10 miles (17 kilometers)

Lodging: Chena Hot Springs, 57 miles (95 kilometers)

Campgrounds:

Mile 27 State Campground, 27 miles (45 kilometers)

North Fork Chena River, 39 miles (65 kilometers)

Chena Hot Springs, 57 miles (95 kilometers)

Fishing: Grayling

Wildlife: Moose and black bears

Chena Hot Springs Road

Winter, summer, spring, and fall, this road is Fairbanks's weekend playground. In the summer there's picnicking, camping, hiking, canoeing, and fishing for grayling along the Chena River. In fall, moose and black bear hunters park at roadside and enter likely looking patches of forest. In the winter and spring, cross-country skiers find terrain to test every skill level. Throughout every season of the year, at the end of the road there's an indoor hot springs pool suitable for soaking away your cares. Finally, about 20 miles up the road is one of the Fairbanks area's finest restaurants, Two Rivers Lodge. Try the barbecued ribs.

You can drive the road in an hour or so; it's only 57 miles from where it leaves the Steese Highway (4.6 miles from Fairbanks) to the end of the road at Chena Hot Springs Lodge. The first 26 miles wind gently through rolling terrain, the land a mix of occasional fields (mostly hay) and boreal forest. After 26 miles, you enter the Chena River Recreation Area for the next 24 miles.

Insider's Tip

A good time to catch Chena River grayling is usually late May (Memorial Day weekend), when the fish are moving upstream to spawning and summer feeding areas. Stand in one spot near the shore, and every time a school of fish swims into view, cast to them. Schools of fish will come along at fairly regular intervals.

Within the recreation area are several possibilities for canoeists, floats of an hour or more to a couple of days if you want to drift all the way into downtown Fairbanks. Popular day trips for canoeists include floating from Mile 39.5 to Mile 37.9, at most a couple of hours on a lazy afternoon. Longer floats with the same take-out site at Mile 37.9 begin at Mile 44 and Mile 52.3. The Mile 44 float is about a 7-hour jaunt, the other about 12–15 hours if you do it in a single day. The river parallels the road for these trips, though it is often out of sight and earshot of the road.

Besides native fish in the river itself, several small lakes at roadside are stocked with grayling. These lakes are at Mile 30, Mile 43.8, Mile 45.5, and Mile 47.9. In the river, grayling should be available at any point where you can reach the riverbank. Check fishing regulations carefully before fishing. Because this is the most popular grayling fishery in the state, bag limits are carefully regulated by the Alaska Department of Fish and Game. There have been periods when grayling numbers were down that fishing was completely closed on the river.

Not every summer, but occasionally, sufficient king and chum salmon enter the Chena River to allow anglers a crack at these big fish.

Along Chena Hot Springs Road, two excellent trails are available for hikers, both suitable for either day hiking or overnight excursions. The first is the Granite Tors Trail, with its trailhead at Mile 39.5. On this trail it's 6 miles to the first tor (a *tor* is a stark outcropping of rock) and 8 miles to the main grouping of tors—the latter a 16-mile round-trip. Be sure to carry water on this trail.

More ambitious hikers will want to check out the Chena Dome Loop Trail. The trailheads are at Miles 48.9 and 50.5. In between, the trail takes a circuitous 29-mile route through the hills and valleys of this part of Alaska. Allow at least two days for hiking the whole loop; three days are even better. As with the Granite Tors Trail, plan to carry plenty of water.

Though the water in the Chena River and elsewhere in Alaska may look quite clear, do not drink from any stream without first boiling the water for several minutes or pumping it through an adequate filter. Giardia (beaver fever) is prevalent in most Alaskan watersheds. Those who have experienced this disease will tell you it's nothing to fool with.

In August, berry pickers delight in vast fields of blueberries and cranberries at various points along the road. In Alaska's Interior, blueberry bushes are low shrubs producing a profusion of tiny, tart, but oh-so-good berries. If you're not sure where to look, watch for cars parked at roadside and people stooped over in the open areas nearby—they're almost certainly picking blueberries.

Human berry pickers along Chena Hot Springs Road will occasionally bump into Mother Nature's most ardent berry picker, a black bear. Usually the bear is just as surprised as the people involved. Stay together in groups of two or more, make lots of noise, and odds are you won't have any unexpected encounters.

Chena Hot Springs Road is a pleasant outdoor playground with a special place at the end of the road, Chena Hot Springs Lodge. Lying back at the end of the day in the pool's naturally warmed water is good for the soul, and afterward there's a great restaurant in the lodge and overnight accommodations available. If you visit the restaurant, be sure to sample the home-baked pies.

For the really adventurous, the owner of Chena Hot Springs Lodge erected Alaska's first-ever ice hotel during the winter of 2003–2004, as well as a couple of winters since. He actually had people paying hundreds of dollars a night to sleep in a building made completely of ice—with ice furnishings. Inside temperature was maintained at about 28°F, and extremely warm bedding was provided. Summer's warm temperatures ultimately finished off the hotel, but the owner has promised to do it again in the future. The ice hotel got him lots of publicity in local papers and on local television stations.

Bears

If you meet a bear that doesn't run away when it realizes you are near, face it and back away slowly, all the while talking in a relatively normal voice. Turning to run may excite the bear into giving chase. If you are charged by a bear, climb a tree if one is available and if you have time. If the bear catches you, drop face forward onto the ground, curl up into sort of a fetal position with your back in the air, and remain perfectly still. This advice has been around for decades. However, it has been determined that this advice works best for grizzly bears that aren't looking to make a meal of you but to eliminate a potential threat. More and more bear experts are saying that if you tangle with a black bear you should fight back with any and every means at your disposal because once you are down, a black bear may consider you its next meal.

Bears are extremely unpredictable. The techniques given here can never be considered 100 percent effective. Statistically, though, these have proven to be the best responses available. Another statistic to consider if you're nervous about bears is that most bear attacks happen to people who are alone or separated from the group. Stick close together with one or more companions and you'll almost certainly be left alone by the bears.

Most bear encounters, and there are thousands every year in Alaska, wind up as non-threatening, even humorous, though they might not seem so at the time they happen.

As an example, one of the funniest bear stories in Alaska came off of the Chena Hot Springs Road about 35 years ago. A young couple from the lower 48 was visiting relatives—the man's brother, who was stationed with the Army at Fort Wainwright near Fairbanks. One weekend they camped out in one of the Chena Hot Springs Road campgrounds. The Alaskan relative offered space in his huge wall tent for his brother and the brother's wife. They declined, preferring instead to try out the tiny backpacking tent they'd purchased just for their Alaskan adventure.

With two people in this tiny tent, their fluffed up sleeping bags pressed lightly against the sides of the tent. Early in the morning a young black bear wandered into camp and sat down beside the small tent, fascinated by the rhythm of the tent wall rising and falling with the woman's breathing. She was sleeping on her stomach, so the most obvious bulge in the side of the tent was over her rear end. After watching for a time, the bear leaned forward against the tent, placed his left front paw on the back of the woman's thighs, his right paw on the small of her back, and nipped her in the behind through the tent fabric and the sleeping bag. Though pinched a little, she was otherwise unhurt.

As you might guess, some screaming ensued, which prompted the curious bear to scamper around to the doorway in front of the tent, where he plopped down to look inside. Only the mosquito netting had been zipped closed, thus the bear could look in and the people could look out. The humans inside the tent wouldn't go out the door with the bear sitting there, so the bear stared at the people, and the people stared at the bear. Things continued in a standoff until the brother in the big tent stumbled outside to see what was going on. At that point the bear scampered away, and the couple in the small tent quickly moved into the big tent for the remainder of the night.

The Steese Highway

Until the Pipeline Haul Road was completed in the mid-1970s, the Steese Highway offered one of only two routes to the shores of the Yukon River in Alaska. Then and now, it is still the most popular route.

When you pull into Fairbanks on the Alaska Highway, you come to a four-way intersection with a stoplight. To the left is downtown Fairbanks and the road to Anchorage, to the right is Fort Wainwright, and the Steese Highway begins if you go straight ahead. The Steese sweeps around the east side of Fairbanks and heads due north at first, gradually swinging to the northeast.

Arguably, gold was responsible for the Steese Highway. Felix Pedro's discovery claim, which resulted in part from the founding of Fairbanks and caused it to become the largest city in Interior Alaska, is just north of the city along the Steese. It's well marked and has a wide graveled area for stopping. Beyond that, about 127 miles from Fairbanks, lies Central, the town that grew up in a region where gold was being mined before it was discovered near Fairbanks. Gold is still mined in the hills and streams around Central, though little of this activity is visible to road travelers.

The Steese Highway

Length: 162 miles (270 kilometers)

Gas Available:

Curry's Corner, 5 miles (8 kilometers)

Miner Ed's Trading Post, 42 miles (70 kilometers)

Miracle Mile Lodge, 66 miles (110 kilometers)

Central, 128 miles (213 kilometers)

Circle, 162 miles (270 kilometers)

Lodging:

Chatanika Lodge, 29 miles (48 kilometers)

Miracle Mile Lodge, 66 miles (110 kilometers)

Central, 128 miles (213 kilometers)

Campgrounds:

Chatanika River Wayside, 39 miles (65 kilometers)

Cripple Creek, 60 miles (100 kilometers)

Bedrock Creek, 119 miles (198 kilometers)

Circle on Yukon River banks, 162 miles (270 kilometers)

Fishing: Grayling

Wildlife: Black bears, moose, caribou (rarely), ptarmigans

However, the lower Steese Highway near Fairbanks offers several things of interest to those wanting to sample Alaska's golden past.

Near Fox and at intervals along the highway, the bottomlands are filled with mounded gravel. These are the tailings left by gold dredges that worked through area streams. A gold dredge is a metal mechanical monster designed to scoop gravel from stream bottoms, process it for gold, and spit all the other stuff out the back. Even the smallest streams in gold-producing areas would get the gold dredge treatment. Dredges worked their way gradually downstream by digging a hole to float in and filling it in behind them. Though they floated, dredges can't be called boats. Before they could move, they had to dig out another place to float. Thus a dredge gradually worked its way downstream crisscrossing the valley, trying to leave no stone or bit of bedrock unscraped in the quest for the precious yellow metal.

Today, environmentalists would have a fit were you to suggest reactivating an inland gold dredge. Without a doubt, these machines significantly altered the landscape. However, it is possible to visit gold dredges today, because when the gold ran out these things were just left where they stopped. Little more than 9 miles from Fairbanks on the Steese Highway sits Gold Dredge #8. Guided tours are available,

Another great spot on Alaska's road system for viewing the Trans Alaska Pipeline is along the Steese Highway just prior to reaching Fox. The pipe is aboveground and right next to the road. A turnout with an interpretive sign is located there.

and you can try your hand at panning for gold. There's also a restaurant, bar, and hotel for those who want to stay a little longer.

Gold Dredge #8 is a National Historical Mechanical Engineering Landmark. (I'll bet that's a designation you've never heard before.) The dredge last operated in 1959. In the 1980s, this five-story, 250-foot-long dredge was restored and opened to the public, rapidly becoming one of the Fairbanks area's most visited attractions.

From the dredge, the Steese Highway winds past Fox, past Pedro's discovery claim, and up to Cleary Summit, a little less than 21 miles from Fairbanks. Atop Cleary Summit (2,233 feet) you look out over the Chatanika River valley, which the road follows upstream for about the next 45 miles. Like the Chena River, there is grayling fishing available in the Chatanika as well as canoeing. The Chatanika, though, is not as heavily used as the Chena.

Insider's Tip

Just past mile 56, fishermen will want to look closely for a one-lane dirt road on the north side of an opening in the forest where the pipe is visible. It leads about 8 miles to Nome Creek. At Nome Creek, turn left on the dredge tailings and a trail winds back and forth across the creek for a couple more miles until the tailings end. (There used to be an abandoned gold dredge at the end of the tailings, but in the late 1970s an enterprising crew tore it apart, hauled it out, and sold it for scrap metal.) Start fishing for grayling right there or in several of the clear pools among the dredge tailings. This is one of the best grayling streams in the Fairbanks area. This road cannot be recommended for any vehicle, but if you want to try it, your best bet is a four-wheel-drive pickup truck.

As far as fishing goes, the Chatanika does have one far-out thing that the Chena lacks—a spear fishery for whitefish, usually about the third week in September, just a few days before freeze-up. Most of the action takes place on a Saturday night at the Chatanika River Wayside, 39 miles from Fairbanks. Otherwise sane adults pull on hipboots, hoist a lighted gasoline lantern in one hand and a spear in the other, and wade into the river. Amid much shouting, consumption of personal antifreeze, and general revelry, these folks stand all night in freezing water trying to spear whitefish, which aren't really very big. Often this event coincides with the first snowfall of the year. If you've got a snug camper or motorhome to sleep in, it's certainly something to see. But be careful: should you get bit by the whitefish bug, you just might find yourself standing in the middle of a rapidly freezing river, all the while trying to think up some believable story for the folks back home.

About 17 miles past Chatanika Wayside, a large pipe is visible to the left. This is part of the Davidson Ditch, built in the 1920s to move water down to the gold dredges. After the dredges shut down, the water flow was used to generate electrical power until 1967, when a flood in Fairbanks flattened more than 1,000 feet of the pipe.

An abandoned gold dredge

Past the Davidson Ditch, the road continues to climb. When the climbing stops this time, drivers will find themselves well above timberline at Eagle Summit, 3,624 feet, 108 miles from Fairbanks. Timberline in this part of the world extends to between 2,500 and 3,000 feet. For folks used to the Colorado Rockies, where timberline starts above 10,000 feet, these numbers are pretty low. But they are handy. Using these numbers, travelers almost always have a means of estimating the heights of various mountains.

For example, say from a distance you note that timberline on a coastal mountain ends about one-third of the way up the mountain. Using that observation, you wouldn't be far wrong to say that the mountain is about 7,500 feet high. You do, however, have to be a little careful and have some sense of where you start in relation to sea level. Say you're sitting at an elevation about 1,000 feet above sea level and you see another mountain where the timbered slopes run one-third of the way up. In this case, the summit would only be about 5,500 feet, because there are only 1,500 feet between you and the timber-line plus the thousand feet above sea level where you already are.

At any rate, Eagle Summit is well above timberline. This is great country for ptarmigan hunting in August or September, but the summit is best known for the summer solstice.

Though it doesn't ever get completely dark during summer nights in Fairbanks, the sun does set at least briefly every night. But, on June 21, if the sky is clear, the added elevation at Eagle Summit means watchers can see the sun that never sets.

At midnight (true midnight, not daylight saving time), the sun dips against the northern horizon but never quite sinks below it. On any given June 21, several hundred Fairbanksans trek to Eagle Summit hoping that the weather will permit them a glimpse of the midnight sun. Weather cooperates about half the time.

From Eagle Summit, the Steese Highway drops rapidly down to Central, one of the Interior's oldest settlements and, these days, one of the smallest. Central services various mining operations in the hills around town, but you won't see many of these folks in town during summer. Those who make their living mining gold have only a few short summer months to extract a year's livelihood.

Just on the northern edge of Central there's a road junction. Straight ahead leads to Circle on the Yukon River. The road to the right leads to Circle Hot Springs, once one of the finest hot springs resorts in Alaska accessible by road. However, the hotel, restaurant, and pool are now closed, and there's no firm information available about the facility reopening in the future.

The last 35 miles of the Steese Highway from Central to Circle (also known as Circle City) is mostly through lowland forests of spruce and birch. Circle, 162 miles from Fairbanks, was erroneously named by area miners in the late 19th century who thought the town site was actually on the Arctic Circle. Unfortunately, the Arctic Circle is about 50 miles farther north.

Circle occasionally floods in May. When the ice goes out on the Yukon River each year, ice jams sometimes form. When one of these jams occurs just downstream from Circle, the water quickly backs up into town. When the ice jam releases, usually within hours to a day, the town quickly drains. At the entrance to the campground on the riverbank in Circle is a large plywood sign welcoming visitors to the campground. The last time the Yukon River flooded the town during breakup, the water reached the bottom of this sign, about 4½ feet above the ground.

The Elliott Highway

This road leads to some wild and remote country. It also passes through active gold mining areas where owners are often adamant about their private property signs. Specific regions of gold-mining activity include the settlement of Livengood (no services available), 71 miles from the road's start at Fox, and Eureka, 131 miles from Fox.

The Elliott Highway

Length: 152 miles (253 kilometers)
Gas Available:
Hilltop Cafe, 5 miles (8 kilometers)
Manley, 152 miles (253 kilometers)
Lodging: Manley, 152 miles (253 kilometers)
Campgrounds:
Lower Chatanika, 11 miles (18 kilometers)
Tolvana River (unimproved), 75 miles (125 kilometers)
Manley, 152 miles (253 kilometers)
Fishing: Northern pike and grayling
Wildlife: Black bears, moose, wolves (rarely)

These liabilities aside, this is a beautiful drive through the heart of Interior Alaska. Most of the route is forested with scraggly black spruce and stands of birch. There is some fairly open country at roadside about 100 miles into the route, country that hosts extensive fields of blueberries, which ripen in early August.

At the start of the road is a picnic area on the left by Fox Spring. Area residents have long cherished the water that comes from the ground year-round at this spot. Many Fairbanks residents make regular trips to the spring for drinking water, ignoring the relatively pure water delivered to the taps in their homes. Take a minute to fill water bottles or just stop and taste the water.

From the spring, it's little more than 4 miles to Hilltop, a café and gas station on the left side. This is a favorite stop for Haul Road truckers. This is also the last gas available before reaching Manley at the end of the road, some 147 miles distant.

The first 73 miles of this road are part of the Pipeline Haul Road, and truck traffic can be particularly heavy. Be exceedingly careful during dry periods because these 18-wheelers kick up blinding clouds of dust. The majority of the northbound truckers turn off on the Dalton Highway, 73 miles from Fox, leaving the second half of the Elliott Highway relatively free of traffic.

Prior to reaching the Dalton Highway junction, the Elliott crosses both the Chatanika and Tolovana Rivers. There's a splendid campground and picnic area next to the Chatanika River bridge (11 miles), though fishing here is mediocre at best, except for a few brief days just after breakup when grayling are moving upstream to summer spawning and feeding areas.

Insider's Tip

Few services are available at any point along the Elliott Highway except at the start and finish. Thus you should start this trek with a full gas tank.

The Tolovana River, 57 miles from Fox, offers slightly better fishing for small grayling, as well as opportunities to catch northern pike. Pike are thrilling sport, particularly on light tackle. Minto Flats, the extensive region of lakes and marsh to the south of the road, regularly produces pike in excess of 30 pounds. River fish will likely be smaller. Generally, big pike need big water.

Minto Flats is also the favorite region for Interior waterfowlers. Best access is usually a 15-minute charter flight from Fairbanks, though it can be reached by road from the village of Minto, accessed by an 11-mile side road that begins at mile 110 of the Elliott Highway. Minto and the surrounding lands are private property belonging to the native village. Strangers are often looked over critically by local residents. Should you elect to drive to Minto and put a boat into the flats to sample the waterfowl hunting or the fishing, be careful out on the water. Native fishermen set gill nets throughout the area, and these are sometimes difficult to spot as you speed through the lakes or marshes in a powerboat. A line of cork floats, usually white, just barely breaking the surface of the water is usually the only indication of a gill net.

Should you wish to stop at Minto just to observe village life or to sample the fishing or waterfowl hunting, it's a good idea to inquire at the Tanana Chiefs' office in Fairbanks prior to setting out. This organization, listed in the phone book, serves

various villages throughout Interior Alaska and can make several suggestions as to timing and activities.

Beyond the Dalton Highway Junction, this is a fairly narrow road and not nearly as well maintained. Though it is open year-round and maintained by the state of Alaska, parts of it can be exceedingly rough.

Probably the best fishing available along the entire road is at Baker Creek, 137 miles from Fox. All summer long this creek is capable of producing grayling to 20 inches in length.

Grizzly cubs

Probably no other fish symbolizes the purity of arctic waters more than the grayling. It's generally found in only the clearest streams. Fresh from the water, there is no finer eating available. The flesh is white, delicate, and smells faintly of thyme. When first pulled from the water the skin shimmers in rich purple hues, though these colors quickly recede to a dark gray with the death of the fish. Prime grayling lures are small silver spinners, various small flies like black gnats, and different mosquito patterns.

Approaching Manley, a side road leads 16 miles to a former mining area known as Tofty. Though there is still some mining around Tofty, the situation is relatively congenial, but visitors should scrupulously obey private property signs. Inquire locally in Manley before driving to Tofty.

Just before entering Manley, Manley Hot Springs is to the right. The lodge there offers a hot springs pool and tours to fish camps, gold mines, and sled-dog kennels.

In Manley, don't be surprised if local residents look you over closely. In the 1980s, a stranger came to town and started randomly murdering people down on the riverbank and throwing their bodies in the river. He then stole a boat and raced upriver. He murdered a state trooper sent to find him and was in turn gunned down by another trooper. This is not a pleasant memory in this otherwise peaceful community.

Insider's Tip

For a real taste of the past, stop in at the Manley Roadhouse, a great place to meet the local citizens—mostly miners, trappers, and mushers—over refreshments. Try the blueberry pie, a house specialty, for a real treat.

Manley rests on the banks of the Tanana River, with about 90 full-time residents. Residents here live a largely self-sufficient lifestyle with few of the amenities most other people take for granted. Some of the vegetable and berry gardens surrounding well-kept homes must be seen to be believed. It takes a fair amount of work to produce these kinds of crops in Interior Alaska.

Fishermen will find pike to 3 feet long in the Manley Hot Springs Slough. A campground on the slough offers a boat launch for those who have the equipment to get away from the immediate shoreline.

Northern pike prefer big pieces of bright hardware—red-and-white or black-and-white spoons are favorites. It's best to use a steel leader in front of the lure, as these fish have mouths filled with jagged teeth that make short work of most fishing line. Fly fishermen will find that big, bright streamers will take pike. On a fly rod, catching a pike best correlates to that old cliché about having a tiger by the tail.

The Dalton Highway

Length: 414 miles (690 kilometers)

Gas Available:

Yukon River bridge, 56 miles (93 kilometers)

Coldfoot Services, 175 miles (292 kilometers)

Deadhorse, 414 miles (690 kilometers)

Lodging:

Coldfoot, 175 miles (292 kilometers)

Wiseman, 188 miles (314 kilometers)

Campgrounds *(no hookups available)*:

Hess Creek gravel bar, 24 miles (40 kilometers)

Yukon River bridge, 56 miles (93 kilometers)

The Arctic Circle, 115 miles (192 kilometers)

Jim River, 139 miles (232 kilometers)

Marion Creek, 180 miles (300 kilometers)

Fishing: Northern pike, burbot, grayling, Dolly Varden, lake trout

Wildlife: Black bears, wolves, moose, Dall sheep, grizzly bears, caribou, musk oxen

The Dalton Highway

Of the various roads described in this guide, the Dalton Highway is far and away the most remote and potentially the most rugged trek available. It is also the one road where carrying a second spare tire might make sense. In the 414 miles of this road there are but three facilities offering limited services.

Also, travelers should carry extra food, plenty of bug repellent, and a complete first aid kit. Help can be a long time coming along this road. Being prepared is the key phrase. Breakdowns will cost you money. Towing services along the Dalton Highway commonly start at $5 per mile.

From its junction with the Elliott Highway, the Dalton Highway is open year-round to general travel, though in the winter months—September through May—it is used almost exclusively by truckers servicing Prudhoe Bay oilfields and the Trans Alaska Pipeline.

Along the Dalton, the speed limit is 45 mph; this is mostly ignored by truckers. The road is lightly patrolled by Alaska State Troopers. If you need police assistance, there is a trooper stationed at Coldfoot, 175 miles from the Elliott Highway junction.

At intervals along the road, you will see one-lane trails leading up to the Trans Alaska Pipeline. These trails are generally barricaded and are not open to public travel. The Trans Alaska Pipeline and its access roads are private property.

Grades along this road are steep, at times exceeding 10 percent. Again, this road was built for industry by industry, and general vehicle travel was not a factor in its construction.

All the cautions aside, this is a spectacular trip, a trip that offers the only road access to the Brooks Range, Alaska's northernmost mountain range. Many Alaskans consider the Brooks Range to be the most beautiful mountains in the world, with good reason. Jagged peaks, stunning valleys, and endlessly varying terrain leave no time for boredom.

Insider's Tip

Stop only where pullouts are available off the road. The Dalton Highway is fairly narrow and used mostly by truckers driving 18-wheelers. Truckers are often unwilling to slow down, which means they raise tremendous clouds of dust during dry periods. If you are engulfed in a cloud of dust at roadside, another trucker approaching may not be able to see your vehicle.

Northbound from the Elliott Highway junction, the terrain is mostly rolling hills with small creeks. The largest of the creeks, Hess Creek, 24 miles from the junction, offers good fishing for whitefish and grayling. You can camp here, if you wish; there is a gravel bar alongside the creek on the north side of the bridge. There are no facilities in terms of tables or outhouses.

From Hess Creek, it's about 32 miles to the Yukon River. The bridge here offers the only vehicle crossing of the Yukon in Alaska. One of North America's mightiest rivers, the Yukon's drainage includes nearly half of Alaska and much of Yukon Territory, Canada.

In July and August it may be possible to obtain fresh-caught salmon from commercial fishermen on the Yukon. Much of the catch is carried upriver to the bridge and shipped by vehicle to Fairbanks. These salmon are the most protein-rich fish in the world, many of them heading all the way to Canada to spawn. No other salmon in North America make such a tremendous journey (1,500 or more miles in fresh water) after leaving the ocean, thus these fish must be stronger than most others. Even at the Dalton Highway bridge, hundreds

The Trans Alaska Pipeline

Carry plenty of water. Drinking water is only available at the Yukon River bridge, Coldfoot, and from an artesian well 5 miles north of the bridge. Water from streams, no matter how clean it appears, must be boiled for several minutes before drinking.

and hundreds of miles from salt water in the Bering Sea, these bright, shiny fish show little evidence of the decay that usually begins when salmon enter fresh water.

The north side of the Yukon River bridge also offers one of only two places to purchase gas or get your car repaired along the Dalton Highway. There is also a restaurant and other travelers' facilities available. Best to fill up here. It's 120 miles to the next gas station at Coldfoot.

About 35 miles north of the Yukon River there's a great camping spot if you can find it and if your rig can get in—the abandoned airstrip that served Old Man Camp, a pipeline construction camp. The only remnants of the camp itself are an overgrown gravel pad near the top of a small rise on the east side of the road. The airstrip is down in the valley before you climb the hill to camp. An unmaintained gravel road leads to the airstrip and may or may not be suitable for your rig. On our last visit there, a friend and I each got our large pickup campers in and out without difficulty. Watch for the gravel road on the right and, if you find it, walk it before trying to drive in a big rig. The airstrip itself offers enough space to dry camp hundreds of rigs. If you can find it and get to it, you'll have a piece of wilderness all to yourself.

Old Man airstrip illustrates one of the great things about the Dalton Highway. If you can find the old gravel pads, gravel pits, and airstrips used to build the road and pipeline right-of-way, you can wind up with a beautiful campsite generally all to yourself. Other opportunities for this kind of camping include Galbraith Lake north of Pump Station 4 (turn left and drive past a still-in-use airstrip until the road ends at a creek coming out of the mountains) and a gravel pit on the east side of the road just south of the now-unused Pump Station 2. This latter one is visible from the road. There are others; you just have to watch closely for them, as none are marked.

Campgrounds along the Dalton Highway are sparsely furnished if furnished at all. Most good camping spots are simply level areas near the fishing streams that have been used by others or the old construction sites as described above. As such, no litter barrels or maintenance is provided. Exceptions include a campground right on the arctic circle, 60 miles north of the Yukon River bridge, and another at Marion Creek just north of Coldfoot. The first campground is about half a mile to the right of the road if you are northbound, and the turnoff is marked. A large, colorful sign denotes the arctic circle for travelers. There is a litter barrel in this campground. The Marion Creek campground is just a short distance north of the Coldfoot gas station. When you camp in other areas, burn all combustible trash in a safe campfire and carry your noncombustible garbage with you until a suitable disposal site is reached.

North of the Yukon, fishermen should also start limbering up their rods. An assortment of streams offers possibilities for burbot, pike, grayling, and Dolly Varden. And, of all the streams at roadside in Alaska, these are the least visited. Good spots to try (and distances from the Yukon River) include: Ray River (15 miles), No Name Creek (24 miles), Kanuti River (50 miles), Fish Creek (59 miles), South Fork Bonanza Creek (69 and 70 miles), Prospect Creek (80 miles), Jim River (bridges at 85, 86, and 89 miles), and South Fork of the Koyukuk River (101 miles).

Sixty miles north of the arctic circle is Coldfoot, a small community more or less at the base of the Brooks Range. Travelers' services here were originally owned by Dick and Cathy Mackey. Dick, one of the North's more colorful characters, won the Iditarod Trail Sled Dog Race from Anchorage to Nome in 1977. He still runs the race occasionally. His son Lance won both the Iditarod and the Yukon Quest in 2007, 2008, and 2009. Dick also organized the Coldfoot Classic sled dog race, which takes place in April in and around the western edge of Gates of the Arctic National Park. The Coldfoot Classic has become one of Alaska's better known middle-distance races for mushers and their dogs and is the last big race of the season for distance mushers.

Also at Coldfoot, the National Park Service has established an information center for Gates of the Arctic National Park, whose eastern boundary is just to the west of the road. One of Alaska's most remote national parks, Gates of the Arctic is only accessible via chartered airplanes or on foot from the road. The hiking is strenuous, and there are no maintained trails.

From Coldfoot north to Pump Station 4, the cliffs surrounding the road offer opportunities for viewing Dall sheep. Look among the rocks and open alpine areas for flashes of pure white. Use binoculars for best viewing.

Insider's Tip

Be extremely careful when planning a campfire. Most of the ground along the Dalton Highway is either tundra or muskeg, both of which are mostly vegetation susceptible to catching fire. Riverbank gravel bars or areas cleared to bare soil or graveled areas left over from road construction are often the only sure places to have a safe campfire. Forest fires are expensive to fight in Alaska, and government agencies have begun presenting bills for firefighting services when the cause can be traced to a person or group of people.

Insider's Tip

Though the streams are ice free in June, good fishing north of the Yukon River usually doesn't arrive until July and August. In June, most rivers are high and muddy from melting snows.

Insider's Tip

Do not feed the bears. Over the years a number of "road bears," both blacks and grizzlies, have been created along the Dalton Highway by people unthinkingly providing handouts. Some bears, particularly grizzlies, will occasionally lie down in the center of the road, force you to stop, and then saunter up to the driver's door looking for a handout. Feeding bears in Alaska is punishable by fines and jail time. It also endangers bears and people. If a bear approaches your vehicle, drive on, and then stop and watch from a distance.

Bears, both black and grizzly, are frequently seen along the Dalton Highway. Black bears generally are found at lower elevations and in wooded regions. Grizzlies most often inhabit the open tundra in alpine areas.

From Disaster Creek north of Coldfoot, the road climbs up into Atigun Pass, which is almost exactly a mile above sea level. This far north, the treeline is about 2,000 feet above sea level, and once you pass it en route to Atigun Pass, there are no more trees in the more than 150 miles of road left to the coast of the Beaufort Sea. North of the Brooks Range, trees cannot grow in the arctic conditions, though they can survive after a fashion. Out in the tundra, if you look closely in the tangled vegetation at your feet, it's often possible to find tiny spruce trees no more than a couple inches tall.

The northbound climb into the pass is probably the longest, steepest grade on the Dalton Highway. Many opportunities for viewing Dall sheep exist along here, and any bears you see from here north will be grizzly bears.

Once across the pass, it's all downhill to Deadhorse, the end of the road for privately owned vehicles. Generally, drivers on this stretch of road will see hundreds of caribou, occasionally a herd of musk oxen, falcons, and with luck, a grizzly bear or two.

All of the oilfields north and west of Deadhorse (the Prudhoe Bay area) are considered private property, and the road is closed to all but authorized vehicles. Since September 11, 2001, tours of the oilfields have pretty much been canceled. Check with the Arctic Caribou Inn, at 866-659-2368, to see if policies have changed and if tours are now available.

An Alaska Legend

If I had a favorite Alaskan—though he might better have been described as a citizen of the world—it had to be a long-distance musher, the late Colonel Norman Vaughan, a fellow who, until just a few years ago, entered the famed 1,049-mile Iditarod Trail Sled Dog Race from Anchorage to Nome each year. That in itself isn't so unusual; several mushers enter the race every year. However, one must take into account that Norm was still entering the race when he was more than 90 years old, and his first great mushing adventure was struggling to the South Pole with Admiral Richard Byrd in 1928.

One of Norm's goals was to live to be 100. He reached that milestone in early 2006 and died a few days later, surrounded by family and friends. He celebrated his 100th birthday in the hospital with a sip of Champagne, which was, according to him, the first alcohol he had ever tasted.

Norm had a cabin in the woods near Trapper Creek, a wide spot in the Parks Highway about 150 miles north of Anchorage. I've never been to his cabin and am not sure I could find it if I tried. In his last years, however, he was forced into an assisted-living arrangement, bedeviled by knees that were not as young as his spirit.

Vaughan's adventures over the years are nothing short of legendary. To fund them, one of his schemes was selling deeds to tiny pieces of the mountain in Antarctica that's named after him. He didn't own it, of course, but he was trying to raise money to fund a huge dog sled expedition to the South Pole. In years past, when not doing that or racing the Iditarod, he spent his time trying to dig some World War II bombers out of the Greenland ice cap. He knew where they were because after the planes crashed in 1943, he mushed in to recover the top-secret bombsights carried aboard the bombers.

I was a guest at his third wedding on New Year's Eve 1989, as was most of the Alaska press corps. It was done in typical Norm Vaughan style. The wedding was held at a backcountry lodge some 7 or 8 miles from the nearest road. Instructions on the invitation told guests to show up at the end of the road in the morning and hop a ride on the next dog sled or snow machine that came along. More than 150 of us did. Later, I calculated that it took about 150 howling sled dogs, 13 dog sleds, and 25 or 30 snow machines to get Norm married. It was an absolute riot of a day, just as Norm intended.

SECTION TWO: Fairbanks to Anchorage

If you wanted to drive from Fairbanks to Anchorage prior to 1971, you first had to backtrack to Delta Junction, and then turn south on the Richardson Highway to Glennallen. From there, you turned west on the Glenn Highway for about 185 miles to Anchorage. All in all, you would travel something on the order of 450 miles on roads that tended toward large frost heaves.

This was also the route to Denali National Park, or Mount McKinley National Park, as it was known back then. In those days you drove south of Delta Junction to Paxon and then west for 135 miles or so on the Denali Highway, which was all gravel, narrow, and less-than-well maintained. If, after visiting the park, you still wanted to go to Anchorage, you had to drive back to Paxon, and then south to Glennallen, and west to Anchorage. The best that could be said of both of these routes is that they were—and are—quite scenic.

The Parks Highway

Certainly the Parks Highway is scenic, as well, but best of all it's a much better engineered road and some 100 miles shorter than the old route. It also crosses some of Alaska's better salmon fishing streams and passes close to others.

Of all the major roads in Alaska, the George Parks Highway joining Fairbanks and Anchorage, Alaska's two largest cities, is the newest, opening for private vehicles in the early 1970s. In the four decades since, it has become Alaska's most-traveled road, and it is continually upgraded and well maintained. Only near the cities, where people use the ends of various highways for commuting to and from work, are any roadways used by more vehicles in the course of a year.

Though this is an all-weather road kept open year-round, winter travelers may occasionally need to wait out blizzards in Broad Pass, where the road crosses the Alaska Range. Complete white-out conditions occur a couple of times a year, making travel exceedingly dangerous.

Probably the greatest reason for the Parks Highway's popularity is that it makes road travel to Denali National Park convenient. The Parks Highway cuts across the park's eastern edge.

Denali National Park is by far the most visited of Alaska's 11 national parks. In fact, more travelers stop at Denali than at all the other national parks in Alaska combined.

The negative side to this is that the small part of Denali National Park that is readily available to visitors has become extremely crowded. For the most part, visitors to this Maryland-size park are restricted to a narrow ribbon of road penetrating about 90 miles into the park. And, with a few exceptions, visitors are not even permitted to drive their own vehicles on the Park Road. To hold traffic to a minimum, in hopes of keeping the park's varied wildlife near the road, a limited number of buses carry visitors into the park.

Two sets of buses operate in the park—green buses and tan buses—and both are operated by Aramark under contract to the US National Park Service. The green buses are essentially shuttle buses. Riders can get on and off at will (space permitting), allowing on-foot exploration of parts of the park. They also carry campers to campgrounds off-limits to private vehicles. These are the cheapest buses available, and the only amenities offered are bathroom stops every hour or so. All the way in to Wonder Lake and back is about an 11-hour day, so bring a lunch and something to drink. As to the oratorical skills and knowledge of the driver, it's pretty hit or miss. Some drivers provide comprehensive commentary; others barely say anything more than fasten your seat belts when the trip begins.

The Parks Highway

Length: 360 miles (600 kilometers)

Gas Available:

Cripple Creek Tire Store, 3 miles (5 kilometers)

Nenana, 54 miles (90 kilometers)

Healy, 109 miles (182 kilometers)

Denali Village, 120 miles (200 kilometers)

Cantwell, 148 miles (247 kilometers)

Chulitna River Lodge, 202 miles (337 kilometers)

Trapper Creek, 243 miles (405 kilometers)

Willow, 289 miles (482 kilometers)

Houston, 301 miles (502 kilometers)

Meadow Wood Shopping Mall, 306 miles (510 kilometers)

Wasilla, 316 miles (527 kilometers)

Peters Creek, 336 miles (560 kilometers)

Lodging:

Cripple Creek Resort (Ester), 6 miles (10 kilometers)

Skinny Dick's Halfway Inn, 30 miles (50 kilometers)

Nenana, 54 miles (90 kilometers)

Rochester Lodge, 78 miles (130 kilometers)

Clear Sky Lodge, 78 miles (130 kilometers)

Healy Hotel, 109 miles (182 kilometers)

Healy Roadhouse, 113 miles (188 kilometers)

McKinley Chalet Resort, 119 miles (198 kilometers)

Harper Lodge, 119 miles (198 kilometers)

Crow's Nest Log Cabins, 120 miles (200 kilometers)

McKinley Village Inn, 127 miles (212 kilometers)

Houston, 301 miles (502 kilometers)

Wasilla, 316 miles (527 kilometers)

(continued on the next page)

Campgrounds:

Skinny Dick's Halfway Inn *(RV parking only)*, 30 miles (50 kilometers)

Tripod RV Park, 54 miles (90 kilometers)

Tatlanika Trading Co., 82 miles (137 kilometers)

McKinley KOA Kampground, 110 miles (183 kilometers)

Mt. McKinley Pioneer RV Park, 111 miles (185 kilometers)

Lynx Creek Campground, 119 miles (198 kilometers)

Denali Grizzly Bear Cabins and Campground, 127 miles (212 kilometers)

East Fork Rest Area, 172 miles (287 kilometers)

Byers Lake Wayside, 211 miles (352 kilometers)

Big Susitna River Bridge, 254 miles (423 kilometers)

Montana Creek, 262 miles (437 kilometers)

Willow Island Resort, 287 miles (478 kilometers)

Nancy Lake Recreation Area, 291 miles (485 kilometers)

Rainbow Acres, 309 miles (515 kilometers)

Big Bear RV Park, 320 miles (534 kilometers)

Fishing: Grayling, rainbow trout, king salmon, silver salmon, chum salmon, pink salmon

Wildlife: Black bears, moose, Dall sheep (rare), caribou (late May–early June is best)

The tan buses are tour buses and cost about twice as much, depending on the tour selected. They are driven by qualified naturalists who offer a running commentary on what you're seeing outside the window. Other than programmed stops, there is no getting on or off these buses to hike around. You go and return on the same bus. Bring your camera, multiple memory cards, and be prepared for some awesome sights. The tan buses only penetrate about 55 miles into the park before turning around at Stony Overlook.

Camping in Denali National Park is similarly complicated in an effort at crowd control. There are only about 200 campsites within the park. The best bet is to make reservations as far ahead of time as possible. Hard-sided RVs can drive in as far as Teklanika Campground (29 miles into the park) if they can get a reservation, or they can camp at Savage River or Riley Creek, both in the small part of the park open to private vehicles. Only tent campers are allowed at Wonder Lake at the end of the road, and to camp at Wonder Lake you must ride the bus; no private vehicles are allowed to drive that far. To make campground and bus reservations by phone, call 800-622-7275 or visit nps.gov/dena and follow the links to make a campground reservation.

However, as driving and camping requirements have become more restrictive within the park during the past decade, a number of businesses have opened up at the edge of the park, including hotels, cafés, and campgrounds for RVs. A short distance north of the park entrance there now exists a thriving mini-city every summer to serve travelers. It is, for the most part, a well-maintained community performing a satisfactory service. Costs, because of demand and the short tourist season, are somewhat higher than normal, though not unfairly so, with the possible exception of gasoline. And, in 2004, for the first time ever, there were two stoplights installed on the Parks Highway in the area of these businesses.

Insider's Tip

If at all possible, avoid buying gas in and around Denali National Park and Healy to the north of the park entrance. Gas prices in and around the park were 40–50 cents a gallon higher than in Fairbanks and Anchorage on our last visit. If you need gas, the best bet is the Chevron station in Cantwell about 28 miles south of the park entrance.

In a sense, this sudden growth of visitor services near the park entrance has taken away some of the magic of visiting Denali National Park for old-timers in Alaska. Not too many years ago, locals wanting to weekend in the park would often spend Friday night camped in a large graveled area near the park entrance, waiting to dash into the park the next morning and sign up for campsites. These impromptu campouts often turned into the most memorable part of the weekend, with spontaneous, shared good times. The mini-city of services that has since grown up in the area took over the gravel pullout. Thus the gatherings so many looked forward to are a thing of the past, replaced by the stricter formalities of individual campsites rented in private campgrounds. The changes are almost certainly a necessity as more and more people visit Denali National Park, but a necessity that leaves some of us with a certain nostalgia.

If you don't have a reservation, to increase your chances of getting a campsite within Denali National Park, leave Fairbanks early in the morning for the three-hour drive to the park. You'll want to time your arrival at Denali between 8 a.m. and 10 a.m. As campers from the previous night depart their sites, those waiting at the park information center will be granted permits as they become available. Most days you must literally be standing in the information center as campsites become available. While you're in the center, you can also sign up for the park service buses departing the center at regular intervals for the interior of the park.

Leaving Fairbanks this early, however, is not without advantages. Wildlife is most active in the early morning, and there are good opportunities to see moose and black bears between Fairbanks and the park. The highway will be less crowded, as well.

From Fairbanks, the road leads through low, rolling hills of spruce and birch forests to Nenana at the confluence of the Nenana and Tanana Rivers. Nenana is a river shipping port accessible to the Alaska Railroad. As you drive across the bridge over the Tanana River, the barge loading docks are immediately on your left. With luck you may see a tug pushing a load of barges downstream toward the Yukon River communities served by the barge company. The Tanana, particularly where it joins the Yukon, is a shallow, braided river that requires the utmost skill by tug pilots and their crews. The deep-water channel changes almost daily, which means tug operators—and private boaters—must have a keen sense of the rivers and their many moods.

If you take time out to explore Nenana, down near the road leading into town, you'll see a large black-and-white tripod—actually a four-legged device but still called a tripod. This is the tripod for the Nenana Ice Classic, Alaska's biggest and most rewarding annual guessing game. Over the winter, the tripod is placed on the Tanana River ice with a cable connecting it to a large clock. When the ice goes out sufficiently to move the tripod enough to stop the clock, ticket holders who guessed the exact day, hour, and minute the ice goes out share a prize that can exceed $200,000. Usually there are several winners each year. Ice has gone out as early as mid-April and as late as mid-May.

Heading south from Nenana, the countryside is fairly flat for the next 50 miles or so, until you approach Healy. For the most part the ground is fairly soggy—almost marshy—and the undergrowth quite thick.

Healy, on the northern edge of the Alaska Range, is a coal-mining town. Off in the mountains to your left is Alaska's primary source of coal for power and for export, the Usabelli Mine. No mining activity is visible from the road.

Nenana Ice Classic tripod in summer storage

The Denali Park Road

If you want to see wildlife, the Denali Park Road is far and away your best bet on the Alaska road system. During a day-long bus trip in summer, passengers will almost certainly see caribou and moose, Dall sheep, probably several grizzly bears, and, with luck, a wolf. Smaller animals like martens, ptarmigan, and fox are common.

Most day visitors board park service shuttle buses at the information center near the park entrance. Seats on buses are either available by reservation or on a first-come, first-served basis. The best buses to take—with the highest chance of seeing wildlife—are the early morning buses (starting at 6 a.m. or earlier) or the last buses in the evening.

Pack a small cooler full of lunch materials, ideally snack food that you can eat at intervals during the day, if you ride one of the green shuttle buses run by the National Park Service. There is no opportunity to purchase food on the trip, and the bus ride to Wonder Lake and back will last eight hours or longer. You'll need food and drink to keep up your strength.

The habitat at roadside, as you move through the park, tends to dictate the type of wildlife you will see. At lower (forested) elevations near the start of the trip and about 30 miles into the trip near Teklanika Campground, moose are more likely to be seen than along any other part of the road.

Past Teklanika, in the mountains near Igloo Creek, Dall sheep should be visible on the steep mountains near the road. Opportunities for grizzlies are most prevalent above the timberline, particularly after passing Igloo Creek. Caribou and wolves, as well, will most likely be seen in the open tundra.

On board the green shuttle buses, things are pretty informal. Anyone seeing wildlife should immediately speak out. The bus driver will stop the bus for viewing whatever animal is spotted and to allow plenty of time for pictures. Most pictures will have to be taken through open bus windows, as passengers are not generally permitted to disembark except at rest stops.

If you wish to get off the bus and hike around in the tundra for awhile, advise the bus driver. He will stop wherever you want, let you out, and then drive away. When you've finished your hike, flag down the next bus in either direction (depending on which way you want to go) and reboard to complete your trip. Those wishing to be dropped off for day hikes should check in at the information center for suggestions and to let the rangers know the area you want to explore. Be sure to take binoculars and plenty of memory cards for your camera . Those wishing to spend time camping in the tundra at remote sites will need to pick up a backcountry camping permit from a building next to the information center.

From Healy the road quickly winds into the heart of the Alaska Range, through a narrow notch in the mountains, and then into the wider expanse of Broad Pass near timberline. As you enter Broad Pass, Denali National Park is to the right. Shortly before reaching the turnoff for park headquarters you will pass the collection of businesses that have grown up to serve area visitors.

The turnoff for Denali National Park along the Parks Highway is the start of the Denali Park Road, or Mile 0 of the Park Road, as it's most often called. If you turn into the park, a short, well-marked drive leads to the park information center. This should be your first stop. If you want a campsite or a seat on one of the park service buses, this is where you get in line.

Past the park entrance, the Parks Highway passes several more tourism-related businesses, among them several companies offering raft trips on the Nenana River, which shares this valley with the road. This is whitewater rafting at its best, and those with a few hours or a day to spare should consider signing up for one of these trips.

A few miles after leaving the park you'll come to two road junctions. The first, to the left, is the Denali Highway, which leads about 135 miles (mostly gravel) through the Alaska Range to Paxon on the Richardson Highway. Much of this road is above the timberline.

The Denali Highway is a spectacular drive, albeit a fairly slow one. There are few facilities along the road other than a couple of BLM campgrounds. It is, however, a wonderful opportunity to penetrate the heart of Alaska's most dominant range of mountains. Allow at least a full day for one-way travel on the Denali Highway; you'll want to stop often to admire the view or wander through the tundra. Wildflowers are at their best in early July; blueberries peak in early August.

Alaska RR Riley Creek Bridge on the edge of Denali National Park

Alaskan Men Versus Oprah

It takes a special breed to live alone in a snowed-in cabin for months on end, and we have more than our fair share of them in Alaska, mostly men.

Back in 1986, an enterprising Anchorage woman started a magazine called *Alaska Men*. In it, she specialized in one-page stories with a photo of single Alaska men, heavily weighted to those supposedly rugged types living a romantic existence in the wilderness. She printed about 1,000 copies of the premier issue. The rest, as they say, is history, and it has been a phenomenal success story. The magazine, a quarterly, got its circulation up to more than 135,000 in the 1990s.

In 1988, a bunch of these men were flown to Chicago to appear on Oprah Winfrey's television show, kind of a meat market in reverse, where the women in the audience were obviously present as potential dates for these "wild-and-wooly" Alaskans.

Both the magazine and the men involved make much of the fact that Alaska is about the only place in the country where there are more men than women. However, in referring to these extra men, one Cordova woman told an Anchorage newspaper reporter, "Yes, the odds are good. But the goods are odd." I guess a subsistence lifestyle in the bush wasn't her idea of communal bliss.

The second junction, with a road leading to the right, is Cantwell Junction. The tiny town of Cantwell is a couple of miles off the main road. Several gas stations, a gift shop, and a convenience store are scattered along the Parks Highway at Cantwell Junction.

Heading south out of Cantwell, the road stays right on the edge of the timberline for quite a few miles. Assuming the weather is clear, as you proceed south, Mount Foraker, Alaska's third highest peak, about 75 miles away, will be visible to the right. Turnouts are provided at many prime viewing spots to allow time out for observation and for taking pictures.

The best views of Denali from the road system are about 80 and 100 miles south of the park entrance on the Parks Highway in Denali State Park. The first, Denali Viewpoint North, also allows overnight camping (no hookups) and can handle the largest rigs. The second, Denali Viewpoint South, does not allow overnight camping but is the more popular of the two, as it is right alongside the road. Both sites can be crowded on sunny summer days, and both sites are well worth a stop on those days when the mountain is visible.

As the road begins dropping out of the Alaska Range into the broad Matanuska–Susitna Valley, fishermen should start getting ready. Between Broad Pass and Anchorage are streams hosting some of the biggest runs of salmon anywhere along the road system in Alaska. Many of these same streams hold large populations of native rainbow trout, though the trout are hard to reach when salmon choke the streams.

Several streams crossed by the Parks Highway offer splendid fishing opportunities, among them Montana Creek, Sheep Creek, and Willow Creek. Even more opportunities are available just off the road system via river charters or fly-in charters.

Your best bet to finding good charter fishing is to inquire at the visitor center in Wasilla, a roadside town about 45 miles from Anchorage. The center is located with the chamber of commerce in the old railroad station right alongside the road. Be prepared for the fishing adventure of a lifetime if you take one of these charters during the height of the king or silver salmon runs.

Before reaching Wasilla, a short spur road leads left to Talkeetna, another source of good charter fishing on area rivers. Also, Talkeetna is the jump-off point for climbers heading for Denali and other nearby peaks. The climbing season is late April through mid-June. If you're in Talkeetna then, it's worth the time to drive out to the airport and watch the almost-frantic activity involved in getting climbers and their equipment to and from the mountain.

The air services that handle the climbers employ some of the finest bush pilots in Alaska. They also offer flightseeing trips in and around Denali. These are great trips in light planes, offering up-close views of the tallest peak in North America. Depending on the air service and your own goals for flightseeing, you can stop off on a mountain glacier (usually Ruth Glacier) for a few minutes of wandering around in an icy wonderland. Most people who take a Talkeetna-based flightseeing trip agree that it's the finest part of their Alaskan adventure.

South of Talkeetna, the road moves ever closer to Anchorage and Alaska's population center. Wasilla, in fact, is more or less Anchorage's northernmost bedroom community, with several thousand area residents commuting 45 miles or more to work in Anchorage each morning and back again in the evening.

In the Wasilla area and near neighboring Palmer are a number of small lakes stocked with trout. These are all pleasant places to spend an afternoon picnicking and fishing. Most are well suited to canoes or other small boats. Again, inquire at the Wasilla visitor center for ideas if you want to sample some of these.

The final leg of the drive to Anchorage from Wasilla takes an hour or a little less, all of it on four-lane highway. If it's late in the day, you may want to stay in a campground or hotel in the Wasilla-Palmer area unless you have a reservation in Anchorage. Campgrounds in Anchorage are fairly limited, and most hotels are booked pretty solid during the summer months. Those wanting either a hotel room or a campsite in Anchorage without reservations should try to arrive early in the day.

January afternoon view of Denali from Denali Viewpont South on the Parks Highway

Critters—Big Critters

Not everybody in Alaska lives in a log cabin and ekes a living out of the fragile wilderness. By far, most Alaskans live in frame houses, condos, or apartments in or near fairly substantial cities. Fully half the state's population, more than 350,000 people, lives within 50 miles of downtown Anchorage. As many say, though, "The only good thing about Anchorage is that it's just an hour away from Alaska." The same can be said of Fairbanks or Juneau, as well, though the time involved to get out of town would be less.

In that telling phrase is everything that explains why people live in Anchorage, or anywhere in Alaska. It is different up here. For instance, grizzly bears live within the municipal boundaries of Anchorage, which tends to inspire a certain amount of awe in city dwellers from other states.

In 1988, 1997, and again recently, one of these bears got lost and wandered out of the mountains on the eastern side of town. All three times, joggers on the coastal trail surrounding the city first spotted a bear near Cook Inlet on the west side of town. In the next couple of days after being spotted, each bear cut right through the heart of the city, crossing major highways, airports, and parking lots as it headed back to the mountains. The first two bears eventually made it safely to the mountains; the most recent bear had to be killed when it popped up in a populated area during a Fourth of July fireworks extravaganza. The fireworks upset the bear, and a police officer at the scene felt he had no choice other than to put the bear down before someone got hurt.

Though grizzlies are rarely seen in town, moose are seen so frequently as to be almost an afterthought. Suburban gardeners go to great lengths to protect their cabbages and other plants. Nothing seems to work very well. After all, how do you tell 1,500 pounds of protoplasm what he can or can't eat? We just gave up one night a few summers back after our resident moose came by and took a single big bite out of each head of cabbage. To our everlasting relief, he didn't know how to dig potatoes. To my son's relief, he also had a taste for broccoli, polishing off all of those plants before starting on the cabbages.

The next year we tried a new technique for keeping moose away from the garden. We were told that moose absolutely detest the smell of Irish Spring soap. So we hung bars of the highly scented soap on our trees and shrubs to keep the moose away during the winter. Looking out the window one frosty morning, I watched a young moose, soap foam dribbling from his chin, gobble up the bar of Irish Spring hanging from the chokecherry tree in the front yard. Then his mother ate the tree.

Whether you consider bears in town and moose in the garden to be privileges or liabilities, these kinds of things make Alaska special. Most of us who live here would probably be quite bored living in more "normal" regions.

SECTION THREE: The Kenai Peninsula

Many of the fishing legends that come from Alaska were born on this peninsula—and some of those legends are true. Here are a couple to whet your appetite: 400-pound Pacific halibut on rod and reel, the world record king salmon (97-plus pounds), ling cod (these look like your worst sea monster nightmare), a total of five species of salmon, and an assortment of saltwater bottom fish. Sadly, the clam beaches have been closed recently, as the clams have all but disappeared. All this is found in a bit of land perhaps 150 miles north and south by about 100 miles east and west. Of course, if you're from the Northeast, that amount of land is bigger than several states. In Alaska, however, it's like a pimple on the coast south of Anchorage.

Because of its accessibility to Alaska's largest city and its popularity, the Kenai Peninsula is almost always crowded on any summer weekend. On Thursday through Saturday nights, campsites may be few and far between near the major rivers and key cities. But, as a visitor, you're not restricted to weekends. It's best to head for the Kenai on Sunday afternoon or Monday, and then clear the area Friday morning before the crowds of weekenders arrive. While it's still likely to be crowded, it won't quite be a madhouse like most weekends.

The Seward Highway

Starting in Anchorage, only one road leads south, the Seward Highway. Those entering Anchorage on the Parks Highway from the north, Anchorage's only other road out of town, intercept the Seward Highway as they pull into town. Where these highways join, 5th and Gambell Streets, is the starting point for Seward Highway mileages given here. Within Anchorage proper, both Gambell Street and Seward Highway signs refer to the same road.

Anchorage, like similar-size cities throughout the nation, has its share of pluses and minuses. Urban sprawl is one of the problems; veiled references by residents to "Los Anchorage" are not made without reason. This town does spread out and requires some sort of a vehicle for getting around conveniently.

On the plus side, there's a first-class performing arts center, plenty of green space, and good museums. Finally, there's the setting. On clear days, mountains are visible whichever way you turn. To the east are the Chugach Mountains; the city edges upward on their lower slopes to the boundary of Chugach State Park, one of the largest state parks in the nation. Across Cook Inlet to the west and around to the north of town is the Alaska Range. Even Denali, nearly 200 miles away, is visible on clear days. Finally, to the south, are the Kenai Mountains of the Kenai Peninsula, certainly not a large mountain range, but the most accessible in Alaska.

The Seward Highway: Anchorage to Seward

Length: 127 miles (212 kilometers)

Gas Available:

BJ Gas, Grocery and Camper Park, 26 miles (43 kilometers)

Girdwood Junction, 37 miles (62 kilometers)

Moose Pass, 98 miles (163 kilometers)

Seward, 127 miles (212 kilometers)

Lodging:

Girdwood, 37 miles (62 kilometers); turn left at junction

Seward, 127 miles (212 kilometers)

Campgrounds:

BJ Gas, Grocery and Camper Park, 26 miles (43 kilometers)

Bertha Creek (USFS), 62 miles (103 kilometers)

Granite Creek (USFS), 64 miles (107 kilometers)

Tenderfoot Creek (USFS), 81 miles (135 kilometers)

Tern Lake (USFS), 90 miles (150 kilometers)

Trail River (USFS), 103 miles (172 kilometers)

Ptarmigan Creek (USFS), 104 miles (173 kilometers)

Primrose (USFS), 110 miles (183 kilometers)

Fishing: Pink salmon, silver salmon, hooligan, rainbow trout, Dolly Varden, grayling

Wildlife: Dall sheep, Rocky Mountain goats, beluga whales, black bears, moose

Turning south on the Seward Highway at 5th and Gambell, the first few miles are fairly typical city driving, complete with traffic lights and turn lanes. The distance between exits begins to stretch out as you enter south Anchorage, primarily a residential area. Suddenly, you crest a small hill, start down toward coastal wetlands, and you're out of town, looking down onto Potter's Marsh, a state wildlife refuge on the left side of the road and Cook Inlet to the right. Winding around to your front is Turnagain Arm of Cook Inlet. Southbound travelers drive completely around Turnagain Arm on a road that drops from four to two lanes as it leaves the city.

Insider's Tip

The best place to watch for both beluga whales and bore tides is, appropriately, Beluga Point, a well-marked turnout with plenty of parking. You may also spot Dall sheep from this point if you look inland. Beluga Point is about 17 miles from Anchorage.

The famed British explorer Captain James Cook named Turnagain Arm during an 18th-century exploration of Cook Inlet. He entered the arm seeking the Northwest Passage, but the shallow waters forced him to turn his ship, time and again, to avoid grounding.

Potter's Marsh is worth a stop, particularly in June. Waterfowl are the most obvious critters in this park, and in June nesting birds bring their down-covered offspring right up to the boardwalk for close viewing. A parking area is provided, but it's not particularly large.

South of Potter's Marsh, the road twists and turns on a narrow strip of land between the Chugach Mountains and Cook Inlet for about 30 miles. In late fall, winter, and spring, avalanches are frequent, as are traffic delays while the road is cleared. In summer, Dall sheep ewes and their lambs are visible on the cliffs near the road, often wandering down to the shoulder of the road. Several turnouts are provided near areas frequented by the sheep.

In Cook Inlet during July and August, beluga whales (small white whales) can be spotted in the inlet chasing salmon as they approach spawning streams. The best whale viewing is at high tide; otherwise, the water's edge is quite far from the road.

Cook Inlet tides are the second-highest in the world, exceeded only by those of the Bay of Fundi in Nova Scotia. During full-moon periods, water levels between high and low tides may vary by 35 feet or more. Of particular interest are bore tides, a moving wall of water that may be as high as 6 feet rolling across Turnagain Arm as the tide changes from low to high.

Along the shores of Turnagain Arm, about 35 miles from Anchorage, the Seward Highway passes a turnoff to Girdwood, the town that serves Alaska's premier skiing area. A dirt road from Girdwood leads to the historic Crow Creek Mine.

Continuing south, 48 miles from Anchorage, another side road leads to Portage Glacier, one of Alaska's most-visited attractions. At the end of this short road is a splendid interpretive center built and managed by the U.S. Forest Service. The center overlooks iceberg-choked Portage Lake. Because it has been receding in recent years, the glacier itself is no longer visible from the visitor center, but a boat excursion is available if you want to see it up close.

Insider's Tip

If you plan to stay in an Anchorage hotel during the summer months, make reservations ahead of time if at all possible. During July and August it is often difficult to find a room on short notice. Information on hotels, motels, lodges, and bed-and-breakfasts can be obtained from the Anchorage Convention and Visitors Bureau, listed in Appendix A of this book.

Insider's Tip

The mud-colored beaches exposed during Cook Inlet's low tides are extremely hazardous. People stuck in this mud, likened to quicksand, are often unable to free themselves before a high tide returns and drowns them. Avoid these mudflats at all costs. If you see anyone stuck in the mudflats, contact state troopers immediately, before attempting a rescue. If you do attempt a rescue, don't complicate things by becoming stuck yourself.

Insider's Tip

Ask one of the rangers about iceworms—believe it or not, they're real, and because they exist in the cold they will "fry" in your hand.

Since the late 1990s, the road to Portage has also become the road to Whittier. Whittier, on Prince William Sound, has been accessible by rail since World War II. In the late 1990s, construction crews finished adapting the longest tunnel to both rail and one-way vehicle travel so it is possible to drive to the city. Driving through the tunnel is thrilling, but the cost can be a bit chilling. If you're in a passenger car, the toll for a round-trip through the 2.5-mile tunnel is $12. A driver with an RV 28 feet long or longer will pay $35.

In and around the Portage Glacier turnoff is considerable evidence of the Great Alaska Earthquake of 1964. The ground in this region sank several feet as a result of the shifting earth. Abandoned, collapsing buildings and dead spruce trees on the right (seaward side) are all victims of this earthquake.

From the Portage Glacier turnoff, the Seward Highway bends around the eastern tip of Turnagain Arm, runs along its south shore for a short distance, and then begins to climb Turnagain Pass through the Kenai Mountains. In winter, this is among the snowiest roadways in Alaska, with snow packs often exceeding 8–10 feet. In summer, the route offers dense forests, clear streams, and a profusion of wildflowers in the open areas. Southbound, the ascent from sea level is rather rapid. Once on top, the descent is gentler, though the road twists and turns through an assortment of narrow river valleys.

Insider's Tip

Because it is relatively unknown, the Johnson Lake Trail offers a perfect Kenai Peninsula getaway during crowded weekends. The last time I hiked this trail was a July 4th weekend, the most crowded weekend of the year on the Kenai Peninsula. In four days on the trail, I saw fewer than 10 other people.

A few miles past the summit a turnoff to the left leads to the Johnson Lake Trail, one of the Kenai's lesser-used hiking trails, but a good one. The trail runs for about 21 miles through the mountains, exiting at Moose Pass, also on the Seward Highway. On the north side of the trail's summit, at about the halfway point, is Bench Lake, with excellent grayling fishing. Little more than a mile south across the pass is Johnson Lake, offering great fishing for rainbows to about 16 inches in length.

About 70 miles from Anchorage, a turnoff to the right leads 18 miles to Hope, founded as a mining community in 1896. Evidence of this activity, which continued well into the 20th century, exists throughout the area. An old-timer or two can frequently be found drinking coffee in Hope's Discovery Cafe and can talk about the heyday of gold mining in Hope.

Just prior to entering Hope is the trailhead for Resurrection Pass Trail, the Kenai Peninsula's most popular hiking route. This 38-mile-long trail leads south to the Sterling Highway. Eight Forest Service cabins along the route are available for rental by hikers traversing the trail, though reservations should be made as early as possible. Cabin costs are low, and reservations can be made up to six months in advance by calling 877-444-6777 or at recreation.gov. For more information on the Resurrection Pass Trail and Chugach National Forest, visit www.fs.usda.gov/chugach.

Eighteen miles past the Hope junction, the Sterling Highway takes off to the right from the Seward Highway. Just past the junction, a marshy lake to the right is often a great place to see moose early in the morning or late in the evening. During June and July, most of the Anchorage weekend traffic will turn off on the Sterling Highway, lessening the crowds on the remaining 39 miles of the Seward Highway.

An assortment of Forest Service campgrounds lies along the final miles of the Seward Highway. Just prior to entering Seward, the highway levels out as you enter town, with the small boat harbor on your left. All travelers' services are available.

Seward is the gateway to Kenai Fjords National Park, a wilderness preserve along the rugged south shore of the Kenai Peninsula. The best way to see the park is via one of the commercial operators offering day-long boat trips from Seward through Resurrection Bay and into some of the glacier-headed fjords. En route, there is an excellent chance of seeing killer whales. Almost certainly, passengers will spy sea lions, sea otters, bald eagles, and thousands of various birds in rocky rookeries at the water's edge.

Glacier near Resurrection Bay

Insider's Tip

The most productive bait for salmon derby fishermen is usually herring trolled slowly behind a boat or "mooched." During August, virtually every store in Seward has frozen bait herring for sale. Fish at varying depths until something bites. Then rig every pole to fish at the depth the fish was caught. If you're going to enter the derby, you must buy a derby ticket prior to fishing, and every fisherman aboard the boat must have a derby ticket.

Seward is an RV-friendly town. Starting near the Alaska Sea Life Center at the end of the road through town and winding almost a half mile to the north along the water's edge is a municipal campground with hundreds of RV sites, designated tent sites, and even RV sites with water and 50-amp power. Virtually every campsite offers a view of Resurrection Bay.

Seward offers two major events each summer: the Mount Marathon race on the Fourth of July, a rugged scramble up and down the mountain that looms over the town, and the Seward Silver Salmon Derby in August. The latter is probably Alaska's biggest and best attended salmon derby, with large cash prizes and an assortment of related activities. Fishing is done from a boat in Resurrection Bay. Party boats are available, or private boats can be launched in Seward's harbor for access to the fishing grounds. Small boat operators should watch the weather carefully. Resurrection Bay's winds can quickly generate heavy waves, making things extremely hazardous on the water.

The Sterling Highway

The Kenai Peninsula is Alaska's most famous fishing area, and the bulk of that fame comes from the streams and shoreline found along the Sterling Highway. There are several reasons for this. The road makes these streams accessible, a relative rarity in Alaska. The king salmon in the Kenai River are the largest of this species in the entire world; the same holds true for the halibut caught from party boats in Homer at the end of the road. In between are hefty runs of red, silver, and pink salmon and rainbow trout. Along this 137-mile route is more fishing adventure than most can imagine, the only liability being the crowds of people that compete for these fish. For the most part, fishing along this stretch of road is not the wilderness experience that most people think of when they dream of fishing in Alaska. However, most of those thoughts are quickly put aside with the first ferocious lunge of an 80-pound king salmon or 200-pound halibut.

It takes about an hour and 15 minutes to drive the Seward Highway from Anchorage to the start of the Sterling Highway. From there, another two-and-a-half hours will take you to the end of the road in Homer, should you not wish to stop. But few people can resist a stop or two at some of Alaska's most popular fishing holes.

Westbound, on the Sterling, the first obvious chance for fishermen is Kenai Lake, though it's illegal to fish for salmon in the lake or its tributaries. Try instead for lake trout or Dolly Varden. The brilliant green color of this lake is caused by glacier silt suspended in the water.

The road parallels the north shore of the lake and then cuts across the Kenai River at the outlet of the lake. In the Kenai River are big kings (already described) in May, June, and July; red salmon in July and August; pinks in August; silvers in August and September; and rainbows to 18 pounds all year. Usually, though, it's difficult to reach the rainbows during salmon runs. Best rainbow fishing is usually late September or early October, but you may have to fight snow to catch rainbows this late in the year.

The best Kenai River fishing is usually from a boat, either a drift boat or a powered boat. A wide variety of operators offer half- or whole-day charters, usually for two to four fishermen to a boat. Boat operators generally furnish necessary tackle and bait. If you want to use your own boat on the Kenai, the largest allowable engines are 35-horsepower outboards, though this may be changing soon to 50-hp motors. The world record king salmon came from the Kenai River in 1985, all 97-pounds, 4-ounces of it. In 1989, a visiting fisherman from Minnesota fought a king believed to be larger for nearly 48 hours before the fish broke the line and got away.

In 1987, a couple of Kenai River guides took time out to pull up the most famous snag in the river, a sunken log in one of the hottest fishing holes. When they wrestled this monster to the surface, stuck to it were thousands of lures and a complete rod-and-reel outfit. Total value of the lost tackle on the log has been estimated at $10,000 or more.

The Sterling Highway pretty much follows the Kenai River from the lake to the town of Soldotna. At Soldotna, the river turns north and the road turns south. South from Soldotna, the road crosses several other streams with opportunities for salmon fishing, among them the Kasilof

Insider's Tip

The best bait on the Kenai River for all salmon and rainbows is usually a glob of salmon roe rigged with some sort of attractor and bounced slowly along the bottom with the current. Fishermen should expect to lose a lot of terminal tackle to snags on the river bottom. If you are not regularly snagging on the bottom, you are not fishing deep enough. Watch the regulations carefully, though. Bait is occasionally prohibited.

("ka-see-loff") and Anchor Rivers and Deep Creek. Off the mouth of Deep Creek, fishermen can also troll for kings from a boat or jig for halibut. If nothing else, stop here long enough to watch crews launch boats in the surf at Deep Creek. Special tractors push large boats into fairly deep water regardless of the wave action. It's pretty thrilling.

The Sterling Highway: Mile 89 Seward Highway to Homer

Length: 137 miles (228 kilometers)

Gas Available:

Sunrise Inn, 9 miles (15 kilometers)

Kenai Lake, 12 miles (20 kilometers)

Cooper Landing, 13 miles (21 kilometers)

Hamilton's Place, 14 miles (23 kilometers)

Sterling, 46 miles (77 kilometers)

Soldotna, 60 miles (100 kilometers)

Treasure Cache, 67 miles (112 kilometers)

Clam Gulch, 83 miles (138 kilometers)

Ninilchik, 99 miles (165 kilometers)

Happy Valley, 110 miles (183 kilometers)

Anchor Point, 121 miles (202 kilometers)

Homer, 137 miles (228 kilometers)

Lodging:

Sunrise Inn, 9 miles (15 kilometers)

Kenai Lake, 12 miles (20 kilometers)

Alpine Inn Motel, 13 miles (21 kilometers)

Cooper Landing, 13 miles (21 kilometers)

Hamilton's Place, 14 miles (23 kilometers)

Gwin's Lodge, 16 miles (27 kilometers)

Sterling, 46 miles (77 kilometers)

Soldotna, 60 miles (100 kilometers)

Clam Shell Lodge, 83 miles (138 kilometers)

Beachcomber Motel, 99 miles (165 kilometers)

Happy Valley, 110 miles (183 kilometers)

Anchor Point, 121 miles (202 kilometers)

Homer, 137 miles (228 kilometers)

Prior to reaching Soldotna, the Russian River joins the Kenai. The Russian is Alaska's premier red salmon fishery in July, and it gets crowded at the few points of public access to the river. Only artificial flies can be used as bait, but this is also combat fishing. Riverbanks will be jammed, and there's little opportunity to practice the delicate art of true fly-fishing. Almost everybody uses a spinning rod with 20-pound test line and ties a fly to the end just below a large weight. When a fish is hooked, it is dragged quickly from the water to avoid tangling with the hundreds of other lines. At the height of the red salmon run, this fishery must be seen to be believed.

Campgrounds:

Sunrise Inn, 9 miles (15 kilometers)

Quartz Creek, 9 miles (15 kilometers)

Cooper Creek (USFS), 15 miles (25 kilometers)

Russian River (USFS), 17 miles (28 kilometers)

Knowlton's, 43 miles (72 kilometers)

Bing's Landing, 45 miles (75 kilometers)

Sterling, 46 miles (77 kilometers)

Scout Lake, 50 miles (83 kilometers)

Soldotna, 60 miles (100 kilometers)

Tustumena Lake, 74 miles (123 kilometers)

Clam Gulch, 82 miles (137 miles)

Ninilchik Recreation Area, 99 miles (165 kilometers)

Deep Creek, 102 miles (170 kilometers)

Stariski Creek, 116 miles (193 kilometers)

Anchor River, 122 miles (203 kilometers)

Homer, 137 miles (228 kilometers)

Fishing: Rainbow and lake trout, Dolly Varden, king salmon, red salmon, pink salmon, silver salmon, steelhead, halibut

Wildlife: Moose, black bears, brown bears, caribou, mountain goats

Past the salmon streams, the Sterling Highway drops down to Homer near the outer edge of Kachemak Bay. Homer is Alaska's favorite halibut fishing site, and a plethora of party boat operators offer day trips after these big bottom fish for about $200 per person. The limit is two fish per fishermen. Annually, halibut in excess of 300 pounds are brought in.

When selecting an operator for halibut fishing, spend some time asking around the docks when fishermen return in the afternoon and evening. Even if few fish are brought to the dock, look for people who obviously had a good time on their day on the water. The rapid growth of this industry has resulted in some skippers providing less service than others. Book your trip on boats that deliver the happiest clients to shore. All bait and tackle should be provided, but fishermen must generally bring their own lunches. Medication for motion sickness is also recommended for those with queasy stomachs. And do not try to sneak a banana on a halibut charter. For whatever reason, bananas are considered bad luck on halibut boats, and skippers will make you get rid of any bananas in your lunch bag before you board.

Premier Kenai Peninsula attractions that are often overlooked by anglers are the Swanson River and Swan Lake canoe trails in the Kenai Wildlife Refuge. The canoe trails are laid out through chains of lakes, some joined by narrow sloughs, others by short portages. Rainbow fishing in this water system can be fantastic, particularly in June and September. Inquire locally in Soldotna for canoe rentals and access points. This is strictly a paddling adventure; no motors are allowed.

One of Homer's most famous attractions is the Homer Spit, a 5-mile-long mini-peninsula jutting into Kachemak Bay. Throughout the summer, a large transient population camps along the spit, and various businesses have grown up near the small boat harbor at the end. Driving out on the spit can be a visual feast during a spectacular sunset.

In recent years, a king salmon fishery has developed at a lagoon on the spit. The Alaska Department of Fish and Game stocks king salmon programmed to return to this lagoon for sport fishermen. Maybe an acre or so in size, the lagoon fills with seawater with every high tide and then empties as the tide recedes. People line the shore of the lagoon casting lures and baits for the returning kings. Late May through early July is the best time. Fish the rising tides. These salmon can't spawn in this lagoon, so the goal is for sport fishermen to catch every one.

Also in Homer, you can board a boat for a short trip across Kachemak Bay to Seldovia on the south shore. Seldovia is a small, tightly knit community, mostly made up of fishermen. It makes for a pleasant one-day outing.

Matanuska River along the Glenn
Highway northwest of Anchorage

CHAPTER 12
Top 10 RV Destinations

Any subjective list like this is rife with danger. Some of my friends will take issue with these—their own lists would almost certainly differ in content and/or priority. That's fine. Everyone is entitled to an opinion. The list that follows happens to be my list of favorite places on the Alaska road system, and it's based on 40-plus years of camping all over the state.

1. SEWARD   This whole town seems designed to attract and cater to RVers—and tent campers too. The entire waterfront, stretching almost from the boat harbor around the west and south side of the city to the Alaska Sea Life Center, is one big RV park and includes a nice grassy spot for tent campers. Hundreds of rigs can set up overlooking the ocean. And once you've set up camp, downtown and the Sea Life Center are a short walk away, as are some of the city's finest restaurants. And if your timing is right, about the middle of August, you can catch a salmon swimming along the shore in front of your rig.

As with all travel, timing can be everything. Two big events over the summer tend to really crowd the town—the Mount Marathon race over July 4th weekend and the Seward Silver Salmon Derby from the second through the fourth weekends of August.

While the salmon derby is pretty self-explanatory, Mount Marathon probably requires some elaboration. Yes, it is a footrace, but beyond that any resemblance to a real marathon is only incidental. Mount Marathon participants run only a few miles—up the 3,000-foot mountain overlooking the town, and then back down. The real excitement is watching the crashes on the way down as various runners try to take shortcuts over cliffs and rock slides and the like. Doctors and medics are standing by and are almost always in demand.

Unless you just have to be there for one of these events, try to come before or after. For example, silver salmon fishing can be quite good from late July through mid-September. Halibut charters are available every day from May through September. In other words, while the marathon and the salmon derby can indeed be fun, finding a place to camp can be difficult. Outside of those two events, however, camping space is available without a reservation at virtually any other time during the summer.

Insider's Tip

At low tide, particularly a minus tide, walk through the exposed rocks in front of Winnebago Point. You should be able to pick up a tackle box full of fishing lures lost by salmon fishermen over the years.

2. THE DENALI HIGHWAY   I've probably had more fun along this 135-mile gravel road between Paxon and Cantwell than anywhere else in Alaska. The fishing is for lake trout and grayling, mostly in high mountain lakes, some alongside the road, and others a few miles in on trails suitable for walking or all-terrain vehicles. The scenery is spectacular, much of it alpine tundra above the timberline. Broad valleys point to the glaciers that give birth to the rivers. Because it is mostly a narrow gravel road, you can't drive it very fast, but that's OK. Unless the weather really socks in, there's something to see around every bend in the road.

There are no RV parks with hookups along this highway, but you will find a couple of Bureau of Land Management campgrounds and innumerable gravel pits for boondocking or tenting. The only crowded conditions you're likely to run into are at Tangle Lakes Campground on the east end of the road over the July 4th weekend. Other than that, you can camp just about anywhere at any time during the summer. Remember, though, that some of these mountain lakes don't thaw until late June. Also, bring plenty of bug spray in the summer months—the mosquitoes in the mountains can be fierce. August will also bring some traffic along the road from caribou hunters; moose hunters will show up around the first of September.

All of the land along this road is managed by the Bureau of Land Management, so there are few restrictions on access. If you use an ATV, check with a ranger or the host at Tangle Lakes for occasional restrictions on when you can or cannot go off the trail with a motorized rig.

3. VALDEZ Much like Seward, this Prince William Sound community provides great accommodations for RVers. Unlike Seward's city-run park along the waterfront, Valdez's RV parks are privately owned.

Privately run parks generally mean more amenities in the form of hookups and staff assistance. All of the Valdez RV parks are well managed, convenient to downtown and the boat harbor, and have staff that can help arrange for sightseeing day boats and fishing charters. As an added plus, the last 25–30 miles of the drive into Valdez is one of the most spectacular stretches of road in Alaska.

Valdez also has a great silver salmon derby in August, though it's not as well hyped as Seward's derby. There's a halibut derby, too, that runs most of the summer. And in July, if you dry camp at Allison Point across the bay from the city (locally known as Winnebago Point because of the mass of motorhomes and trailers parked there from late June through August), you can walk to the rocky shoreline outside the door of your rig and catch a pink salmon on every cast, as millions of these fish swim along the shoreline headed for spawning grounds. In August you can catch silver salmon in the same place, though these won't be as numerous as the pinks in July.

Insider's Tip

While the fishing can be quite good in Silver Lake, it's even better in Van Lake. Paddle a canoe about two-thirds of the way up the right side of the lake. A hard-to-see trail leads a couple hundred yards over a low ridge to Van Lake. Portage your canoe over the trail and fish the arm of Van Lake where you first approach it—throw small lures or flies from the canoe toward the structure along the shore.

4. SILVER LAKE   This one's hard to find, and the accommodations might not suit the real big rigs, but it's worth the hunt if you want to tangle with feisty rainbow trout and kokanee. To get to Silver Lake, turn south toward Valdez from Glennallen. About 32 miles south of the road junction, follow the signs that point east to Kenny Lake and Chitina. The pavement lasts all the way to Chitina. Keep going across the bridge over the Copper River and another 9 or 10 miles on the gravel road that has replaced the old railbed of the Copper River and Northwestern Railroad.

Silver Lake is on the right; there is no longer a campground available. Access to the lake is on foot only, but you should be able to carry a canoe down to the lake. The scenery is pretty special too. This particular spot is absolutely my favorite place for catching rainbow trout.

5. MINTO FLATS NEAR FAIRBANKS   The two big draws here are fishing for tackle-busting northern pike and waterfowl hunting in September. Easiest access is via floatplane from a Fairbanks-area flying service; it's only about a 15-minute flight. Many of these operators will also be able to provide you with a small boat for moving about the marsh as part of the package.

Heavy spinning tackle is usually the preferred gear for pike, though more and more people are going after these toothy predators with fly rods. Fly fishers will require heavier rods using number 7 or number 9 line with a fast-sinking tip. Big, bright streamers with carefully sharpened hooks are the flies of choice. Spin fishermen can throw almost any piece of hardware from their tackle boxes and catch pike, though red-and-white spoons seem to be preferred.

6. KENNICOTT/MCCARTHY   This is a long, slow, bumpy, 60-mile ride on a narrow gravel road. While it is possible to make this trip in a big rig, it must be done slowly and carefully. Allow at least three hours to drive this road one way. It's worth every bit of time and effort you put into getting there.

The road ends at a footbridge crossing the Kennicott River. Just before the road ends there's a ranger station, café, and campground. Cross the bridge and walk into the town of McCarthy (year-round population of about 65 people). From there it's a 5-mile walk on a good gravel road–trail to Kennicott. You can also ride to Kennicott in locally owned buses or vans for a fee.

Kennicott is a slice of Alaskan history frozen at the moment of its abandonment in the 1930s. It was a thriving mining town supporting the Kennecott Copper Mine built by the Guggenheim-Morgan syndicate in the 1920s.

As part of that mining operation, the Copper River and Northwestern Railroad was built to haul ore from the mines to tidewater at Cordova. The road leading to the footbridge is built on the old roadbed of the railroad. In fact, if you watch closely at roadside as you drive along, you'll see an occasional piece of bent rail off to the side or possibly an old railroad spike.

At any rate, when the price of copper crashed in the 1930s, the town abruptly shut down. Everybody left at virtually the same time on the last train out of town.

When I first visited Kennicott in the mid-1980s, you could enter most of the buildings. The blacksmith's tools were still laid out around the forge; the smell in one building indicated that it could only have been a hospital, and much of the machinery for the mill was still intact. In recent years, more and more of the buildings have been locked up to prevent theft and as a means of preserving them for potential restoration. Even if you can't get into the buildings, though, walking around this ghost town is not to be missed. Tours that may allow entrance into some of the buildings are available.

Get there by following the directions to Silver Lake given earlier in this chapter. Once you reach Silver Lake, just keep driving another 50 miles or so.

7. MATANUSKA-SUSITNA VALLEY   OK. I'm prejudiced. I live in the Mat-Su Valley and happen to think it one of the most beautiful spots on Earth, but there are plenty of reasons to stop here for a visit.

First, if you are driving a big RV and Anchorage is on your itinerary, the RV parks in and around Palmer make a great base for exploring Alaska's largest city. Anchorage offers relatively few RV parks but is a quick 45 minutes from Palmer on a four-lane highway. Either use your tow vehicle if you pull a trailer, your towed vehicle if you drag one behind your motorhome, or rent a car locally for getting around. Like all large cities, Anchorage is not a friendly place when it comes to getting around in big rigs.

Kennecott Copper Mine

For the best silver salmon stream fishing anywhere in Alaska, sign up with Mahay's Riverboat Service in Talkeetna to be dropped off for the day on Clear Creek. Pick a day late in August when the crowds have thinned out. Cost is about $60 per person; the riverboat handlers will put you off on a wide gravel beach just downstream where Clear Creek flows into the Talkeetna River, and you'll catch silver and chum salmon until your arms hurt.

Besides visiting Anchorage, though, the Mat–Su Valley has plenty of offerings in its own right. A large number of rivers offer superb king and silver salmon fishing, as well as some fabulous trout streams. The best views of Denali from any road in the state are from the Parks Highway toward the northern end of the Mat–Su Valley. River rafting on the Matanuska River attracts others, and more than 150 hiking trails of all levels of difficulty are available. There's also the Iditarod Trail Sled Dog Race Headquarters in Wasilla, a musk ox farm, a reindeer farm, accessible glaciers, and some top-drawer flightseeing trips to Denali from Talkeetna about 70 miles north of Palmer. Come to think of it, you could spend your whole vacation in the Mat–Su Valley and never get bored.

8. TEKLANIKA CAMPGROUND, DENALI NATIONAL PARK   The only people who can drive the 29 miles of the park road to this point are those who have a reservation at this campground. Reservations can be made at the visitor center when you arrive if you are lucky, but it's better to make them ahead of time by calling 800-622-7275 or visiting reservedenali.com. Reservations are accepted beginning December 1. The campground is usually open from late May to early September. Normally, the earlier you make your reservations, the better.

Once you have a site at the campground, you'll need a bus ticket to explore the rest of the park. Arrange these at the same time you make a reservation for a campsite. The bus will pick you up at the entrance to the campground and transport you—with frequent stops for wildlife viewing—to either the Eielson Visitor Center at Mile 66 or to Wonder Lake, about 20 miles farther on, depending on which bus ticket you purchase. After stops long enough for a quick lunch at either of these destinations, the bus will bring you back to the campground. Although the bus ride to Wonder Lake and back is only little more than 100 miles round-trip from the campground, expect to spend the entire day on the bus, so pack a lunch of easy-to-carry-and-eat snacks and drinks.

9. PRINCE OF WALES ISLAND   You are going to have to work to get to this one, and it will cost you some money, but it is worth all the trouble and expense.

Drive your rig aboard an Alaska Marine Highway System ferry in either Bellingham, Washington; Prince Rupert, British Columbia; Haines, Alaska; or Skagway,

Alaska, for a trip to Ketchikan. At Ketchikan, drive off the ferry and catch a smaller interisland ferry for the 3-hour trip to Hollis on Prince of Wales Island.

The island offers a 300-mile road system winding through a temperate rain forest. Though you'll see old clear-cuts from past logging days, the scenery is mostly spectacular. Be sure you leave Ketchikan with a full water tank and empty holding tanks (a dump station is available in Ketchikan not far from the ferry dock) because you'll be dry camping on the island.

Insider's Tip

Black bears and deer are plentiful all over Prince of Wales Island. And, as much as it pains me to admit it, the best place to see the bears is at the town dump just outside of Hydaburg, one of several small towns on the island.

Several small U.S. Forest Service campgrounds are available at intervals along the road system, most close to a clear stream or lake that may host cutthroat trout, rainbows, steelhead, or several species of salmon, depending on the timing of your visit.

Whales can often be seen from a campground on the northern end of the island—you'll have to walk a little way to the beach—and I've spotted several bears at a distance on that beach over the years.

Most roads on the island are well-maintained gravel roads. The worst driving problem you're likely to have is a muddy rig from driving in the rain on these roads.

10. SKAGWAY   Probably the best Fourth of July party in Alaska takes place in Skagway. Not that the town is not fun on any other day.

You can get to Skagway either on an Alaska Marine Highway System ferry or via a 99-mile paved road that heads due south from Whitehorse on the Alaska Highway. Driving this road on a sunny day is pretty spectacular. From Whitehorse south, it gradually climbs to the summit of White Pass, about 3,300 feet above sea level. From the top of the pass (the border between Alaska and Canada), the road careens down to sea level in Skagway in a mere 14 miles.

Skagway and the surrounding area combine to form a National Historic Park celebrating the Alaska Gold Rush at the end of the 19th century. It was here that would-be miners unloaded their gear at sea level and trekked over 3,290-foot Chilkoot Pass to the headwater of the Yukon River in Canada to build a boat and then drift more than 400 miles downstream to the Klondike goldfields. Many of the century-old buildings remain and are still in use. The White Pass and Yukon Route Railway still runs excursion trains north on its narrow-gauge rails to Lake Bennet near the top of White Pass and back.

And Skagway sees hundreds of cruise ships each summer, most disgorging a thousand or more passengers for a day of sightseeing. It is not unusual for three ships or more to visit Skagway on any given summer day. This generally means that downtown streets are jammed with pedestrians. Though it is well worth a visit, it is almost impossible to make a summer visit to Skagway and not be in danger of being swallowed up in the crowd.

This, then, is my list of favorite Alaskan attractions. Probably where most others will disagree with me is my reluctance to put Kenai Peninsula streams on my list. My reasoning is simple. I don't live in Alaska so I can spend my weekends standing shoulder to shoulder with the entire city of Anchorage hoping to catch a salmon. There are plenty of quieter places to fish and plenty of other fish for the catching.

That the Kenai Peninsula is beautiful and worth your time as a visitor is without a doubt. But, to paraphrase my late father about the fishing, "When you have to bring your own rock to stand on, much of the magic is gone." I'm lucky enough to live in Alaska. I can visit the Kenai in late spring before the crowds arrive or in early fall after the crowds have disappeared. The best prescription I can provide for visiting the fabled Kenai Peninsula salmon streams during the summer months is to head out of Anchorage on Monday morning and be out of the way of the weekenders by Friday noon.

RV camping , Matanuska Glacier

CHAPTER 13
Heading Back

If getting there is supposed to be half the fun, followed by lots of fun while you're there, what's left for the trip back? In the case of a drive to and from Alaska, plenty. This alternate routing, starting from Anchorage, will take you deep into Yukon and British Columbia. You can do this by repeating only about 25 miles of your journey north on the real Alaska Highway. Over the years an alternate route of sorts has been created.

As an overview, this routing, broken down by days, is as follows:

- Anchorage to Tok: Glenn Highway
- Tok to Dawson City, Yukon: Taylor and Top of the World Highways
- Dawson City to Carmacks: Klondike Highway
- Carmacks to Watson Lake: Campbell Highway
- Watson Lake to Yellowhead Highway 16 in British Columbia: Cassiar Highway (two days)

Once past Tok, this routing offers long legs through remote regions. A couple of the side trips available offer you the opportunity to really poke into the wilds. Be sure of your fuel status and the distance to the next gas station at all times.

Finally, this is a much longer route south, taking about six days if you don't stop to explore Dawson City or sample the fishing or try a couple of side trips. If you've dawdled longer than planned on your way north or in Alaska and need to hurry home, the Alaska Highway offers the fastest route.

From Anchorage, the only way to go south to a lower-48 state or a home in Canada is to first drive north several hundred miles to intercept the Alaska Highway at Tok or the Taylor Highway a few miles east of Tok. If you take the Taylor Highway, as suggested in this chapter, you'll drive even farther north before turning south.

Just getting to Tok from Anchorage is one of Alaska's most breathtaking drives through two major mountain ranges and across broad expanses of Alaska's Interior.

The Glenn Highway

From Anchorage, you'll retrace your route you took into Anchorage for about 35 miles on the Glenn Highway to its junction with the Parks Highway. Keep to the right on the Glenn Highway, following the signs to Palmer. An alternative route to Palmer, now known as the Old Glenn Highway or the Palmer Alternate, turns off Glenn Highway 28 miles from Anchorage. This is a fairly scenic but winding road along the base of the Chugach Mountains. In August, at about mile 13 of the Old Glenn, look for sockeye salmon in full spawning colors (brilliant red with olive green heads) in the creek at roadside to the right.

In a sense, Palmer is unique in terms of American communities. During the depression of the 1930s, President Franklin Roosevelt's administration colonized the region with farmers from the northern Midwestern states, transporting several hundred farming families to the Mat-Su Valley in an attempt to make Alaska self-sufficient in terms of food production. Families were given 40 acres of land to clear, and homes and barns were built under government contract. Many of the old barns, locally called Colony Barns, still stand. Essentially, a Midwestern-style barn was erected on top of a lower story of logs to create these buildings.

Whichever route you take to Palmer, several attractions are worth checking out once you get there. First is the Musk Ox Farm, actually on a side road about 2 miles out of town along the route to Tok. Musk oxen are shaggy beasts of about 600 pounds normally found in the most extreme arctic regions. They were wiped out in Alaska by meat hunters around the turn of the century, and the musk oxen now in Alaska— both wild and at the farm—are descendants of animals imported from Canada. The underfur of these animals, carefully combed from them each spring, is a warm wool (qiviut; pronounced "ki-vee-oot") suitable for spinning into yarn, then weaving into a host of winter clothing. Various items are for sale at the farm and a downtown Anchorage store, the latter also named Qiviut. Because this wool is in rather short supply and somewhat difficult to recover, these garments are fairly expensive.

Probably Palmer's premier annual attraction is the Alaska State Fair, held the 10 days in late August and early September leading up to Labor Day. On display will be the massive vegetables that the Mat-Su Valley has become famous for—such as cabbages in excess of 80 pounds. Most of the usual state fair–type activities are on the menu as well, but with decidedly Alaskan twists and turns. The biggest crowds show up on Labor Day weekend. Come early on a weekday to enjoy the less-crowded days and before the big vegetables (some of which are judged the first day of the fair) begin to wilt. But if you want to see the grand champion cabbage, you will have to wait until the last weekend, as these are judged the last Friday of the fair.

The author's granddaughter poses with the grand champion cabbage at the Alaska State Fair.

Anchorage to Tok

Our Starting Mileage:

MIleage: 328 miles (545 kilometers)

Driving Time: 7–8 hours

Towns En Route:

Palmer, 42 miles (70 kilometers)

Glennallen, 187 miles (312 kilometers)

Tok, 328 miles (545 kilometers)

Gas Available:

Palmer, 42 miles (70 kilometers)

Sutton, 63 miles (105 kilometers)

Chickaloon General Store, 78 miles (130 kilometers)

Eureka Lodge, 128 miles (213 kilometers)

Glennallen, 187 miles (312 kilometers)

Hub of Alaska, 190 miles (317 kilometers)

Trailside, 191 miles (318 kilometers)

Gakona Junction, 205 miles (342 kilometers)

Sinona Creek Trading Post, 238 miles (397 kilometers)

Midway Services, 265 miles (442 kilometers)

Mentasta Lodge, 281 miles (469 kilometers)

Tok, 328 miles (545 kilometers)

Campgrounds:

Palmer, 42 miles (70 kilometers)

Pinnacle Mountain RV Resort, 70 miles (116 kilometers)

Long Lake, 85 miles (142 kilometers)

Matanuska Glacier State Campground, 101 miles (168 kilometers)

Glacier Park Resort, 102 miles (170 kilometers)

Grand View Cafe and RV Campground, 109 miles (182 kilometers)

Tolsana Wilderness Campground, 174 miles (290 kilometers)

Dry Creek State Campground, 192 miles (320 kilometers)

Gakona RV Park, 209 miles (347 kilometers)

Gridley Lake RV Park, 256 miles (427 kilometers)

Doubletree RV Park, 264 miles (440 kilometers)

Midway Services, 265 miles (442 kilometeers)

Porcupine Creek State Wayside, 267 miles (445 kilometers)

Eagle Trail State Wayside, 312 miles (520 kilometers)

Sourdough Campground, 326 miles (541 kilometers)

Tok, 328 miles (545 kilometers)

Lodging:

Palmer, 42 miles (70 kilometers)

Long Rifle Lodge, 103 miles (171 kilometers)

Sheep Mountain Lodge, 114 miles (190 kilometers)

Eureka Lodge, 128 miles (213 kilometers)

Nelchina Lodge, 144 miles (240 kilometers)

Tazlina Glacier Lodge, 157 miles (262 kilometers)

Tolsana Lake Resort, 171 miles (285 kilometers)

Glennallen, 187 miles (312 kilometers)

Gakona, 205 miles (342 kilometers)

Mentasta Lodge, 281 miles (468 kilometers)

Tok, 328 miles (545 kilometers)

Major Terrain Features: Chulitna Pass (Chugach Mountains), Mentasta Pass (Alaska Range), muskeg, boreal forest, tundra

Fishing Available: King salmon, red salmon, grayling, lake trout, Dolly Varden, northern pike

Wildlife: Black bears, caribou, moose, grizzly bears, Dall sheep

Also in the Palmer area is the Hatcher Pass road, leading through a gold-mining area to an abandoned mine site high in the mountains. The mine is a state historic site, and tours are available. The last few miles of this road are extremely narrow. Signs to Hatcher Pass, the Musk Ox Farm, and the wolf kennels are prominent along the Glenn Highway.

For winter travelers, Hatcher Pass offers tremendous cross-country skiing and great sledding adventures. Snowmobilers also find huge tracts of land to explore at length.

From Palmer, the Glenn Highway twists through Chulitna Pass in the Chugach Mountains with few opportunities to pass slow-moving vehicles for about 70 miles. If a line of five cars or more builds up behind your vehicle, Alaska law requires that you pull over at the first opportunity and allow them to pass.

This is rugged, beautiful country, climbing from Alaska's south coastal climatic zone into the drier Interior climate. The Matanuska Glacier can be seen from roadside, and a turnoff at Glacier Park Resort leads to the face of the glacier. This is a private road, and there is a fee for driving up to the glacier.

Insider's Tip

In and around Palmer (the Mat-Su Valley) are more than 150 known hiking trails, many of which can also be used for cross-country skiing and snowmobiling in the winter. Those who want a day hike, an overnight, or an expedition of several days—on dirt or snow—can investigate the possibilities by inquiring at the Mat-Su Borough natural resources office in the Borough administration building in downtown Palmer.

The animals most frequently seen between Palmer and Glennallen (187 miles from Anchorage) are Dall sheep, moose, and caribou, though occasionally a black bear crosses the road. The sheep, appropriately enough, are usually visible on Sheep Mountain on the north side of the road near Sheep Mountain Lodge, about 114 miles from Anchorage. Best times for sheep viewing are in June and July. In August, when sheep hunting season opens, the sheep usually go deeper into the hills.

But in August chances are good for seeing caribou once you cross the summit of Chulitna Pass. The fairly flat land from the summit to Glennallen hosts the Nelchina caribou herd each fall, almost certainly the most accessible caribou herd to overland travelers. The animals will be mostly in scattered bands of two or three to about ten animals, and they're not above standing in the road trying to stare down passing cars.

Between Palmer and Glennallen, the clear streams along the route offer fair opportunities for grayling and Dolly Varden throughout the summer months, as do some of the lakes at roadside. Most fish caught near the road won't be large, but diligent nimrods should be able to catch enough for a meal or two.

Glennallen, the largest community between Palmer and Tok, is primarily a service center for this portion of Alaska's Interior. Full services are available. Glennallen also

hosts the headquarters for Wrangell–St. Elias National Park, the largest national park in the United States. Approaching Glennallen on a clear day, drivers can get an idea of the scope of this park by looking at the eastern skyline. Three major peaks—Mount Sanford, Mount Drum, and Mount Wrangell—dominate the horizon, though still many miles in the distance. And these are not the tallest peaks in the park. Mount St. Elias, on the Canadian border and too distant to be visible, rises 18,008 feet, making it the second-highest summit in both Alaska and Canada.

Matanuska Glacier, Alaska

A Legend in His Own Mind

Long-distance mushers are a unique breed, though not as rare as they once were. With the 1,049-mile Iditarod and later the Yukon Quest, another 1,000-miler between Fairbanks and Whitehorse, long-distance mushing has developed into a spectacular sport, embracing all kinds of people. And it's more than just mushers. The Iditarod, for example, involves more than 1,200 volunteers from all walks of life, bringing them together for a couple of short weeks each March across a huge slice of the Alaskan wilderness.

One of these volunteers some years back was Don Burt, a short guy, then in his 50s, with almost-white hair and a beard to match. A good friend once described Don as "a sawed-off Santa Claus gone bad." Don lived in a cabin off the Glenn Highway, again about 150 miles from Anchorage, this time to the northwest. You could spot his driveway by looking for the candy-apple-red mailbox next to the road.

Don led the Iditarod trail breakers on snow machines for several years. Four or five snow machines towing sleds leave a day or so ahead of the mushers to make certain the trail is clearly marked. They attempt to stay at least a day ahead of the leaders, though on a couple of occasions some fast-running mushers have actually caught up with the snow machines. It is, to say the least, a wild ride across Alaska's major mountain ranges and massive rivers, but breaking trail on the Iditarod is an unforgettable experience, made all the more so by Don's antics.

I drove one of the snow machines with Don in March of 1989. That year, at the bottom of one particularly steep hill, Don hung up a sign that said FREE TOWING—CALL 376-5155, the number for Iditarod Headquarters. A couple of years prior to that, he erected a plywood palm tree on a beach outside of Nome, a sandy beach blown clear of snow by the wind. If you didn't realize how cold it was outside, the tree perched on the sand dune looked almost like it belonged there. Nobody who has raced a trail marked by Don Burt has ever forgotten the experience.

His greatest claim to infamy in recent years was volunteering to be at the center of an explosion. At the Alaska State Fair, he lay down in a wooden box and allowed an "expert" to detonate several sticks of dynamite all around him. He told me later that he always wanted to do that. Living alone in the bush does strange things to people, I guess.

Past Glennallen the Glenn Highway joins the Richardson Highway, which runs from Valdez to Fairbanks. Turn left at the stop sign to continue on to Tok; turn right for Valdez on Prince William Sound.

Northbound, for 16 miles from the junction, the Glenn and Richardson Highways are the same road. At Gakona Junction, Tok-bound travelers turn right to continue on the Glenn, and Delta- or Fairbanks-bound travelers continue straight ahead on the Richardson.

If you wish to view the most spectacular mountain pass in Alaska, alter your route to Tok and take the Richardson Highway to Delta. Then turn right on the Alaska Highway for Tok. Isabel Pass, on the Richardson, can be spectacular when the weather is good. But when the weather is bad, it can feature frightening winds and wind-driven rain, snow, or sleet at any time of the year.

Mentasta Pass, on the Glenn Highway to Tok, is beautiful, though it falls short of the rugged magnificence that is Isabel Pass. The terrain is much gentler through Mentasta Pass, and the road stays well within the timberline.

Approaching Tok, one of the best campgrounds in the area is Sourdough Campground, about 2 miles before you reach the junction with the Alaska Highway in downtown Tok. A small restaurant adjoining the campground office puts on a wonderful feed of sourdough hotcakes every morning.

If you don't stop at Sourdough Campground, several suitable facilities for RVs are in Tok, as well as an assortment of lodges and motels. Travelers continuing north on the Taylor Highway to Dawson City, Yukon, or back down the Alaska Highway to Beaver Creek, Yukon, should be sure to top off their gas tanks in Tok. The gas available beyond Tok is usually very expensive.

The Taylor Highway

Though driving distance on this day is fairly short, allow plenty of time. The road is narrow in places, twists like a sidewinder in other places, and sometimes suffers both problems. Also, the road turns to gravel about 80 miles in when you pass the town of Chicken—it's hot and dusty when dry, cool and gooey when wet. And much of the pavement has been repaired with extensive gravel patches over the years.

Leaving Tok, head southeast on the Alaska Highway for 12 miles to Tetlin Junction. At the junction, turn left (north) onto the Taylor Highway. This highway, more or less paved up to Chicken, was originally a trail that over time has evolved into a road and leads into the heart of active gold-mining country. In fact, the Fortymile Country, as it's called, was the scene of a thriving gold-mining economy almost two decades before the Klondike Gold Rush of 1898. The small Yukon River town at the end of the Taylor Highway, Eagle, was the judicial and military center of Interior Alaska before gold was discovered in Fairbanks.

Valdez

Valdez, made infamous by the 1989 grounding of the tanker Exxon Valdez, offers much more than just an oil terminal—or an oil spill. In fact, despite many assumptions to the contrary, Valdez itself and the broad bay to its front were untouched by the spilled oil.

Salmon fishing can be tremendous in and near Valdez, and the protected waters of Valdez Arm and Prince William Sound make the fish fairly easy to get to, though boaters should keep a weather eye out—things can blow up fast in this country. In July, pink salmon can be caught one right after the other just by fishing from the shore at Allison Point (aka Winnebago Point), across the bay from town. In August, silver salmon are available from a boat or from selected spots along the shore (try some of the rocky areas along the road leading to the Trans Alaska Pipeline terminal).

From the Glenn–Richardson Highways junction just outside of Glennallen, it's 115 miles south to Valdez on a good road. The route takes you over Thompson Pass, a gentle slope upward for southbound travelers, but almost a plunge from the summit to the small coastal plain where Valdez sits. Worthington Glacier comes almost down to roadside near the summit of the pass, and visitors can walk up to the face of it and chip ice for the cooler if they desire. Try chilling your evening cocktails with a bit of clear glacier ice—if you listen closely, you can hear it fizzle and pop as air trapped centuries ago escapes from the melting ice.

Thompson Pass holds one distinction that summer travelers probably won't notice—it's the snowiest place in Alaska, receiving as much as 1,000 inches of snow or more a year.

Probably Valdez's major attraction, outside the fishing, is Columbia Glacier, the largest of the few tidewater glaciers in Alaska that are reasonably accessible. Several charter operators in the harbor offer day trips to this glacier and others in large, comfortable boats. The best known and most experienced is Stan Stevens Glacier & Wildlife Cruises (866-867-1297, stephenscruises.com). These trips can last eight hours or more, and besides the glacier, passengers will almost certainly see bald eagles, seals, sea lions, and—with a little luck—killer whales.

Lodging can be a problem in Valdez during the summer months. If you need a room for the night, have a travel agent in Anchorage make you a reservation before you head for Valdez. Campground space is usually not too much of a problem, though the RV park across the street from the small boat harbor fills up quickly on most summer days.

Tok to Dawson City, Yukon

Our Starting Mileage:

Mileage: 187 miles (312 kilometers)

Driving Time: 5–6 hours

Towns En Route:

Chicken, 77 miles (129 kilometers)

Boundary, 118 miles (197 kilometers)

Dawson City, 187 miles (312 kilometers)

Gas Available:

Tetlin Junction, 12 miles (20 kilometers)

Chicken, 79 miles (132 kilometers)

Boundary, 118 miles (197 kilometers)

Campgrounds:

Tetlin Junction, 12 miles (20 kilometers)

Walker Fork (BLM), 94 miles (157 kilometers)

Lodging:

Tetlin Junction, 12 miles (20 kilometers)

Boundary, 118 miles (197 kilometers)

Major Terrain Features:

Low, rolling, forested hills gradually giving way to alpine tundra

Fishing Available: Grayling, sheefish

Wildlife: Moose, black bears, grizzlies (rare), caribou (in the fall)

Except for miners and a few others, mostly hunters in the fall and tourists in the summer, the country along the Taylor Highway is pretty well deserted these days. Chicken, about 90 minutes driving time from Tetlin Junction, is the only town along the route, and some would say describing this collection of a few residents as a town is being charitable. But these are fine folks, and the party-picnic they throw on July 4th is well worth attending if you're in the area. Most of the miners come in from the creeks for this event, the only time off during the summer that they allow themselves.

A delightful story surrounds the naming of Chicken. The miners in the area during the 1880s wanted to name the town after the ptarmigan (grouse-like birds, and the word is pronounced with a silent *p*) that lived in the area. However, none of the miners then working in the area could spell *ptarmigan*. Thus they settled on Chicken as the closest word for describing an edible bird.

A great way to get a feel for Chicken's history is a book by Ann Purdy, *Tischa*. Purdy came to Chicken as a young schoolteacher in the 1920s, reaching the town after an arduous horseback ride of several days. She fell in love with the region, married a local resident, and spent the rest of her life living in Chicken. She died about 15 years ago, but her book lives on. Many of the people she wrote about are still in the area. The title of her book comes from the way the young Indian children struggled to pronounce the word *teacher*.

Insider's Tip

Top off your fuel tanks in Chicken. The gas will be expensive, probably upward of 50 cents a gallon more than in Tok, but it is still the cheapest gas you are likely to see for several days. The one other gas station in Alaska just before you enter Canada at Boundary has prices almost on a par with Canadian stations and may or may not be open when you get there.

Before reaching Chicken and after passing it, the road crosses various forks and tributaries of the Fortymile River, an excellent stream for canoeists. Most popular is putting in at one of the Fortymile River access points, floating downstream into Canada, and then floating into the Yukon and downstream to Eagle. It's a great four- or five-day trip, with occasional Class III water but mostly no more threatening than Class II. The Fortymile River and its tributaries are also a draw for fishermen, who pull grayling at breakup in the spring and just before freeze-up in the fall. Sheefish to 10 pounds are occasionally caught in July and August—try the slower water.

Past Chicken, the road is gravel and the surrounding country becomes a bit more rugged with evidence of bygone mining days. Included in this are old log cabins, a gold dredge abandoned right next to the road, and various pieces of equipment left lying around, mostly near the streams. Avoid trespassing on posted mining claims. Area miners can be extremely protective of their property rights. If you want to try your hand at gold panning, plenty of places along the streams are accessible and not part of any active mining claim.

Chicken Post Office, Taylor Highway

After winding through the river valleys for a short distance, the road begins to climb up to Jack Wade Junction. At the junction, the Taylor Highway goes left (north) to Eagle; the Top of the World Highway turns east to Dawson City, Yukon.

The road to Eagle is even narrower and less traveled than the lower stretches of the Taylor Highway. However, if you have time, Eagle is fun to visit. Several clear streams meet the road close to Eagle; almost all have hungry grayling about 17–18 inches in length. These fish are rarely bothered, so it should be easy to entice a few to a hook.

In Eagle, there's an excellent museum, a campground near the old Army barracks, a gas station, a restaurant, and a lodge. John McPhee spent considerable time living and observing life in Eagle for his book, *Coming into the Country*. Though things have changed to some extent in the nearly three decades since McPhee was in residence, his book offers an interesting portrait of the town and its people. McPhee is not particularly popular in Eagle, as many longtime residents regard his description of the town as something less than flattering.

Top of the World Highway

Those electing not to go to Eagle continue on the Top of the World Highway to Dawson City, Yukon, 79 miles from the junction. You'll quickly see why this is called Top of the World Highway—much of it is above the timberline or right on the edge of it, and on clear days you can see for miles and miles. Plenty of blueberries are along this road in August. In June, unmelted patches of snow can provide ammunition for a summer-day snowball fight.

Boundary, just inside the Alaska border, is not so much a town as it is the reflection of a man who died some years back. Action Jackson was the only name anyone ever knew him by, and his bar—the Boundary Lodge, then more popularly known as Action Jackson's—was a riotous frontier establishment. Jackson tended the bar with a six-shooter on each hip, and he wasn't above pumping a round or two into the ceiling when things got a little out of hand. A lot of young people from Dawson City used to drive to Boundary looking for action on Friday and Saturday nights. Things are quieter these days, but that quiet is often a minor distinction.

Leaving Boundary, there is a combined US and Canadian customs station. You are required to stop before entering Canada. Clearing customs in either direction should take no more than a minute or two for US and Canadian citizens. See Appendix C for customs requirements.

This station is normally open from about May 15 to October 1, and closed the rest of the year. Hours are usually 8 a.m.–8 p.m. on the Alaska side and 9 a.m.–9 p.m.

on the Canada side, which reflects the fact that this is a time-zone change at the border. Canada's 9 a.m. is Alaska's 8 a.m.

Once you're in Canada, there are actually some stretches of pavement on this road. The road seemingly stays on the ridgeline until the last possible minute when it drops steeply down to the Yukon River and Dawson City. There is no bridge at Dawson, but a free ferry hauls people and vehicles across the river to Dawson.

Abandoned gold dredge, Dawson City

Campers should check out the Yukon public campground (no hookups) on the Alaska side of the river, across from Dawson. This is an excellent site laid out along the banks of the Yukon. After camp is set up, take a walk to the riverbank beside the campground and walk downstream a short distance. You'll suddenly come upon the graveyard of several of the old stern-wheelers that used to ply their trade on the Yukon. When they had outlived their usefulness, these boats were just abandoned where they were put up for the winter. There's not much left of them these days, but it's still interesting to look them over. However, do not climb aboard the remains of these boats; they are in an advanced state of deterioration, and you risk injury doing so.

Looking across the river to Dawson, try and imagine the steep hill behind the town covered with log cabins. Indeed it was, less than 100 years ago. Brush has overrun these sites since, and you will have to walk the ground to find these old areas of habitation.

Dawson itself is enjoying a rebirth as a historic park. City ordinances require anyone building within the city limits to erect false fronts and generally give their structures a turn-of-the-20th-century appearance. Many of the surviving old buildings have been restored, some are under restoration, and at least one or two have been rebuilt from the ground up using the original plans.

Insider's Tip

Two great events highlight the summer season in Dawson: Canada Day on July 1 and Discovery Days in mid-August. The latter features a parade, dances, and even an outhouse race. It's a rollicking good time.

Great 1900-era theater with a professional cast can be found each summer night in the Palace Grand Theatre. Legalized gambling, complete with can-can show, is on every night at Diamond Tooth Gerties, and a wide variety of other attractions tempt visitors at all hours of the day. Dawson City is a great place to spend a day or two.

The Klondike Highway

Dawson City, created by the Klondike Gold Rush (often referred to as the Alaska Gold Rush), sprang into being just upstream on the Yukon River above its confluence with the Klondike River. Within a couple of years of gold's discovery in August 1896, this previously barren stretch of riverfront became the North's largest city. In its heyday, it was called the "Paris of the North" and the "largest city north of San Francisco."

The Klondike Highway leading south from Dawson retraces the steps of the argonauts who rushed to the gold fields on the "Trail of '98." However, there wasn't much of a road or even a trail in those days. Most came to Dawson by boat, floating down the Yukon River in craft built from lumber hastily whipsawed from green trees. The boats leaked, were dangerously unstable, and often sawed in half when partners began to argue. But most of them eventually made it to Dawson, where the lumber used to build the boats was put to use for cabins and furnishings.

The Yukon River, the transportation artery that carried these fortune hunters, is the primary terrain feature visible along the Klondike Highway. For the most part it's a fairly gentle stream, though the current is respectable. Downstream from Whitehorse en route to Dawson, the only major river obstacle is Five Finger Rapids, visible from a highway turnout. The rapids upset a number of the home-built boats and later contributed to the destruction of some of the stern-wheelers plying this water road between Whitehorse and Dawson. A trail with 239 stairs leads to a viewing platform on a cliff above the rapids. It is a great walk of about 1.2 miles round-trip, and the views are stunning.

Leaving Dawson, the highway crosses the Klondike River. Evidence of the region's golden past are all around, including mile after mile of tailings from the gold dredges that worked through area streams. Several businesses and government agencies offer different activities near the Klondike River bridge to provide a glimpse of the past.

Dawson City to Carmacks

Our Starting Mileage:

Mileage: 225 miles (375 kilometers)

Driving Time: About 5 hours

Towns En Route: Pelly Crossing, 158 miles (263 kilometers)

Gas Available:

Klondike River Lodge, 25 miles (42 kilometers)

Moose Creek Lodge, 98 miles (163 kilometers)

Stewart Crossing Lodge, 113 miles (188 kilometers)

Pelly Crossing, 158 miles (263 kilometers)

Midway Lodge, 183 miles (305 kilometers)

Carmacks, 225 miles (375 kilometers)

Campgrounds:

GuggieVille, 3 miles (5 kilometers)

Klondike River Campground, 11 miles (18 kilometers)

Moose Creek Campground, 98 miles (163 kilometers)

Stewart Crossing Lodge, 113 miles (188 kilometers)

Ethel Lake Campground, 121 miles (202 kilometers)

Minto Campground, 179 miles (298 kilometers)

Tatchum Campground, 208 miles (347 kilometers)

Carmacks Campground, 225 miles (375 kilometers)

Lodging:

Klondike River Lodge, 25 miles (42 kilometers)

Moose Creek Lodge, 98 miles (163 kilometers)

Stewart Crossing Lodge, 113 miles (188 kilometers)

Midway Lodge, 183 miles (305 kilometers)

Carmacks, 225 miles (375 kilometers)

Major Terrain Features: Low, rolling hills, mostly forested; Yukon River valley

Fishing Available: Grayling, lake trout, northern pike

Wildlife: Black bears, moose

After passing the Klondike River, the road swings well to the east of the Yukon River and doesn't come within site of it again until near Minto, four to five hours driving time from Dawson. This is pretty country, though it can be hot and dry during the summer months, with only occasional thunderstorms providing some measure of relief. I spent a long, hot July 4th weekend in Dawson a few years back, with daytime temperatures exceeding 100° Fahrenheit. At the time, the most popular activity was waterskiing on the Yukon River.

About halfway between Dawson and Minto is Stewart Crossing. If you stay at the RV park there, the towns of Mayo and Keno are 32 and 69 miles away, respectively. Keno, in particular, is a great place to visit, especially the museum in town dedicated to mining in the region. After looking through the museum, drive to the top of the hill and look out over the surrounding countryside; the view is magnificent. This side trip will take an extra day, assuming you stay at the RV park at Stewart Crossing or the one in Mayo.

Fishermen will want to check out Ethel Lake, 121 miles from Dawson, for lake trout. It's best to fish from a boat, trolling slowly at different depths until you find the fish. The lake and campground with a boat launch are about 17 miles off the highway. Good to excellent fishing for grayling is available at Crooked and Moose Creeks. Crooked Creek also holds northern pike, a fish that's often ignored in the North and is usually pretty easy to entice to a lure or a really big fly.

Travelers planning to overnight in or near Carmacks will have to backtrack about 3 miles the next day if they desire to drive the Campbell Highway to Watson Lake, as suggested in the next section of this chapter.

Those wishing to continue south to Whitehorse, and intercept the Alaska Highway there, have an additional 103 miles to go on the Klondike Highway. En route, the road passes Lake Laberge ("la-barge"), made famous by one of Robert Service's best-known poems, *The Cremation of Sam McGee:* "Twas on the marge of Lake Laberge . . ."

Some years back, my family was camped on Lake Laberge with friends from Whitehorse. While we were sitting in the sun, a troop of Boy Scouts from New Hampshire showed

Yukon from Dawson Dome, Klondike Highway

up en route to Alaska. The kids immediately changed to swimming trunks and headed for the water. Upon entering, one screamed, "Now I know why he cremated Sam McGee." Swimming in the chilly waters of Lake Laberge is not for the faint of heart.

Dempster Highway

Twenty-five miles south of Dawson, heady adventurers with a taste for the remote can turn north on the Dempster Highway, which runs 466 miles to Inuvik at the apex of the Mackenzie River delta. This road leads as far north as it's possible to drive in Canada.

Be absolutely certain you can go halfway (234 miles) without refueling before setting out for Inuvik. There are no fuel or auto repair facilities for the first half of the drive.

At Peel River and Arctic Red River, free ferries carry you and your vehicle across. However, early and late in the season, during breakup and freeze-up respectively, there is no way to cross these rivers. It's best not to try to cross prior to June 15 and after September 1. Also, these ferries do break down occasionally, and it's not unusual for travelers to have to wait for a day or longer while they are repaired. Be prepared for cold weather, high winds, and limited visibility at all times.

Insects can also be a severe problem—black flies, mosquitoes, and gnats. Carry plenty of repellent; there are few places to purchase it en route.

Early and late in the season, a caribou herd migrates across the highway. Other wildlife is abundant as well—grizzlies, moose, fox, wolves, and all manner of birds. If caribou are in the area, look carefully for wolf packs hovering on the fringes of the herd hoping to pick off injured animals or those that stray too far from the herd. Few things can compare to watching this fundamental part of nature as a wolf pack assaults and brings down prey.

There is good to excellent grayling fishing available in several streams crossed by the Dempster simply because few travelers tackle this road. It's not unusual to drive for hours without seeing another vehicle.

Allow a minimum of two days each way for driving the entire length of the Dempster. Slow down during rainy periods. Much of this gravel road is surfaced with a material rich in clay. It becomes extremely slick when wet.

Horay marmot near Keno, Klondike Highway

The Campbell Highway

Those planning on taking the Campbell Highway to Watson Lake should figure on getting an early start if they want to drive the entire route in a single day. Little, if any, of this road is paved, and there are few facilities along the 365-mile route.

This road should prove an absolute delight to fishermen. Probably the best roadside fishing in all of Yukon Territory awaits, simply because so few travelers drive this route. Lake trout lurk in the depths of Frenchman's Lake (25 miles), Little Salmon Lake (Drury Creek campground, 72 miles), Frances Lake (260 miles), and Simpson Lake (316 miles). Other streams and lakes along the way offer fishing for stocked rainbows and kokanees, northern pike, and grayling. This is truly a road where a fisherman could invest a week or more without getting bored.

But the fishing is not what brought this road into being. Like most northern roads, mining led to its creation. Much of that mining is still going on today, and all of the towns along the Campbell Highway are supply points for mining activities.

For the first 106 miles to Faro, there may be heavy truck traffic—ore trucks carrying rock to Carmacks—depending on whether or not the mines are open, which has been an off-and-on thing in recent years. This lead, silver, and zinc ore is trucked from Faro to Carmacks, to Whitehorse, and finally to Skagway, where it is loaded aboard ships for transport to processing sites.

Ross River, though situated near coal fields, offers more in the line of visitor services, particularly to big-game hunters. Several outfitters are active in the region, all offering hunts deep into Yukon and Northwest Territories. Also, canoeists interested in floating the Pelly River often start their trips in Ross River and float downstream to where the river intersects the Klondike Highway at Pelly River. Officials recommend camping on islands and gravel bars to avoid bears and the dense hordes of mosquitoes. Usually there's a breeze in the open areas to help keep the bugs away. There are two sets of rapids along the way. Inquire locally for river conditions before setting out.

Lapie Canyon

Carmacks to Watson Lake

Our Starting Mileage:

MIleage: 365 miles (608 kilometers)

Driving Time: 8–10 hours

Towns En Route:

Faro, 106 miles (177 kilometers)

Ross River, 139 miles (232 kilometers)

Gas Available:

Faro, 106 miles (177 kilometers)

Ross River, 139 miles (232 kilometers)

Campgrounds:

Frenchman's Lake Campground, 25 miles (42 kilometers)

Salmon Lake Campground, 51 miles (85 kilometers)

Drury Creek Campground, 72 miles (120 kilometers)

Fisheye Lake Campground, 104 miles (173 kilometers)

Lapie Canyon Campground, 138 miles (230 kilometers)

Frances Lake Campground, 260 miles (433 kilometers)

Simpson Lake Campground, 316 miles (527 kilometers)

Lodging:

Faro, 106 miles (177 kilometers)

Ross River, 139 miles (232 kilometers)

Major Terrain Features: Pelly River, many large lakes

Fishing Available: Grayling, lake trout, northern pike

Wildlife: Black bears, moose

After leaving the turnoff for Ross River headed for Watson Lake, be absolutely certain of your fuel supply. There are no services for the next 205 miles, and it is a pretty rugged gravel road. This road is reminiscent of the Alaska Highway in the 1950s and 1960s, though services were never that far apart even on the old Alaska Highway. Help can be a long time coming in this part of the North Country.

Tamarack, a type of larch, can be seen near the Watson Lake end of the road. Though a member of the pine family, this tree loses all its needles in winter. For the most part, tamarack is fairly rare in the Yukon.

The Campbell Highway joins the Alaska Highway in Watson Lake at the Sign Post Forest. Travelers following the route recommended here will turn northwest on the Alaska Highway for 12 miles to intercept the Cassiar Highway. Alternately, the Alaska Highway leads southeast to Fort Nelson and Dawson Creek.

The Cassiar Highway

Though more remote and much less traveled, the Cassiar Highway offers the shortest route to and from Alaska. Using Watson Lake on the Alaska Highway as a base, it's several driving hours shorter to use the Cassiar than to go via Dawson Creek and the regular Alaska Highway.

There are some liabilities, though. A couple of lengthy sections of the Cassiar are gravel, and these parts of the road quickly become nasty in heavy or prolonged rains. Potholes develop quickly, and the road surface becomes slick. Services, too, are few and far between. Also, some of the long-haul truckers headed for Whitehorse or Alaska tend to prefer the Cassiar because it cuts down their driving time. Be alert, too, for ore trucks near the northern end of the road between Cassiar and Watson Lake and for logging trucks on the southern end. Except for the southernmost 100 miles or so, this road is a pretty narrow one, and oncoming trucks must be handled very carefully. Many of the stream crossings are only one-lane bridges.

> **Insider's Tip**
>
> Though the Cassiar Highway from Watson Lake to Yellowhead Highway can be done in one long driving day (10 to 12 hours), it's far better to take two days. Major portions of this drive are slow going and extremely fatiguing for drivers.

That said, many travelers believe the scenery along the Cassiar superior to that along the Alaska Highway, with the Coast Range looming to the west, and several glaciers distantly visible. There's probably a better chance of seeing black bears along this road than most other northern roads. Of several trips on the Cassiar, I have never failed to see at least one black bear on every trip.

Those who like to fish will find much to interest them, though it's best if you have some sort of boat available. Much of the fishing is fairly tough to get to, requiring some walking off the road or negotiating narrow, twisting, rutted, and unmaintained trails to reach a lakeshore. Car-top or other easily transportable boats are probably best. There is good fishing for rainbows in several spots south of the mountain pass near Dease Lake, and for lake trout in most of the large lakes along the way.

From Dease Lake, about midway along the Cassiar Highway, a gravel road leads 74 miles to Telegraph Creek on the Stikine River. Charter boat trips are available on the Stikine, and hardy souls may want to float the river all the way to its mouth near the southeastern Alaska town of Wrangell. Access in and out of Wrangell is via Alaska Airlines or the Alaska Marine Highway ferries. No roads lead to Wrangell. From the mouth of the river, an open-water crossing of several miles is necessary to reach Wrangell. Kayaks are much better than canoes for this trip.

Watson Lake to Yellowhead Highway 16

Our Starting Mileage:

Mileage: 476 miles (793 kilometers)

Driving Time: 2 days

Towns En Route:

Cassiar, 88 miles (147 kilometers)

Dease Lake, 160 miles (266 kilometers)

Kitwanga, 468 miles (780 kilometers)

Gas Available:

Cassiar Highway Junction, 13 miles (22 kilometers)

Good Hope Lake, 74 miles (123 kilometers)

Dease Lake, 160 miles (266 kilometers)

Forty Mile Flats, 203 miles (338 kilometers)

Iskut, 211 miles (352 kilometers)

Tatogga Lake Resort, 220 miles (367 kilometers)

Meziadin Lake Junction, 375 miles (625 kilometers)

Kitwanga, 468 miles (780 kilometers)

Highway 16 Junction, 476 miles (793 kilometers)

Campgrounds:

Boya Lake Provincial Park, 66 miles (110 kilometers)

Mighty Moe's Place, 107 miles (178 kilometers)

Tanzilla River Campground, 166 miles (276 kilometers)

Forty Mile Flats, 203 miles (338 kilometers)

Tatogga Lake Resort, 220 miles (367 kilometers)

Kinaskan Lake Provincial Park, 236 miles (393 kilometers)

Meziadin Lake Provincial Park, 376 miles (627 kilometers)

Cassiar Campground, Kitwanga, 468 miles (790 kilometers)

Lodging:

Dease Lake, 160 miles (266 kilometers)

Iskut Valley Inn, 213 miles (355 kilometers)

Tatogga Lake Resort, 220 miles (367 kilometers)

Meziadin Lake Junction, 375 miles (625 kilometers)

Major Terrain Features: Rugged mountains with glaciers to west

Fishing Available: Lake trout, rainbows, grayling, Dolly Varden

Wildlife: Black bears, grizzly bears, moose, deer

A second great side trip along the Cassiar leads from Meziadin Lake Junction (375 miles from Watson Lake) to Stewart, British Columbia, and Hyder, Alaska. Hyder is unique for a US community in that the medium of exchange is Canadian currency. There are no banks in Hyder, thus the few local businesses keep their accounts in Stewart, a couple of miles away. Because the banks are Canadian, it's much easier for most business to keep track of things in Canadian currency. The exception, of course, is the US Post Office.

Of particular interest on the Stewart-Highway Access Road is Bear Glacier, which terminates in a lake a few hundred yards away from the highway. It's possible to sit at roadside and watch the glacier calve icebergs into the lake at almost any time during the summer. Several other hanging glaciers in the mountains above the road can be seen along this route. Only at Worthington Glacier near Valdez can travelers drive this close to a glacier on a public road anywhere on a trip to and from Alaska.

Just south of the Meziadin Lake Junction, Meziadin Lake Provincial Park offers one of the most beautiful settings for a campground anywhere in northwestern Canada or Alaska. Campsites are right on the lakeshore, and a summer sunset here must be seen to be believed.

Both north and south of Meziadin Lake Junction are extensive regions of clear-cut forest. These deforested lands are not, however, just meant to line the pockets of the logging industry or to create an eyesore. In the 1980s, area spruce trees suffered from a heavy infestation of spruce bark beetles, which kill virtually every tree they touch. As the dead trees dry, they become major forest-fire hazards. Rather than accept the hazard or allow a resource to go to waste, local authorities allowed extensive clear-cutting of the infected forests. The extensive cutting seems to have drastically reduced or even eliminated the beetle infestation, and the replanted forest seems to be recovering nicely. Environmental zealots who don't believe in cutting trees for any reason might learn a lesson or two if they were to look over this new forest with an open mind and compare it with the vast tracts of beetle-killed trees in Alaska, trees that are just waiting for a spark.

On the plus side, these clear-cuts just burst into vibrant colors in July when the fireweed blooms. Whole mountainsides turn a reddish lavender. From high ground, these brilliant fields of flowers can be seen extending for miles. The best time to see the fireweed is the latter half of July.

Near the southern end of the Cassiar Highway, several small Indian communities offer a broad assortment of totem poles. Kitwanga, off on a side road less than half a mile from the end of the highway, has the most-visited and accessible totems. There's also a nice RV park in Kitwanga, the Cassiar RV Park, that made its way onto our top 10 roadside favorites as described in Chapter 10.

Once you complete your trip on the Cassiar, you are on Yellowhead Highway 16, which leads 307 miles east to Prince George. From Prince George you can either turn south on BC 97 toward Washington or continue east on the Yellowhead Highway to Jasper and Edmonton, both in Alberta. Except for isolated areas of road construction, the Yellowhead Highway is paved.

Insider's Tip

Several of the logging roads used in the clear cutting lead into the relatively treeless hillsides. These offer excellent access for those who want a close look at the fireweed. Be careful, however, as these roads are not maintained and are likely to be narrow or washed out in spots.

CHAPTER 14
The Mackenzie Loop

Why drive this route? No "great" scenery is obvious; most of the roads described in this chapter wind through some fairly flat country. Perhaps the best excuse is simply that it's there and few others have even attempted this swing through the southern edge of Northwest Territories.

Most of the ground is soft limestone, a prehistoric coral reef that has been uplifted into a plateau over thousands of centuries. Rivers coursing through the region cut deep into the soft stone, gouging out canyons. In these canyons, below the level of the surrounding terrain, roaring rivers cascade over towering cliffs. For the most part, you'll have to drive a short distance off the main road to find these; most are marked with some sort of sign indicating where to turn. Follow these signs and the rewards are many, as are the opportunities for photographs.

Insider's Tip

There are some awesome sights, though you'll have to do a little extra work to seek them out. Specifically, this otherwise flat terrain hides some of the most magnificent waterfalls in the North Country.

Plan well your drive along this loop, which begins in British Columbia, winds north into Northwest Territories, and then takes you east and south into Alberta. Gas stations and lodging—even campgrounds—are spaced at lengthy intervals for most of the route. And the last time we drove this loop we found that a gas station listed in another popular travel guide, and one that we were counting on, had been closed for years. While I am reasonably confident that the gas stations listed here are open, I can never be 100 percent certain from year to year.

From Fort Nelson, the turnoff for the Liard Highway is 17 miles west of town on the Alaska Highway. From here on, this is paved for 85 miles until you reach the Northwest Territories border. From there it is a gravel road until you get close to Great Slave Lake several hundred miles farther on.

As you left Fort Nelson, you were approaching the Rocky Mountains. However, as you turn north on the Liard Highway, the Rockies generally recede to the northwest as each mile you drive takes you farther from the peaks of North America's greatest mountain range. After a hundred miles or so the Rockies can no longer be seen, and from the higher points on this stretch of gently rolling terrain you can see for miles and miles on a clear day.

Insider's Tip

Liard Highway is a well-maintained gravel road, but it can be exceedingly dusty during dry periods and slick and muddy when it rains.

The highway generally parallels the path of the Liard River, though the river is rarely seen from the road—it's a little too far to the west. The Liard is a major tributary of the Mackenzie River, the largest drainage system in northwestern Canada.

The first major tributary of the Liard River is the Fort Nelson River, which you'll cross in about 30 minutes' driving time after you leave the Alaska Highway. The Fort Nelson River Bridge is the longest Acrow bridge in the world, a bridge type better known as a Bailey bridge in honor of Sir Donald Bailey, the British engineer who designed it. The steel truss panels on this particular bridge have been in use on various northern bridges since World War II. As the other bridges were rebuilt or replaced, the salvageable panes were stored until needed for bridging the Fort Nelson River. There's a turnout with a picnic table and an excellent view of the bridge on the north side of the bridge if you want to stop and look it over more carefully.

Fifty-five miles farther on, the road crosses the Petitot River, reputed to have the warmest water in British Columbia. From here, canoeists might want to attempt the 10-hour trip to Fort Liard, down the Petitot to the Liard River. The village is at the confluence of the two rivers. Sheer rock canyons and rapids make this an adventurous trip, but one that is easily done in a day. Freshwater clams, pike, and pickerel provide limited offerings for those seeking a meal from the wild.

Insider's Tip

The only community along the Liard Highway, Fort Liard, is accessed by a side road that turns off some 125 miles from Fort Nelson. Take the time to fill your tank at the gas station at this junction just in case some of the ones ahead aren't open when you get there. The nearest guaranteed gas from here is in Fort Simpson, some 200 miles ahead.

Past the river the road climbs rapidly with a 10-percent grade for about a mile and a half. A mile past the crest you cross into Northwest Territories, formerly Canada's largest province but now only second in size after it was divided into two separate provinces. The population of this still-huge land mass is only about 20,000 or so.

The only campground on the actual Liard Highway is at Blackstone River, about 194 miles from Fort Nelson. When we visited, the caretaker ran a small visitor center and had plenty of time to talk about the area.

From Blackstone River, it's 107 miles to Fort Simpson, 67 miles to the junction with the Mackenzie Highway, and then 40 miles to the west. To reach the town, a free vehicle ferry carries you and your rig across the Liard River. Be aware, though, that when water levels are low, usually in late August and early September, the ferry may not be able to make the crossing.

The last time we made this trip, the ferry skipper was a jovial sort with all kinds of stories about the local area and the folks who live there. He offered up one story after another for the few minutes we were on his boat, and every one had a punch line worth waiting for.

Fort Simpson is primarily a community of Dene (an Indian word meaning "the people"), and the region is rich in history. The town's name comes from the Royal Canadian Mounted Police post that was established here in the 1880s. Now the people in the area take an active interest in native rights and sovereignty. They are organized and active in local politics.

The visitor center was located with the newspaper office when we visited. It's a great place to stop and learn what is going on around town and what you should see while you are there. The Dene, for instance, are extremely proud that Pope John Paul II singled out their community for a visit back in the 1980s and will encourage you to visit the spot where he spoke. They go to great lengths to keep this site attractive.

Leaving Fort Simpson, you'll have to retrace your route for 40 miles back to the Liard Highway junction. From there, the road runs due east to Enterprise, where it turns south for Alberta. Along the way, however, are some of the spectacular water-falls mentioned earlier. Some of the best of these, in order as you are eastbound, are Whittaker Falls, Lady Evelyn Falls, and Louise Falls.

Insider's Tip

Photographers should visit Lady Evelyn Falls in the early morning when the angle of the sun creates a fabulous rainbow in the mists engendered by the falling water.

Campgrounds, though still relatively few, are slightly more frequent along this stretch of road leading to Enterprise—there are four along the 245 miles between Enterprise and Fort Simpson. Gas is available at the junction where a road leads north to Yellowknife, about 180 miles from Fort Simpson. Yellowknife is the capital of Northwest Territories and is on the north shore of Great Slave Lake.

Ducks in Alberta

Alberta is one of the world's great duck "factories." The potholes in the northern part of the province provide some of the finest waterfowl nesting areas in the world. Almost every roadside pothole will have ducks in it if you look carefully. For the most part these birds will not take flight at your approach but will instead try to hide in the vegetation ringing the pond. Look closely and you should be rewarded with frequent sightings of ducks and ducklings.

Detouring off the Mackenzie Highway to Yellowknife is a two-day affair. It's about a six-hour drive, one way, to Yellowknife from the road junction and includes another free ferry, this time crossing the Mackenzie River. Yellowknife is a modern city in every sense of the word, with full facilities for travelers and many new buildings. As the center of government for the province, it is primarily a service center—and probably the only community in the province where one regularly sees men wearing jackets and ties and women in skirts and dresses suitable as office wear.

For those who want to see Great Slave Lake, the tenth largest lake in the world, and don't want to drive to Yellowknife, turn left and follow the signs to Hay River when the Mackenzie Highway reaches Enterprise. Hay River is a shipping point and railhead on the south shore of the lake. Here, goods for Yellowknife and other points in the Interior are delivered by rail and transshipped across the lake in ocean-size freighters. There's also a great swimming beach, complete with white sand, just outside the port.

Insider's Tip

If you're traveling with kids, Hay River offers the first opportunity in several days to buy a pizza or an ice cream cone—the latter important for the mental health of adults, as well—on a hot summer afternoon.

At Enterprise, the Mackenzie Highway turns south for Alberta, gradually leaving the wilderness behind as you drive farther into one of Canada's prairie provinces.

As the road runs deeper into Alberta, much of the swampy land turns into fields of hay, wheat, and other grains. In a sense, Alberta and neighboring Saskatchewan are Canada's breadbasket. The economies of farming in this day and age, however, are such that few of the typical family farms exist anymore. Most of the acreage under cultivation is in the hands of large conglomerates or huge private holdings created by acquiring and combining a number of small farms as they become available for sale. Watching the harvest on these massive farms in the fall is awe-inspiring, as huge phalanxes of combines sweep through fields of grain whose borders are measured in miles. That, combined with the colors of fall, makes for unforgettable photographs.

The end of the Mackenzie Highway—or the beginning if you choose this route to start your trip—is at Grimshaw in central Alberta. From Grimshaw, you can turn west for Dawson Creek or southeast for Edmonton. Dawson Creek is less than a two-hour drive from Grimshaw; Edmonton is about five hours away.

Wood Buffalo National Park

Leading east from Hay River is NWT 5, which takes you to Fort Smith and Wood Buffalo National Park. The park is named for the last survivors of this particular strain of bison, which are slightly larger than the plains buffalo so familiar to most people.

Wood Buffalo National Park also offers one other distinct claim to fame—snakes, the most northern population of common garter snakes known in North America. The only snakes found in Alaska, Yukon, or Northwest Territories are found in Wood Buffalo.

Park naturalists are generally reluctant to direct visitors to the snake habitat. The population is fairly limited, and it's believed that the survival of these reptiles is best ensured by keeping disturbances to a minimum.

They will, however, gladly direct you to the buffalo, if they are accessible—and also to what might be the park's other major attraction, whooping cranes. Wood Buffalo is the last natural nesting ground for this endangered species. Again, naturalists aren't too keen on these birds being disturbed. But keep a sharp eye out and you might get lucky and catch sight of this rare fowl.

At the Salt River, about 150 miles from Hay River, fishermen can try for inconnu (sheefish), one of the few places in the North where road travelers get a chance at this spectacular game fish, often called the tarpon of the North. If the sheefish aren't biting, pike and walleye are available.

Headquarters for Wood Buffalo National Park is in Fort Smith, a town of about 2,400 people approximately 167 miles from Hay River. All travelers' services are available in Fort Smith. From Fort Smith, two narrow roads lead deep into Wood Buffalo National Park. Be sure you carry enough gas for a round-trip if you attempt either of these drives.

CHAPTER 15
The Alaska Marine Highway

One of Alaska's most scenic regions cannot be reached by road, but if you get your vehicle to southeastern Alaska, you can explore a lot of places. The state of Alaska subsidizes a system of sea-going ferries, which allows vacationers to do just that.

Ferry travelers can bring their vehicles—up to and including the largest RVs—to the densely forested fjords of Alaska's Panhandle, or they can use the ferries to speed and ease the drive to Fairbanks or Anchorage. Frankly, there's so much to do and so many places to visit that a ferry-hopping vacation in southeastern Alaska might better be a separate vacation, rather than combined as part of a we'll-do-it-all-this-summer-or-else trip.

Northbound travelers can board Alaska Marine Highway ferries in Bellingham, Washington (about an hour's drive north of Seattle, traffic permitting), or in Prince Rupert, British Columbia, the western end of Yellowhead Highway 16, described elsewhere in this book. Those wishing to use a ferry to speed their way to Fairbanks or Anchorage should book passage to Haines or Skagway, the northernmost communities in southeastern Alaska served by the ferry system. From Haines, it's a little more than a 650-mile drive—two fairly easy days—to Fairbanks and about 750 miles to Anchorage. Distances from Skagway are about 75 miles farther.

In recent years, a new twist has been added to the ferry routes. It is now possible to board a ferry, the *M/V Kennicott,* and have it transport you and your vehicle all the way to Whittier in south-central Alaska. Whittier is about a 90-minute drive from Anchorage. The road goes through a railroad tunnel and passes within sight of Portage Glacier. During the summer there are two sailings per month of the *M/V Kennicott* scheduled into Whittier.

Typically, there are two ferries northbound to southeastern Alaska from Bellingham each week in the summer, normally leaving on Tuesdays and Fridays. These ferries dock early Sunday morning and late Monday afternoon, respectively, in Haines after a 65-hour passage with brief stops in Ketchikan, Wrangell, Petersburg, and Juneau. Northbound ferries are available almost daily from Prince Rupert in British Columbia. From Haines, northbound ferries typically continue on to Skagway, which is the turnaround point for the ships to begin their southbound voyages.

Sample one-way fares for ferry transportation from Bellingham to Haines, effective through April 30, 2017, are given below. These will almost certainly increase for the summer season beginning May 1, 2017. Visit ferryalaska.com for the most up-to-date fare information.

- Adult: $440 per person (meals and berth not included)

- Vehicle 20 feet long: $1,613 (includes driver)

- Cabin (two-berth, full facilities): $416

Prince of Wales Island

The ferries from Bellingham to Haines are just a tiny part of a big story. Besides those ferries, a host of other ships are continually working routes throughout southeastern Alaska. One of the best of these is the Ketchikan to Hollis (Prince of Wales Island) route, which is run by the Alaska Inter-Island Ferry Authority (interislandferry.com or 866-308-4848).

Prince of Wales Island (PWI) offers a splendid driving vacation in southeastern Alaska. Over the past several decades, roads built by the logging industry have been joined throughout the island, ultimately producing a network of several hundred miles of roads. These roads are rarely traveled; they pass some of the finest fishing streams in Alaska; bald eagles by the score nest in the tall, stately Sitka spruce at roadside; and large numbers of black bears and deer travel barely discernible trails through the rain forest.

Though Prince of Wales Island can be explored by tent campers with a car, the rain forest climate makes a camper or travel trailer more desirable. For those without an RV, however, the U.S. Forest Service maintains about 160 cabins in scenic spots in the Tongass National Forest throughout southeastern Alaska. Dozens of these are on Prince of Wales Island and can be rented for $25 a day—bring your own food and sleeping bags.

Most cabins are on a lake or stream teeming with fish and have rowboats available. On PWI, a couple of cabins can be reached by vehicle, others require a short hike, and the rest are best reached by floatplane chartered out of either Ketchikan or Craig, the latter being the largest community on Prince of Wales Island.

For an affordable wilderness experience that you'll remember all your lives, these cabins can't be beat. For details on renting a cabin on Prince of Wales Island, or for anywhere in southeastern Alaska for that matter, write to Tongass National Forest, Ketchikan Ranger District, 3031 Tongass Avenue, Ketchikan, AK 99901, call 877-444-6777, or visit recreation .gov. The Forest Service will send you a packet of information that includes a map of cabin locations, information on fishing and other attractions, and instructions for reserving a cabin for your use. Reservations are on a first-come, first-serve basis and can be made up to six months in advance. If you have a special cabin in mind, make your reservations as early as possible—the more popular cabins tend to fill up fast.

Thus two adults and a typical pickup-size vehicle would travel from Bellingham to Haines for about $2,469, plus the cost of their meals in the cafeteria. The two and a half days spent on the ferry would cut three or four driving days out of a trip to Fairbanks or Anchorage.

Fares are somewhat cheaper in the off-season, October through April, and there is less urgency for reservations during these months.

During the summer months, space is usually at a premium and reservations for vehicles and cabins are strongly recommended. Generally there is no problem for walk-on passengers. There are occasionally a few available spots for last-minute vehicle loadings at most destinations, but if you're on a tight schedule it would not be wise to rely on bringing a vehicle onboard on a space-available basis.

It is also possible to do this trip for even less money. Cabins are not really necessary unless you desire complete privacy. Sheltered solarium decks on the larger ferries, which include the ships on the Bellingham schedule, offer room to erect freestanding tents for those who want to "boat-camp." Shower and toilet facilities are available. Also, the observation lounges aboard the ships are equipped with reclining chairs, much like airline seats only with much more legroom, and many people choose to sleep in these.

What you cannot do, though, is sleep in your RV, which will be parked on the vehicle deck. You'll be allowed down to your vehicle at each stop to check things out, to retrieve any items you might want to use, or to exercise a pet, but that's all.

It is also possible just to walk on the ferry with only your luggage and pay just the per-person fare; one does not need to bring a vehicle aboard to utilize the ferries. Every summer, many young people enjoy cheap vacations in southeastern Alaska doing just that. They hop from town to town as the mood strikes them. At the end of the summer, most have had an experience beyond compare. As they

Ketchikan, Alaska

travel, these young men and women, college students for the most part, pass away the hours at sea planning their futures, staging sing-alongs on the decks where their tents are pitched—there's always at least one with a guitar—and, in the manner of young people the world over, make the first struggling attempts at understanding and correcting the imperfect world that surrounds them. Perhaps some of the most pleasant evenings of an Alaskan vacation can be spent sitting with these folks as they explore southeastern Alaska on their limited budgets.

What else, then, awaits the vacationer in southeast Alaska? Quite a lot, as demonstrated by the following brief descriptions of some of the more popular ports of call in southeastern Alaska for Alaska Marine Highway System ferries.

KETCHIKAN

Until the 1990s, the major industries in Ketchikan were fishing, logging, and tourism. It can be fairly said that the policies of the Clinton administration killed the logging and pulp industries in Ketchikan and that fishing is hurting these days because of competition from farmed salmon raised in pens in Chile and Canada. Thus tourism is now the mainstay of Ketchikan's economy, though fishermen did get a boost in the form of higher-than-expected prices in recent years.

Most tourists visiting Ketchikan arrive by cruise ship. Several ships reach the city each summer day, and each disgorges 1,000 or more people for 8–10 hours. These people disembark into the heart of the action on the city dock, where any number of vendors await with charter fishing opportunities, flightseeing excursions, bus tours, and so on. Arriving at the ferry dock a couple of miles away, however, is a little different. Assuming you have your vehicle, you'll drive into town if you want to visit the city dock, or out to Saxman to see the totem poles, or to a campground to spend the night, or to wherever else you want to go in the Ketchikan area.

Ketchikan is not very RV friendly. The campgrounds for the most part are U.S. Forest Service facilities with few amenities other than outhouses and picnic tables,

Insider's Tip

To make ferry reservations—and these ships are booked solid during the summer months—go online to dot.state.ak.us/amhs or call 800-642-0066. You can request a printed schedule of sailings or review this information online. Printed rate schedules are no longer available, and you have to calculate your costs by filling out an online form. This is not a good option if you're sort of window-shopping for a destination. And as I found out while working on this section with this new method, the cost may depend on whom you talk with. The price quoted on page 238 was provided by whomever answered the phone when I called the 800 number. When another agent priced the trip in response to an e-mail I sent, the price was $2,104, some $365 less. The e-mail and the call were less than 24 hours apart.

and the individual campsites are pretty small for the most part. If you drive off one of the ferries late at night and need a site in one of these campgrounds, plot your escape from the ferry dock well in advance. Others leaving the ferry will be of the same mind, and it's often a race to see who gets the remaining campsites.

Probably one of Ketchikan's more infamous attractions on the walking tour is the restored part of the old town built on a boardwalk over the water and called Creek Street. This used to be the rowdy part of town, and a favorite saying that evolved over the years was that Creek Street was "where men and salmon came to spawn." The houses of ill repute are now historical fixtures and no longer offer their former services. The salmon, however, unencumbered by the laws of man or the finer points of human etiquette, still fill the creek under the boardwalk as they complete their life cycle.

Ketchikan is on an island, specifically Revillagigedo ("ra-VEE-a-gi-GEE-doe") Island, named by English Captain George Vancouver for an 18th-century viceroy of New Spain, the Count of Revillagigedo, Don Juan Vicente de Guemes Pacheco di Padilla y Horcasitas. Thank goodness Vancouver stuck to the guy's title and not his full name. For the sake of convenience, locals tend to shorten the name of their island to Revilla in informal conversation.

Last but not least, it does rain in Ketchikan, so much so that the city maintains a liquid-sunshine gauge on the dock. Check in to see how much ahead or behind the annual average of 165 inches of rain the city is during your visit—and bring a rain jacket. Wet or dry, Ketchikan is lots of fun, but you'll enjoy it more if you stay dry.

Liquid sunshine gauge, Ketchikan, Alaska

WRANGELL

This is another town whose economy is in the doldrums due to the virtual shutting down of the logging and pulp industries. And, unlike Ketchikan, Wrangell has not been discovered by the cruise ships, so times are pretty lean. A few visitors get off the ferries for a day or two, and some people fly into town, but otherwise things are pretty quiet in Wrangell these days.

Unlike Ketchikan, however, Wrangell is somewhat better equipped to handle RVs. There are campgrounds with limited hookups available and enough room to park big rigs properly.

Charter fishing and sightseeing cruises up the Stikine River dominate the offerings for visitors, but perhaps the best of Wrangell is free. Hundreds of years ago, local natives etched detailed petroglyphs into rocks just below the high-tide line north of town. A 10-minute walk from the ferry dock or a short drive (parking is limited) brings you to a narrow access road. At the end of the access road, a wooden stairway leads down to the beach. Turn right at the bottom of the stairs and walk a few hundred yards. (Check locally for the timing of low tide, the best time to hunt for these petroglyphs.) Note that most of the land above the high tide line is private property.

Once you find some of the petroglyphs, you'll want to make rubbings of the replicas provided to preserve what you have found. These things are pretty hard to photograph, being uncolored indentations in flat, gray rocks. Take some rice paper (available from Norris Gifts on Front Street) with you to the beach and strip several handfuls of ferns from the dense growth along the access road. Lay the paper flat over the petroglyph replica, wad up a handful of ferns, and rub the wadded up ferns vigorously across the rice paper. It usually works best with two people—one to hold the paper and one to do the actual rubbing. It also seems to work better if you rub in only one direction. After you're done, the marks on the rice paper will appear green, but as the residue dries the markings will turn brown. This becomes your own personal recording of early Alaska native art.

An Alaska Marine Highway System ferry unloads at Hollis on Prince of Wales Island.

Replicas of the petroglyphs were made for the rubbings because damage to the real petroglyphs was becoming a problem as more and more people discovered them. You can still see the real thing, but you cannot use the real petroglyphs for rubbings.

PETERSBURG

Just a few miles outside of town, Blind Slough ranks high among my favorite fishing holes in Alaska. If your timing's right—generally around July 4th—it's possible to stand in one spot at the mouth of this small stream and catch king salmon weighing up to 40 pounds or more on every cast. This is the only place I know of where this is possible for kings.

Insider's Tip

If you need a hotel in Petersburg, try the Scandia House downtown. Rebuilt after a fire burned the old building, it is a first-class facility in every sense of the word.

Then, too, once you're tired of catching salmon or if your timing is off, Petersburg has lots more to offer.

Founded by an immigrant Norwegian fisherman in 1898, Petersburg is still known as Alaska's Little Norway. People greet you with "velkommen" instead of "welcome." The annual visitors guide published by the local paper is known as The Viking Visitors Guide, which is always available in plenty of time for the Little Norway Festival that takes place each year in mid-May. Part of the festivities include a replica of a Viking boat sailing in the harbor, and, as the town's promotional brochure states, it's a time when "Vikings and Valkyries go marauding."

For a small town not connected to the road system, Petersburg is surprisingly well equipped to handle RVs, with at least two campgrounds offering some hookups.

SITKA

A number of years ago some women in Sitka came up with the idea of performing traditional Russian and Ukrainian dances for local festivals and for visitors. Local men at the time shrugged off efforts to recruit them and left the women to their own devices. Thus, both the men's and women's parts in these dances are performed by women. Now that the group is a major success, often giving 100 or more performances a year, some men have asked to join. They have been bluntly refused. The group is still completely female, and if a performance is scheduled at any time during your visit to Sitka, be sure not to miss it.

The Russian dancers are just part of Sitka's deliberate capitalization on its history. Sitka was the last capital of Russian America, and it was here in October 1867 that Russia handed over control of Alaska to the United States of America.

Here, too, is an Alaska native culture that flourished for centuries before the Russians showed up, and a native culture that at least tried to drive the Russians away. Sitka National Historic Park on the south side of town is built on the site where the Tlingits fought the Russians. Walk through the brooding rain forest in this park and you can almost feel the emotions of that moment some two centuries ago when Russian technology triumphed over an ancient culture.

Though there are plenty of good hotels and a couple of small U.S. Forest Service campgrounds, Sitka is not particularly RV friendly. Streets in town are pretty narrow, and the road system is fairly limited.

JUNEAU

Unique among state capitals in the United States, Juneau cannot be reached by road. You must arrive either by air or sea. And when the weather closes in, which it does with distressing frequency during the winter months, either way can be chancy at best. Almost all longtime Alaskans have tales of setting off for Juneau by air and winding up sitting out the weather in the Seattle airport for days at a time.

It's quite easy in Juneau to start an argument—just say out loud something to the effect that Alaska should move its capital somewhere more readily accessible to the people in the state, maybe Anchorage. Folks in Juneau tend to get riled up about this subject, which surfaces in some form of ballot measure once every decade or so. In the 1970s, in fact, Alaskans voted to move the capital to Willow, a wide spot along the Parks Highway about 60 miles north of Anchorage. A few years later we voted down the money to move the capital, so it is still in Juneau, which suits most residents of the capital city just fine.

Many of these people work for state government—good, solid jobs relatively immune to twists and turns in the private-sector economy. And, with the capital all but inaccessible to most residents, these government bureaucrats don't have to spend much time dealing with their constituents on a face-to-face basis. Working for the state of Alaska in Juneau is more or less the perfect government job: good pay, regular hours, plenty of benefits, and relatively little direct interference from those whose lives are most affected by the rules and regulations spewing forth from Alaska's various government agencies. The thought of moving the capital to make it more accessible to the people or of putting in a road so you can drive to Juneau horrifies most of these people and inspires them to go to great lengths to fight any possibility of moving the capital. Moving the capital would, in a phrase, upset their perfect little worlds.

Bureaucrats aside, Juneau can be a delightful place to visit. Like Ketchikan, the core area downtown is heavily geared toward thousands of cruise ship passengers arriving every summer day, but, unlike Ketchikan, Juneau has a strong winter economy. In early January the state legislature and its entourage show up and hang around until the first of the year's cruise ships arrive. This tends to keep the hotels, restaurants, and bars hopping all year.

Juneau offers lots to see and do. A tram near the cruise ship docks transports visitors way up the side of a mountain overlooking the city, Mendenhall Glacier is within the city limits, and fishing and sightseeing businesses abound.

Insider's Tip

There is an RV park at Auke Bay, near the ferry terminal a few miles north of town. If you take a big rig to Juneau, park it here and use taxis or a small rental car to get around. Downtown streets are narrow and steep, no place at all for a motorhome or fifth-wheel trailer.

To my mind, the best sightseeing opportunity is a helicopter glacier tour. You board a helicopter near the Juneau airport, and in a few minutes' flying time the pilot drops you off high on the Juneau Icefield where qualified guides show you around the glacier. After 20 or so minutes on the glacier, you reboard the helicopter for a short aerial tour of the area before returning to the heliport. Of the various helicopter tours available throughout Alaska, I consider this one the best of the lot.

GLACIER BAY NATIONAL PARK–GUSTAVUS

You can't get here by ferry. You have to fly in from Juneau, Skagway, or Haines or observe the park from the decks of a cruise ship. Assuming you're in one of the three towns named above, this is a side trip that's well worth the cost and effort, even if just for a few hours.

Guided ocean kayaking trips are best for those who want to spend a few days touching the vast wilderness of this national park. Those who prefer their wilderness in smaller doses with clean sheets in lieu of sleeping bags every night should plan to stay in Gustavus. Kayaking services, day boats for sightseeing, and fishing charters can all be arranged in Gustavus, a small town and airstrip at the edge of the park. To start planning, call the Gustavus Inn at 907-697-2254 and talk about what is available and what you would most like to do. Also visit their website at gustavusinn.com.

HAINES

Until about 25 years ago, Haines was the final northern destination for Alaska Marine Highway System travelers who had their vehicles along. From Haines it is about 150 miles north to Haines Junction in Yukon Territory, where you can connect to the Alaska Highway to continue on to Fairbanks or Anchorage.

The opening of the road from Whitehorse, Yukon, to Skagway, Alaska, in the late 1970s changed everything by offering another option—and Skagway is technically farther north than Haines. However, of the two ports, Haines still offers the shortest drive to the Alaska border by about 75 miles.

Whether you drive into Haines from the north or arrive from the south by ferry, Haines generally means eagles, specifically up to 10,000 or more bald eagles gathering in the fall to feast on the decaying remains of the region's last run of salmon in the Chilkat River. In October it is not at all unusual to see a dozen or more of the stately birds perched in a single tree overlooking the river, each watching intently for its next meal.

Beyond the eagles, the scenery is great, there's plenty of history in town, and a wide assortment of offerings is available for visitors. Haines offers superb facilities for RVs, unusual in most southeastern Alaska towns.

SKAGWAY

Those of us who can remember studying the Klondike Gold Rush back in the dim and distant past of high school almost always conjure up a specific image of the event printed in almost every textbook: a long, thin, single file of overburdened men struggling up the steep face of a snow-clad cliff. Those men were toting part of the 2,000 pounds of supplies Canada required each man to have before allowing him across the border to head for the Klondike goldfields. It took each man a minimum of 10 trips up and down the mountain to get all of his personal gear to the top.

Now people hike this trail for recreation, and to do so they must first come to Skagway, just like the would-be miners of more than a century ago. As before, after landing in Skagway, today's hikers head down the road a few miles to the old town site of Dyea, perhaps camp for a night or so at the National Park Service campground near the foot of the trail, then start the arduous climb up the Alaskan side of the route. Thankfully, Canada no longer requires each person to tote 2,000 pounds of foodstuffs and gear across the border.

Not only do today's hikers have lightweight gear and emergency services available if needed, but they also no longer have to deal with Soapy Smith and his band of thugs on the streets of Skagway. Soapy and his gang swindled would-be miners out of their grub-stakes with various confidence games or just plain stole their supplies.

Skagway was pretty lawless in those days and remained so until a local hero arrived. Frank Reid killed Soapy in a Wild West–style gunfight down on the dock, but in so doing was mortally wounded himself. Reid hung on for a couple of days before dying and was laid to rest in the same cemetery as his antagonist. After Soapy's death, some semblance of order began to take hold in Skagway, and the gang gradually broke up and left town.

These days Skagway's entire summer seems devoted to reliving the revelry of the "Days of '98." The wooden, false-fronted buildings remain downtown, as do the boardwalks. The Red Onion Saloon still dispenses copious quantities of spirits, and mannequins leering at you from the second-story windows are a reminder that this building was once a profitable bordello. If you want to see the upstairs bedrooms, which have been restored and turned into a museum, you'll need to book a tour. Visit redonion1898.com for more information.

RV facilities in Skagway are at least adequate, with the largest down by the docks. Hookups are available. The road north to Whitehorse, Yukon, is well built and well maintained all year. From Skagway to the summit of White Pass (and the Canadian border), the road is extremely steep. You go from sea level to about 3,000 feet in 14 miles.

How Did Skagway Get Its Name?

There's some confusion as to the actual Tlingit word from which Skagway was derived, and this confusion subtly illustrates the attitude of the town. First there's *Ska-gua,* meaning home of the north wind, and it is indeed windy in Skagway much of the time. Then there's *Sch-kawai,* meaning the end of salt water, which is true as well because this is the head of Lynn Canal.

Local groups prefer two other possible definitions. One insists that this is the sound a sled runner makes when it breaks loose from snow and ice. Another favorite story in the local pubs is that Skagway is an Indian word meaning "lady relieving herself on a rock." Variations on the name include "rough water" and "cruel wind." Pick whichever legend you like best and be prepared for a good-natured argument.

Haines Junction

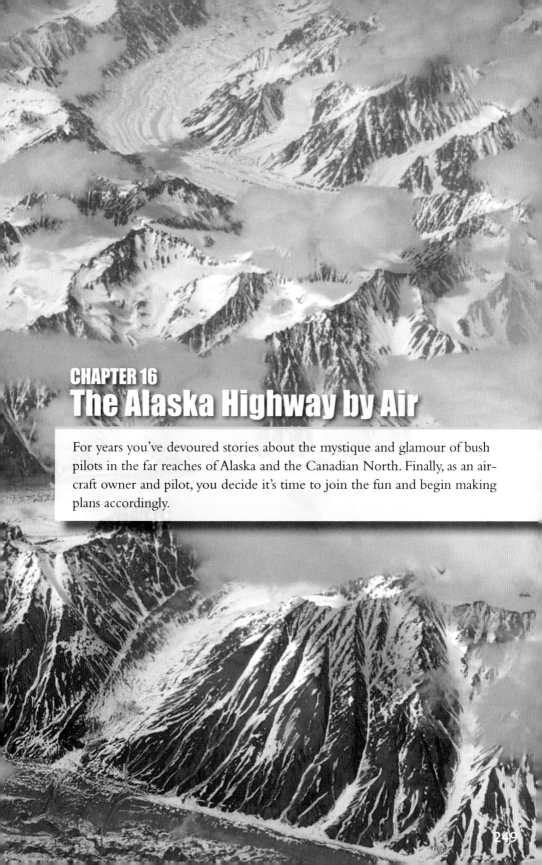

CHAPTER 16
The Alaska Highway by Air

For years you've devoured stories about the mystique and glamour of bush pilots in the far reaches of Alaska and the Canadian North. Finally, as an air-craft owner and pilot, you decide it's time to join the fun and begin making plans accordingly.

First and foremost, forget about the mystique and the glamour. Bush flying is hard, precise work that utilizes skills developed over years and many thousands of hours of flying over uninhabited terrain and dealing with the worst weather in the world. The saying that "there are no old, bold pilots" is more true in Alaska than anywhere else on Earth. If nothing else, the aviation accident statistics from Alaska make this glaringly apparent.

Flying your own light plane to Alaska, through Alaska, and back takes more time and effort in planning than any other flight you're likely to make in your lifetime. Margins for error are razor thin, and waiting for help in the wilderness can test all of your existing survival skills—and probably make you wish you had a few more upon which to draw.

Don't Forget to Pack the Alarm Clock

Sometimes the strangest thing can turn out to be a piece of survival gear in an aviation incident. Back in 1980, a wind-up alarm clock helped save my neck. It was early winter on the North Slope (mid-October), and I had been hauling sling loads by helicopter all day at the aptly named settlement of Lonely, about 100 miles west of Prudhoe Bay on the edge of the Beaufort Sea. The original plan was for me to stay there that night and fly back to Prudhoe in the morning. However, I finished a little early and thought I had time to get back.

Dusk found me out over the Beaufort Sea in a whiteout blizzard with no horizon and few immediate prospects. Using my radar altimeter, I eased down to about 50 feet above the surface and turned due south toward land. A few minutes later I spotted a dark line of frozen mud above the tide line and gratefully landed on the snowbank above it. I was out of radio range and nobody knew where I was. I had to keep the aircraft from freezing up through a 14-hour night so I could start it in the morning to get back, and I had less than two hours of fuel in the tanks.

Sifting through my personal gear and my survival gear, I came across the alarm clock—why it was there I'll never know. But it was my answer. I'd set it to allow a couple hours of sleep in an arctic sleeping bag, then get up and run the helicopter for 10 minutes or so to warm everything up and charge the battery. Two hours was just long enough to keep the oil from thickening too much in the cold.

Five times that night I crawled out of my bag and fired up the engine—once scaring the dickens out of several caribou that had come by to investigate, and me as well when I saw them move suddenly in the glare of the landing light. When the new day brought a firm horizon to the featureless landscape, I fired up the helicopter one more time, took off, and flew about 50 miles to Prudhoe Bay and a warm bed.

PILOT QUALIFICATIONS

A private pilot with little or no training in instrument flying has no business flying in Alaska. Even if you plan to make your trip strictly under VFR (visual flight rules) conditions, avail yourself of the opportunity to qualify for an instrument rating before you head for Alaska. Weather in the North's remote areas is extremely variable and exceedingly difficult to predict. Consider an instrument ticket as insurance. While you may not need it, it is sure nice to have if conditions deteriorate, as can happen with little warning.

Besides an instrument ticket, training and practice in mountain flying are essential for flying to Alaska. You will be flying around, through, and alongside the most extensive mountain ranges in North America on this trip, and knowing how to deal with mountainous terrain and the weather it can generate is imperative.

AIRPLANE EQUIPMENT

As a minimum, your aircraft should carry sufficient fuel for 350 miles of flight with an adequate reserve. More is better.

Your instrument panel should include all basic flight instruments, a radio compass (magnetic compasses are notoriously unstable and often unreliable in northern latitudes), an operational ADF receiver, an operational VOR receiver (ideally one with DME), and a first-rate attitude indicator as a minimum. Other nice-to-have features include either LORAN or GPS, a vertical-speed indicator, and a radar altimeter. Two VHF radios for voice communications are better than relying on one.

An ELT (emergency locator transmitter) with fresh batteries should be properly mounted to the airframe so that it transmits upon impact in a crash or can easily be switched on by the pilot or a passenger. If something does go wrong, an ELT is the best possible insurance that you will be found quickly. Test the ELT frequently to make certain it is operating properly. The Alaska Supplement prominently lists times and procedures for properly testing ELTs.

Survival gear is required by law for flights in Alaska and Canada, and sufficient quantities should be carried to adequately serve each person on board in the event of a mishap. As a minimum, here's what you'll need:

- ax
- fishing lures and line
- fire-starting materials
- food for each occupant of the aircraft for several days

- insect repellent
- lightweight shovel
- raingear
- tent and sleeping bag for each occupant of the aircraft
- warm clothing (including hat and gloves)
- water container
- wire for small-animal snares

A firearm and ammunition are required in Alaska to be on board, and most pilots operating only in Alaska carry some sort of handgun. It is, however, illegal for foreigners to have possession of a handgun in Canada. Thus, you should carry some sort of long gun and ammunition for it. Several breakdown survival rifles are available (usually .22 caliber), and these will do nicely as long as they can only be operated as a rifle. Any firearm that can be effectively used with one hand will likely be questioned by Canadian authorities. And there will be certain paperwork requirements even for your survival rifle. Check Appendix E on firearms to understand completely your responsibilities for transporting a firearm in Canada.

PUBLICATIONS

In addition to the charts and publications you routinely carry in your aircraft, you should obtain all VFR and IFR charts for Canada and Alaska as appropriate to your flight, an Alaska Supplement, instrument approach plates for western Canada and Alaska, and one or more of the various booklets listing aerodromes and related facilities. A particularly handy VFR chart covers the Alaska Highway in Canada as a single map. This is essentially a strip map covering the highway itself and terrain 50 or so miles on either side of the road. It can be ordered wherever you purchase your charts, as can any of these other publications. Never has the term "flying bookkeeper" been more appropriate than for a pilot heading to Alaska.

ROUTES

Essentially there are two VFR air routes leading to Alaska. One follows the coast north from Seattle through British Columbia and Alaska's Panhandle; the other follows the Alaska Highway through British Columbia and Yukon Territory.

The coastal route can be a real problem because of weather. This is wet country with at least one coastal community on Admiralty Island, Port Alexander, receiving upward of 300 inches of rain a year. All that rain means lots of low clouds and poor visibility in a region famed for its towering mountains and narrow, twisting fjords.

For pilots of single-engine aircraft there's another hazard—there are virtually no suitable forced-landing areas along the route for wheeled planes. Any pilot attempting to fly this route to Alaska is best advised to use either a multi-engine aircraft, a floatplane, or an amphibian in lieu of a single-engine wheeled plane.

For obvious reasons, the route following the Alaska Highway is the preferred course for most who fly private planes to Alaska. With a little common sense and application of the basic rules learned early in ground school, a competent pilot should be able to fly to Alaska from Seattle in just a couple of days, given decent weather.

When flying along the road, treat it just as if you were driving it. Stay to the right side. Northbound, choose an altitude of even thousands of feet plus 500 feet (2,500, 4,500, etc.), just as you learned in ground school when your heading is in the western half of the compass rose (180 degrees–359 degrees). Southbound, use odd thousands plus 500 feet (1,500, 3,500, etc.) for the same reason (headings of 0 degrees–179 degrees). Within reason, higher altitudes offer more options in an emergency than lower altitudes, especially in the mountains.

For those with limited mountain flying experience, the mechanical turbulence associated with winds blowing over mountains is perhaps the most difficult condition to understand and overcome. On a clear day there may be few visual clues, although any time you're flying near mountains on a windy day you should be particularly alert. The one primary visual clue that should send you scurrying to the nearest landing strip is a lenticular cloud clinging to the top of a mountain or in the sky just downwind of a peak. When you see this kind of a cloud, the wind is really howling near the summit because these clouds are made up of tiny ice crystals blown off the mountain. Mechanical turbulence associated with the winds causing these clouds can be experienced 50 or more miles downwind of the mountains. Thus, it's sometimes possible to get through a mountain pass and be flying over relatively level ground 15–30 minutes later and suddenly get hammered with turbulence.

Insider's Tip

Whatever you do, don't push the weather. If you experience the slightest doubt, land at the earliest opportunity, even if it means turning back. Thunderstorms, severe clear air turbulence, high winds, icing conditions, and other weather hazards are all possible in any summer month in the North. With the possible exception of thunderstorms, all these conditions occur even more often in the winter months.

My own worst turbulence experience in Alaska came on New Year's Eve 1972. I was flying a large Army helicopter out of Fairbanks and had gone to Anchorage to pick up the Army band for that night's party in the officer's club—obviously an important mission. The weather wasn't great—it was clear but windy for the return trip, and all the weather forecasts we could get were for severe turbulence, effectively grounding us. But this was one of those must-do missions, and we finally cajoled a weatherman into grudgingly admitting that there might be only moderate turbulence at altitudes of 6,000–9,000 feet through Broad Pass in the Alaska Range.

Insider's Tip

One particular bit of sage advice I received from an old pilot early in my flying career had to do with mountain turbulence. He told me that whenever he approached a mountain range and hit an updraft, he immediately applied power and climbed even higher because he knew that as soon as he crossed the ridgeline he would hit a downdraft of equal or even greater intensity. Nothing is quite so frightening as a severe downdraft when you are flying close to the ground.

With that, we blasted north out of Anchorage at dusk (about 3 p.m.) for the two-and-a-half-hour flight to Fairbanks. Things were going great until we approached the first major ridgeline near Talkeetna. Heading across the ridge, we were flying at 6,500 feet and the ground was about 2,000 feet beneath us.

A massive updraft seized the helicopter and shot us upward at an unbelievable rate. Even putting the aircraft into a screaming dive (I hadn't yet learned about climbing in updrafts) had no effect on our upward progress. Seconds later the updraft spit us out at more than 12,000 feet. In the clear night we could see the lights of Fairbanks some 200 miles distant. At 12,000 feet, much higher than we normally flew in our helicopters, the air was smooth as silk. We stayed there for another half hour or so, and then eased down to 10,000 feet to complete the trip.

Taking the band back to Anchorage the next day was a snap. The air was calm all the way, though it was a trifle cold in Fairbanks—66 degrees below zero—when we took off at dawn, sometime around 10 a.m. or so.

INSURANCE

Check carefully with the company that insures your airplane before departing for Alaska. Insurance rates are higher in Alaska, and you may have to pay a little extra for suitable coverage. Also check and see if your policy has a clause, common to aircraft policies, about crossing the Arctic Circle. Many aircraft policies are void north of this latitude.

FLIGHTSEEING AND FLIGHT PLANS

In a nutshell, common sense and prior planning will make a flying trip to Alaska a success. And having a plane in Alaska opens up possibilities that most people in a vehicle can only dream about.

For example, Lake Minchumina on the north side of the Alaska Range is about 150 miles southwest of Fairbanks. It offers an excellent gravel landing strip, one end of which is just a few steps from the lake. Park off this end of the strip, unlimber your fishing rod, and start catching northern pike up to three feet long. Or fly west to Nome, inaccessible by road and an excellent place to soak up a little of Alaska's gold rush history and revelry.

If salmon fishing is your goal, try King Salmon or Iliamna, southwest of Anchorage near the head of the Alaska Peninsula. Be careful with the weather here, as you'll probably fly through Rainy Pass, one of Alaska's more unpredictable places concerning weather. The fishing on the other side of the pass is great.

Other flightseeing possibilities include Denali National Park, Wrangell–St. Elias National Park, a variety of glaciers, and wilderness of every description.

Finally, always file a flight plan. Make it as specific as possible. Controllers in Alaska are used to maintaining and following flight plans for people flying over remote areas and probably know the landmarks about as well as anyone. Don't be afraid to list your route of flight as following a river or stream, or from a mountain peak to a valley. Pilots do it all the time in Alaska, and for good reason. We want somebody, somewhere to know when and where to start looking if something goes wrong.

Muncho Lake Floatplane

Appendixes

APPENDIX A: Visitor Information

ALASKA (STATEWIDE)

Alaska Division of Tourism
P.O. Box E-101, Juneau, AK 99811; travelalaska.com
(free travel guide/vacation planner available)

Alaska Travel Industry Association
2600 Cordova Street, Suite 201, Anchorage, AK 99503; alaskatia.org

ALASKA MARINE HIGHWAY

Alaska Marine Highway System
6858 Glacier Highway, Juneau, AK 99801-7909
Reservations: 800-642-0066; ferryalaska.com or dot.state.ak.us/amhs/

Inter-Island Ferry Authority (Ketchikan and Prince of Wales)
P.O. Box 470, Klawock, AK 99925
907-755-4848; interislandferry.com

SEAtrails
*(collaboration of the AK Marine Highway, communities, and land managers
throughout the Inside Passage)*
seatrails.org

ALASKA'S RAILROADS

Alaska Railroad
327 W. Ship Creek Avenue, Anchorage, AK 99501
907-265-2300; 800-321-6518; alaskarailroad.com

White Pass & Yukon Route
P.O. Box 435, Skagway, AK 99840
907-983-2217; 800-343-7373; wpyr.com

GENERAL INFORMATION BY CITY/TOWN

Anchorage Convention and Visitors Bureau
524 W. Fourth Avenue, Anchorage, AK 99501-2212
907-276-4118; 800-478-1255; anchorage.net

Chugiak–Eagle River Chamber of Commerce
P.O. Box 779353, Eagle River, AK 99577
907-694-4702; cer.org

Cordova Chamber of Commerce
P.O. Box 99, Cordova, AK 99574
907-424-7260; cordovachamber.com

Delta Junction Chamber of Commerce
P.O. Box 987, Delta Junction, AK 99737
907-895-5068; 877-895-5068; deltachamber.org

Denali National Park and Preserve
P.O. Box 9, Denali Park, AK 99755
907-683-2294; nps.gov/dena

Eagle Historical Society & Museums
P.O. Box 23, Eagle, AK 99738
907-547-2325; travelalaska.com/Destinations/Communities/Eagle.aspx

Fairbanks Convention and Visitors Bureau
101 Dunkel Street, Suite 111, Fairbanks, AK 99701-4806
907-456-5774; 800-327-5774; explorefairbanks.com

Greater Copper Valley Chamber of Commerce
P.O. Box 469, Glennallen, AK 99588
907-822-5555; coppervalleychamber.com

Haines Convention and Visitors Bureau
P.O. Box 530, Haines, AK 99827
907-766-2234; 800-458-3579; visithaines.com

Homer Chamber of Commerce Visitor Information Center
201 Sterling Highway, Homer, AK 99603
907-235-7740; homeralaska.org

Iditarod Trail Headquarters
P.O. Box 870800, Wasilla, AK 99687-0800
907-373-6998; iditarod.com

Juneau Convention and Visitors Bureau
Centennial Hall Visitor Information Center
101 Egan Drive, Juneau, AK 99801
907-586-2201; 888-581-2201; traveljuneau.com

Kenai Convention and Visitors Bureau
11471 Kenai Spur Highway, Kenai, AK 99611-7757
907-283-1991; visitkenai.com

Kenai Peninsula Tourism Marketing Council, Inc.
35571 Kenai Spur Highway, Soldotna, AK 99669
907-262-5229; 800-535-3624; kenaipeninsula.org

Ketchikan Visitors Bureau
131 Front Street, Ketchikan, AK 99901
907-225-6166; 800-770-3300; visit-ketchikan.com

Kodiak Island Convention and Visitors Bureau
100 Marine Way, Suite 200, Kodiak, AK 99615
907-486-4782; 800-789-4782; kodiak.org

Nome Convention and Visitors Bureau
P.O. Box 240, Nome, AK 99762
907-443-6555; visitnomealaska.com

North Pole
125 Snowman Lane, North Pole, AK 99705
907-488-2281; northpolealaska.com

Palmer
Greater Palmer Chamber of Commerce
550 S. Alaska Street, Palmer, AK 99645
907-745-2880; palmerchamber.org

Palmer/Wasilla
Matanuska-Susitna Convention and Visitors Bureau
7744 E. Visitors View Court, Palmer, AK 99645
907-746-5000; alaskavisit.com

Petersburg Visitor Information Center
P.O. Box 649, Petersburg, AK 99833
907-772-2626; 866-484-4700; petersburg.org

Prince of Wales Chamber of Commerce
P.O. Box 490, Klawock, AK 99925
907-755-2626; princeofwalescoc.org

Seldovia Chamber of Commerce
Drawer F, Seldovia, AK 99663
907-234-7612; seldoviachamber.org

Seward Chamber of Commerce
2001 Seward Highway, Seward, AK 99664
907-224-8051; sewardak.org

Sitka Convention and Visitors Bureau
P.O. Box 1226, Sitka, AK 99835
907-747-5940; sitka.org

Skagway Convention and Visitors Bureau
P.O. Box 1029, Skagway, AK 99840
907-983-2854; 888-762-1898; skagway.com

Talkeetna Chamber of Commerce
P.O. Box 334, Talkeetna, AK 99676
907-733-2330; talkeetnachamber.org

Tok Chamber of Commerce
P.O. Box 389, Tok, AK 99780
907-883-5775; tokalaskainfo.com

Unalaska/Dutch Harbor Convention and Visitors Bureau
P.O. Box 545, Unalaska, AK 99685
907-581-9612; 877-581-2612; alaskatravel.com/alaska/unalaska.html

Valdez Convention and Visitors Bureau
200 Chenega Street, Valdez, AK 99686
907-835-2984; Toll-free: 800-770-5954; valdezalaska.org

Wasilla
Greater Wasilla Chamber of Commerce
415 E. Railroad Avenue, Wasilla, AK 99654
907-376-1299; wasillachamber.org

Whittier
whittieralaskachamber.org

Wrangell
Wrangell, AK 99929
907-874-2381; wrangell.com

ALBERTA

Travel Alberta
P.O. Box 2500, Edmonton, AB T5J 2Z4 Canada
800-252-3782; travelalberta.com

Central Alberta
888-414-4139; travelalbertacentral.com

Banff
Banff and Lake Louise Tourism
224 Banff Avenue, Banff, AB T0L 0C0 Canada
403-762-8421; banfflakelouise.com

Calgary
Tourism Calgary
200, 238–11 Avenue SE, Calgary, AB T2G 0X8 Canada
403-263-8510; 800-661-1678; visitcalgary.com

Edmonton
Edmonton Tourism
Main Floor, World Trade Center, 9990 Jasper Avenue, Edmonton, AB T5J 1N9 Canada
780-496-8400; edmonton.com

Grande Prairie Visitor Information Center
Suite 114–11330 106 Street, Grande Prairie, AB T8V 7X9 Canada
866-202-2202; gptourism.ca

Hinton
hinton.ca

Jasper Park Chamber of Commerce
discoverjasper.com

Lethbridge
Chinook Country Tourist Association
2895 Scenic Drive, Lethbridge, AB T1K 5B7 Canada
800-661-1222; exploresouthwestalberta.ca

Peace River
800-215-4535; mightypeace.com

Tourism British Columbia
800-435-5622; hellobc.com

British Columbia Ferries
(Port Hardy, Prince Rupert, Vancouver, Victoria)
888-223-3779; bcferries.com

Central British Columbia
Cariboo Chilcotin Coast Tourist Association
204–350 Barnard Street, Williams Lake, BC V2G 4T9 Canada
250-392-2226; 800-663-5885; landwithoutlimits.com

Atlin Visitors Association
877-399-2665; discoveratlin.com

Dawson Creek Visitor Information Centre
900 Alaska Avenue, Dawson Creek, BC V1G 4T6 Canada
250-782-9595; 866-645-3022; tourismdawsoncreek.com

Dease Lake
deaselake.net

Fort Nelson
fortnelson-bc.worldweb.com

Fort St. John Visitor Centre
10631–100th Street, Fort St. John, BC V1J 3Z5 Canada
250-785-3033; 877-785-7181; fortstjohn.ca

Kamloops Visitor Centre
1290 West Trans-Canada Highway, Kamloops, BC V2C 6R3 Canada
250-372-8000; 800-662-1994; tourismkamloops.com

New Hazelton
new-hazelton.travel.bc.ca

Okanagan
okanagan.com

Prince George
Tourism Prince George and Area
101–1300 First Avenue, Prince George, BC Y2L 2Y3 Canada
250-562-3700; 800-668-7646; tourismpg.com

Prince Rupert Visitor Info Centre
P.O. Box 669, Prince Rupert, BC V8J 3S1 Canada
250-624-5637; 800-667-1994; tourismprincerupert.com

Smithers
Tourism Smithers
P.O. Box 2379, Smithers, BC V0J 2N0 Canada
250-847-5072; 800-542-6673; tourismsmithers.com

South Cariboo Visitor Centre
Box 340, 100 Mile House, BC V0K 2E0 Canada
250-395-5353; 877-511-5353; southcaribootourism.ca

Terrace
4511 Keith Avenue, Terrace, BC V8G 1K1 Canada
250-635-4944; 877-635-4944; kermodeitourism.ca

Vancouver
vancouverinfocenter.com

Vancouver Island
Tourism Vancouver Island
501–65 Front Street, Nanaimo, BC V9R 5H9 Canada
250-754-3500; vancouverisland.travel

NORTHWEST TERRITORIES
Northwest Territories Tourism
P.O. Box 610, Yellowknife, NT X1A 2N5 Canada
800-661-0788; spectacularnwt.com

Fort Liard
Hamlet of Fort Liard
General Delivery, Fort Liard, NT X0G 0A0 Canada
867-770-4104; fortliard.com

Inuvik
Box 1160, Inuvik, NT X0E 0T0 Canada
867-777-8600; inuvik.ca/tourism

Yellowknife
Northern Frontier Visitors Association
4 4807–49th Street, Yellowknife, NT X1A 3T5 Canada
867-873-4262; 877-881-4262; northernfrontier.com

YUKON
Tourism and Culture Center
100 Hanson Street, Whitehorse, YT Y1A 2C6 Canada
867-667-5036; tc.gov.yk.ca

Carmacks
P.O. Box 113, Carmacks, YT Y0B 1C0 Canada
867-863-6271; carmacks.ca

Dawson City
Klondike Visitors Association
P.O. Box 389C, Dawson City, YT Y0B 1G0 Canada
867-993-5575; dawsoncity.ca

Mayo
P.O. Box 160, Mayo, YT Y0B 1M0 Canada
867-996-2317; yukonweb.com/community/mayo

Watson Lake
Watson Lake Sign Post Forest
yukoninfo.com/watson/signpostforest.htm

Whitehorse
whitehorsetourism.ca

Yellowhead Highway Association
107 4990–92 Avenue, Edmonton, AB T6B 2V4 Canada
780-429-0444; 877-469-3556; yellowheadit.com

APPENDIX B: Currency Exchange

Canadians measure their wealth just as do US citizens, in terms of dollars and cents. I once asked a youngster in Whitehorse which currency she preferred, Canadian or US. She pondered the question for a moment, then replied, "I like US money because it spends better, but I think the Canadian money is prettier."

Canadian businesses will occasionally accept US currency, but be prepared to pay a premium for this service. Your best bet is to stop at a national bank or currency exchange facility, either before leaving the United States or as soon as you get into Canada, and exchange your money.

Credit card users can freely charge to VISA, MasterCard, Discover, American Express, Diners Club, and gasoline cards. The companies issuing the cards will adjust for the differences in exchange rates prior to sending you a billing statement. VISA and MasterCard are the most frequently accepted cards in western Canada.

The exchange rate in June of 2016 was approximately 25 percent, which is to say a Canadian dollar was worth about $0.75 in US currency. I usually stop at the first ATM I see, insert my debit card, and withdraw several hundred Canadian dollars. Like all banks, my statement will be adjusted to reflect the actual value of the Canadian money in US funds.

APPENDIX C: Border Crossings

Though US and Canadian citizens used to be able to travel freely across each other's borders without a passport, that is no longer the case. You will need a valid, current passport to both enter Canada and reenter the United States. (Children age 15 and younger, or students age 18 and younger traveling with a school or religious organization, are exempt from the passport requirement and need only a copy or original birth certificate.)

For most people, border crossings are completed through the car window by answering a few questions from a customs agent. Occasionally one of these answers will result in a customs inspector asking to examine certain items. Cooperation is the key to any border crossing. Customs officers do have the authority to completely search you, your vehicle, and all your possessions should your answers be unsatisfactory. Items that cause the most problems at border crossing include:

- **Firearms:** Foreigners may not possess handguns or fully automatic rifles in Canada. Do not attempt to cross into Canada with these items in your possession; they will be seized, and you will be jailed. Manually operated, shoulder-fired shotguns and rifles can be brought into Canada if they are properly registered. Registration will cost $50 (Canadian) and can be done by mail before you leave or in person at the border crossing.

- **Alcoholic beverages:** Up to 1.2 liters of hard liquor, 1.2 liters of wine, and 8.5 liters of beer per adult can be transported legally across the border. More than that is subject to seizure.

- **Items for resale in Canada:** Items carried across the border for sale to Canadian citizens are subject to duty.

- **Tobacco:** Up to a carton of cigarettes per person for personal consumption can be carried into Canada. Larger amounts are subject to duty.

- **Insurance:** Be prepared to demonstrate proof that your automobile insurance is valid in Canada. If you ask, your auto insurance company will send you a rider noting that your coverage is valid in Canada. You must carry at least $200,000 of third-party liability insurance.

- **Identification:** Each adult member of your party must carry a valid, current passport. If you are traveling with children age 15 and younger who are not your own—grandchildren, for example—have a birth certificate for each child, as well as a notarized letter from a parent authorizing you to travel in Canada with the child. (A power of attorney from the parent to allow you to seek medical treatment and so forth for a child other than your own is also handy to have.)

- **Length of stay:** We are almost always asked how long we plan to be in Canada and what we plan to do while there.

- **Food:** The only things we have ever had seized during border crossings are various foodstuffs. When mad cow disease was a problem, customs officers seized our hot dogs. Once we had to dispose of some fruit. Read the paper before entering Canada to determine what particular food item is being fought over at the moment.

- **Pets:** If you are traveling with a pet, be prepared to show a copy of a health certificate prepared and signed by a veterinarian within the previous 10 days.

Travelers bound for Alaska may also be asked how much cash they are carrying. Canadian authorities are concerned that people not run out of money en route, particularly in the event of an emergency.

APPENDIX D: Pets

The family dog or cat is certainly welcome to join you on your vacation to and from Alaska. However, out of consideration for your pet, and for the citizens of the states and provinces you will be passing through, certain things should be done in advance.

Within 10 days of your departure, make sure your pet's shot records are up to date and ask your veterinarian to prepare a health certificate. Customs officers may ask to see this health certificate and can, if uncertain about the health of your pet, place it in quarantine. The key item of interest on an animal's health certificate will be a current vaccination for rabies.

Be sure to allow sufficient time for your pet to get exercise. And remember, courtesy requires that your pets be leashed in public areas such as campgrounds or parks and that you properly clean up after your pet every time it defecates in a public-use area.

Provide plenty of water at regular intervals for your animals. Traveling on hot, dusty days can be dehydrating for animals just as it is for people.

Those traveling via the Alaska Marine Highway should note that pets are not permitted in passenger areas aboard ship. Pets are confined to their owners' vehicles except for twice-daily exercise periods on the vehicle deck. Be sure to clean up after your pet on these excursions. Pets can also be exercised when the ship stops at various ports along the way.

Finally, keep your pet under control at all times. Wildlife officials have a special distaste for dogs that chase wild animals and, in many cases, may shoot any dog found doing so. Your pet is your responsibility.

APPENDIX E: Firearms and Ammunition

For whatever reason, driving trips to and from Alaska inspire people to carry guns, usually in the name of personal protection from bears or whatever. For the most part, these weapons are unnecessary. Most bear problems in campgrounds are avoided simply by keeping a clean camp, and officials work hard to keep bears away from campgrounds, often trapping and relocating bears that are a problem.

If you do choose to carry a gun on your trip to Alaska, be completely familiar with its operation. Probably the most dangerous weapons anywhere are those in the hands of people who don't know how to use them.

In your vehicle, keep guns and ammunition separate so a child or an intruder can't easily get hold of both together. For safety's sake, do not, under any circumstances, travel down the road with a loaded gun in your vehicle.

Hunters traveling to Alaska or any of the Canadian provinces should keep their firearms packed away until it's time for the hunt. After a lengthy road trip, all rifles should be test-fired in a safe area to ensure that the sights were not jarred during transit. Most guides and outfitters can recommend a nearby rifle range or other safe area for this activity.

Carrying guns into Canada has also become much more problematic over the years. Foreigners, which include citizens of the United States, are absolutely forbidden to possess handguns or automatic weapons in Canada. Possession of one of these will get you thrown in jail. Manually operated rifles and shotguns can be carried through Canada only if they are registered. Registration will cost $50 (Canadian) per gun and can be done by mail prior to departing or at the border. Registration must be updated and paid every year.

APPENDIX F: Time Zones

Geographically, Alaska spans five time zones. However, in the early 1980s, Alaska's politicians decided that two were sufficient. Virtually all of the populated parts of the state now run one hour earlier than the Pacific Coast. Only the extreme western part of the Aleutian Islands runs on a clock that is two hours earlier than the Pacific Coast. Thus, noon in New York City is 11 a.m. in Chicago, 10 a.m. in Denver, 9 a.m. in Los Angeles, and 8 a.m. in Anchorage, Fairbanks, and Juneau. Daylight saving time is observed in Alaska and Canada.

Canadian provinces operate with a little more knowledge of functional geography. Both Yukon Territory and British Columbia keep to Pacific Coast time; Alberta and Northwest Territories run on Rocky Mountain time, the same as Denver.

APPENDIX G: Public and Private Campgrounds

Private campgrounds are those on private land operated as a business serving the traveling public. Fees for usage are generally higher than for public campgrounds, but usually there are more facilities available, such as showers, coin-operated washers and dryers, electrical service, and water and sewage hookups for RVs.

Public campgrounds are those operated by a national, state, provincial, or local government. Samples of these would be the U.S. Forest Service, the Bureau of Land Management, the National Park Service, British Columbia's provincial parks, Yukon's territorial campgrounds, and Parks Canada facilities. Usually these are in more remote areas well away from towns, and facilities are usually limited to picnic tables, level parking sites, and pit toilets. While many such campgrounds in the lower 48 often offer water, sewer, and electrical hookups, few of the public campgrounds in Alaska, Yukon, and northern British Columbia do.

Fees for public campgrounds range from about $8 to $15 per night, depending on the location. Fees for private campgrounds generally start around $15 for a tent site and go up to $30 or more for a site with hookups for electricity, water, and sewage.

Dump stations for RVs are usually found in private campgrounds and in some service stations. Drinking water may or may not be available in public campgrounds, or if available it may require boiling before drinking.

APPENDIX H: Fishing

Some of the most fabulous freshwater and saltwater sport fishing on Earth is available in northwestern Canada and Alaska. However, each state and province has its own regulations governing the take of fish from various waters. In many cases, these regulations are stream or lake specific. Be absolutely certain you have a valid fishing license for the particular state or province you are in, and that you understand the regulations governing that body of water. For additional information, check with the following agencies:

ALASKA
The Alaska Department of Fish and Game
P.O. Box 25526, Juneau, AK 99802-5526
907-465-4100; state.ak.us/adfg/adfghome.htm

BRITISH COLUMBIA
Ministry of Agriculture, Food and Fisheries
Box 9058, Stn. Prov. Govt., Victoria, BC V8W 9E2 Canada
www.env.gov.bc.ca/fw

NORTHWEST TERRITORIES
Wildlife and Fisheries, Department of Resources
P.O. Box 1320, Yellowknife, NWT X1A 2L9 Canada
867-920-8064; enr.gov.nt.ca/programs/fishing

YUKON TERRITORY
Fish and Wildlife, Yukon Government, Department of the Environment
P.O. Box 2703, Whitehorse, YT Y1A 2C6, Canada
867-667-5652; environmentyukon.gov.yk.ca

APPENDIX I: Hunting

Alaska and northwestern Canada offer unmatched opportunities for hunting a wide variety of big-game animals, including Dall sheep, Stone sheep, caribou, moose, black bears, brown bears, grizzly bears, mountain goats, and wolves. As with the fishing, however, the taking of these animals is carefully regulated by each state and province.

In Alaska, out-of-state or foreign hunters must be accompanied by a state-licensed guide or master guide while hunting Dall sheep, brown bear,s or grizzly bears. US citizens hunting big-game animals in Canada must almost always be accompanied by an outfitter or guide.

Guided hunts, however, are no assurance of success and are also expensive, with fees typically averaging $750–$1,000 a day or more. Finally, guided hunts are usually booked a year or more in advance.

Beyond big-game hunting, there are spectacular opportunities for small-game hunts in Alaska and northwestern Canada, specifically for waterfowl in September and October, and for grouse or ptarmigan—usually with an August to March season. Bag limits are liberal, up to as many as 20 ptarmigan and 15 grouse per day.

For additional information on hunting opportunities and regulations, contact:

ALASKA
The Alaska Department of Fish and Game
P.O. Box 25526, Juneau, AK 99802-5526
907-465-4100; state.ak.us/adfg/adfghome.htm

BRITISH COLUMBIA
Ministry of Agriculture, Food & Fisheries
P.O. Box 9058, Stn. Prov. Govt., Victoria, BC V8W 9E2 Canada; gov.bc.ca/agf

NORTHWEST TERRITORIES
Wildlife and Fisheries, Department of Resources
P.O. Box 1320, Yellowknife, NWT X1A 2L9 Canada
867-920-8064; nwtwildlife.rwed.gov.nt.ca

YUKON TERRITORY
Fish and Wildlife, Yukon Government, Department of the Environment
P.O. Box 2703, Whitehorse, YT Y1A 2C6, Canada
867-667-5652; environmentyukon.gov.yk.ca

APPENDIX J: Gas Prices—Converting Liters to Gallons

Gasoline in Canada is measured and sold by the liter. It takes approximately 3.7 liters to equal 1 US gallon. To determine the number of gallons purchased, divide the number of liters measured out by the gas pump by 3.7.

To determine the price paid per gallon in US funds, first multiply the cost per liter by 3.7 to obtain the cost per gallon in Canadian funds. Then multiply the cost per gallon in Canadian funds by the conversion rate obtained when you exchanged your money. The formula below uses the price and conversion rate effective in June 2016.

For example, if you pay $1.259 (Canadian) per liter of fuel—the most common price along the Alaska Highway in 2016—and the conversion rate is 0.75, the math works like this:

$1.259 x 3.7 x 0.75 = $3.49 (US) per US gallon

Index